Most questions commonly asked about international politics are ethical ones. Should the international community intervene in Bosnia? What do we owe the starving in Somalia? What should be done about the genocide in Rwanda? Yet, Mervyn Frost argues, ethics is accorded a marginal position within the academic study of international relations. In this book he examines the reasons given for this, and finds that they do not stand up to scrutiny. He goes on to evaluate those ethical theories that do exist within the discipline – order-based theories, utilitarian theories and rights-based theories – and finds them unconvincing. He elaborates his own ethical theory – constitutive theory – which is derived from Hegel, and highlights the way in which we constitute one another as moral beings through a process of reciprocal recognition within a hierarchy of institutions which include the family, civil society, the state, and the society of states.

CAMBRIDGE STUDIES IN INTERNATIONAL RELATIONS: 45

Ethics in international relations

CAMBRIDGE STUDIES IN INTERNATIONAL RELATIONS

Series list continues after index

Ethics in international relations

A constitutive theory

Mervyn Frost
University of Kent

CAMBRIDGE
UNIVERSITY PRESS

PUBLISHED BY THE PRESS SYNDICATE OF THE UNIVERSITY OF CAMBRIDGE
The Pitt Building, Trumpington Street, Cambridge, United Kingdom

CAMBRIDGE UNIVERSITY PRESS
The Edinburgh Building, Cambridge CB2 2RU, UK
40 West 20th Street, New York, NY 10011–4211, USA
10 Stamford Road, Oakleigh, VIC 3166, Australia
Ruiz de Alarcón 13, 28014 Madrid, Spain
Dock House, The Waterfront, Cape Town 8001, South Africa

http://www.cambridge.org

First published 1996
Reprinted 1997, 2000, 2001

Ethics in international relations succeeds and replaces *Towards a normative
theory of international relations*, published by Cambridge University Press in
1986 (0 521 30512 8)

Printed in the United Kingdom at the University Press, Cambridge

A catalogue record for this book is available from the British Library

Library of Congress Cataloguing in Publication Data
Frost, Mervyn.
  Ethics in international relations: a constitutive theory/by Mervyn Frost.
    p.   cm. – (Cambridge studies in international relations: 45)
Includes bibliographical references.
ISBN 0 521 55505 1 (hc)
1. International relations–Moral and ethical aspects. I. Title.
II. Series.
JX 1255.F76   1996
172′.4–dc20   95-31520 CIP

ISBN 0 521 55505 1 hardback
ISBN 0 521 55530 2 paperback

WV

Contents

Preface

When I wrote *Towards a Normative Theory of International Relations* (1986) there was a dearth of books dealing with the ethical issues which arise in international relations. International ethics was not a recognized sub-field within the discipline of international relations, and there was a general scepticism as to whether ethics had any place at all within the discipline. This scepticism was surprising given the fact that there was a great deal of scholarly activity directed at ethical issues that arose within states. Some of the key debates concerned justice, liberty, equality, political obligation and democracy. In *Towards a Normative Theory of International Relations* I explored the reasons (either assumed or expressed) which scholars in international relations had for eschewing normative theory. I found that all the arguments offered (or assumed) did not stand up to close scrutiny. Indeed, I went on to argue that all scholars in the field could do no other but become involved with ethical issues (either expressly or tacitly). This then led me on to examine some of the major ethical positions which tacitly informed much of the scholarship at that time. The key ones were order-based theories, utilitarian theories and rights-based theories. I found all these to be wanting in one way or another, and in their place I put forward a secular Hegelian ethical theory which I called "constitutive theory".

Subsequently there has been a surge of interest in ethics in international relations as reflected in the publication of several major books, the appearance of many journal articles, the establishment of conference panels on the subject, and the modification of university curricula to include components dealing with ethics in world politics. Yet, in spite of all these developments, ethics remains at the fringes of the discipline, together with feminist and environmental approaches. I welcome the growing interest in international ethics. But I am greatly perturbed, first, by the way in which scholars continue to place it at the periphery, and, second, by the continued reliance that scholars place on order-based, utilitarian or rights-based theories. These considerations have prompted me to rework *Towards a Normative Theory of International Relations* and to publish it as *Ethics in International Relations: A Constitutive Theory*. For I am as convinced as ever that normative theory is central to the discipline of international relations. The arguments advanced for denying it this central status are weak ones. Similarly I am convinced that constitutive theory has much to offer us as we confront new and increasingly complicated ethical problems in world politics.

In this book I have sought to strengthen my case by writing a new and longer Introduction that traces some recent developments with regard to the standing of normative theory *vis-à-vis* the mainstream of the subject. I have also added a seventh chapter showing how constitutive theory may be applied to the ethical puzzles which have come to light in the Bosnian conflict. In the body of the book I have honed my arguments as best I can and in many cases I have changed the examples in order to make them more appropriate to the present times.

I read early drafts of the revised introduction at postgraduate seminars at Selwyn College, Cambridge and at the graduate seminar of the Department of Politics and International Relations at the University of Kent. A draft of chapter 7 was read at the seminar on International Political Theory at the London School of Economics and Political Science. I am indebted to many of the participants of these seminars for their valuable comments.

This book was revised during a term spent at the Centre for International Studies at the London School of Economics and Political Science. I would like to thank my colleagues in the Centre and in the Department of International Relations who, as always, managed to create what I consider to be an ideal academic environment. In particular I would like to thank James Mayall, Robert Jackson, John Charvet, Chris Brown and Justin Rosenberg for the invaluable conversations I had with them.

I am grateful to the Human Sciences Research Council, Pretoria, South Africa and to the University of Natal, Durban, for the financial assistance they provided while I was writing this book.

Finally I would like to express my appreciation to Lola, Sarah and Anna Frost who enjoy academic conversation as much as I do. Living with them while writing is a pleasure indeed.

Introduction

In this book I argue that although normative questions regularly arise in the day-to-day practice of international politics the discipline of international relations has not accorded ethical theory a central place within it. I examine the reasons which are given for this neglect of normative theory and find that they are not convincing. Having made the case that normative theory ought to be central to the discipline, I turn to the business of constructing a substantive ethical theory which will enable us to answer the difficult questions we encounter in the practice of international relations. I do this by first examining the theories which are dominant in the field. These turn out to be seriously flawed.

Second, I turn to the more positive task of presenting a theory which I hold is better able to answer the pressing ethical questions we encounter in international relations. This theory I call *constitutive theory*. In the final chapters I show how constitutive theory may be applied to normative questions which arise with regard to the use of unconventional violence in international affairs and to questions about the self-determination of nations.

Normative questions in the practice of international relations

We, as individuals or in association with others, are all regularly called upon to seek answers to the following questions: Where different nations claim the right to self-determination in the same territory, whose claim should we support? What should we do about famine in other states? What should we do about other states, groups or individuals who seriously damage the global environment? How should we treat people (possibly tens of thousands) who arrive in our country as political and economic refugees? Where a government engages in genocide against a minority in its territory what ought we to do about it? What may we legitimately do against a state which infringes another state's rights? May we use force of arms to stop human rights abuses in other states? Daily our newspapers furnish examples of states within which these problems arise.

The kind of problem which faces actors in the realm of international relations is well illustrated in the conflicts which have arisen in what was Yugoslavia.[1] In Bosnia rival nationalist groupings are warring about the final form and shape of the state of Bosnia-Herzogovina, indeed the survival of that state itself is in question. Each movement claims that its right of self-determination entitles it to draw the map according to its preferred plan. Each directs a request to the international community, based on the supposed strength of its moral case, requesting economic, political and military support. We in the international community (both politicians and citizens) are called upon to evaluate these requests.

These problems are all *normative* in that they require of us that we make judgements about what *ought* to be done. Normative questions are not answered by pointing to the way things are in the world. The normative nature of these problems is not dissolved by suggesting that the actors involved (including us) always do (and will) act according to our (or their) respective self-interests. For what is to count as self-interest is partially determined by normative considerations. For example, what the Bosnian Muslims put forward as their self-interest is underpinned by a normative claim about their right to self-determination. Their notion of self-interest is also supported by human rights claims – these rights, they argue, are being grossly infringed by the other parties to the dispute. Other nationalist movements throughout the region (and elsewhere in the world) make similar normative claims. The nub of the matter is that any concept we may have of our own self-interest is partially determined by normative ideas about what we are entitled to.

These normative questions pertaining to international relations press in on us every day. That they are urgent questions for prime ministers, presidents, foreign ministers, and generals is clear. But they are also important for ordinary citizens. For the most part citizens may not think deeply about these matters because they feel relatively

2

powerless to do anything about them. Yet there are occasions when they, too, have to make up their minds on such matters. Political leaders, from presidents to warlords, have to elicit the support of their followers if they are to achieve their aims. People (as citizens and/or soldiers) have to decide whether to support or oppose their leaders.

Normative theory

In order to give rational answers to these questions we need to engage in normative theory. It may seem as if normative theory should be directed in the first place to the question: What should I, as citizen (or we the government, or we the nation, or we the community of states) do? But finding an answer for this kind of question usually depends on finding an answer to a prior question which is quite different. This prior and more important question is about the ethical standing of the institutions within which we find ourselves (and the ethical standing of the institutions within which others find themselves). Thus, for example, before we are able to answer the question "What ought South Africa's foreign policy be with regard to its neighbouring states?" we need some answer to the question "What is the ethical importance of states as opposed to other institutions such as families, churches, corporations, trades unions and the like?" For if we find, for example, that from a moral point of view states are more important than families, corporations, or churches, we might judge that under certain circumstances it might be appropriate to risk our lives to protect states, but be quite inappropriate to do so for families, corporations or churches. Whereas, if we judged churches to be primary from an ethical point of view, risking our lives to protect these would make more sense than doing this for the protection of states. Let us explore the importance of investigating the moral standing of social institutions in more detail.

We all live our lives in the context of social institutions, such as families, markets, companies, churches, trades unions, political parties, social movements, states, and international organizations. The major events of international relations such as wars, revolutions, wars of national liberation, terrorist campaigns, interventions, secessions, irredentist activities, and the like, usually turn on disputes about the structure and powers of these institutions and their relations to other institutions. (For example, those who lived in colonies fought wars of national liberation with the metropolitan states. The colonial peoples rejected the subordination of their government to the imperial one.) Precisely which institutions are the primary focus of such disputes varies from one historic period to another. During the medieval period, for example, churches were centre stage. In the modern period the focus shifted to disputes about the form, functions, territorial scope, internal organization, and so on of the *state* and also to the relationship between states and sub-state institutions such as trades unions, political parties, and the host of other pressure groups which are to be found in civil society.

With regard to the institutions within which we live (and the institutions within which others live) the fundamental normative question is not in the first place, "What ought we to do?" but rather is "What is the ethical standing of these institutions?" In order to answer this we need some measures with which to evaluate different institutions such as the family, civil society, states, and international organizations. Within these institutions, which values ought to be primary – should freedom be held more valuable than equality? Is justice more important than both of these? Where do human rights fit in? And where should democracy be placed in the pattern of values?

Theories which give a satisfactory account of the *raison d'etre* of states and other institutions, of the proper structure of these institutions, and of the relationships which ought to hold between them, will, of course, indicate what institutions like the state might legitimately do *vis-à-vis* other states and *vis-à-vis* other social institutions such as those found in civil society.

Normative theory in the discipline of international relations

A decade ago in *Towards a Normative Theory of International Relations* (1986) I wrote "One very striking feature of the modern discipline of International Relations is that in spite of the fact that most scholars within the discipline claim to be motivated by an urgent moral concern for the well-being of the world polity, there has been very little explicit normative theorizing about what ought to be done in world politics."[2] There had been some normative theorizing, but it was an activity confined to the fringes of the discipline. The mainstream of international relations focussed on description and explanation which, it was understood, could be undertaken in a way that was independent of normative theory.

Since then, there have been dramatic developments in both theory and practice which I had hoped would open the way for normative theory to take its place as a central feature of the discipline. Some progress has been made. There has been, of late, something of a flowering of normative theory in international relations.[3] Several major books on the topic have appeared, a number of journals regularly carry articles on topics which fall broadly within this field, and some universities offer modules covering normative topics.[4] But, by and large, things are as they ever were. Normative theory is to be found on the fringes of the discipline. Scholars in the discipline do not consider that normative theory is fundamentally necessary to the study of world politics. It is to be found instead next to the other marginal sub-groupings within the discipline, namely post-modernism, feminism, and ecological approaches.

I had hoped that the disappearance of a set of pre-existing factors which were clearly inimical to the development of a normative approach to international relations would open the way for normative theory. For example, the Cold War could clearly be seen as blocking the emergence of ethical theories within the discipline.

Cold War politics was such that there seemed little point in studying international ethics. The public rhetoric of those times portrayed the other side as fundamentally immoral (or even amoral). In a "life or death" struggle there did not appear to be much point in spending time and effort discussing the shape of a just world order – for the battle was portrayed as being about survival. And survival was understood to take precedence over justice. For talk about justice, it is commonly supposed, only arises within minimally cooperative social systems. Given that the relationship between the super powers was not a cooperative one, it was not surprising that normative theory was seen as largely irrelevant.

The little normative theorizing that did take place in international relations was not about possible worlds, but about the justice of the means to be used against such an enemy. In particular, a body of normative theory developed with regard to the nuclear deterrent. Some argued that using nuclear weapons would be wrong whereas others held out that even threatening the use of such weapons was ethically impermissible.[5] However, these debates were seen by those in the mainstream as being confined to the eccentric fringe of the discipline. In confronting an enemy who opposed every aspect of one's cultural, economic, social, and political system, ethical discourse could be presented as trivial.[6]

During that time the Third World seemed a more promising area for normative theory. Here, questions about the protection of rights, about securing the self-determination of peoples from colonial rule, and, more importantly, about establishing a more just distribution of resources were quite clearly important to many people. But even here the Cold War put a damper on the salience of normative theory. Most political disputes in the underdeveloped world were immediately subsumed into international politics in Cold War terms. Once again, in practice there appeared to be no room for taking ethical questions seriously when the implacable foe – the total "other" – was seeking to use every opportunity to defeat the enemy.

In short then, that period of our history was presented to us, both by politicians and by the bulk of international relations theorists, in stark realist terms as a naked battle for power between the super powers. The core function for those studying international relations, understood in these terms, was to provide policy-makers with good information so that they could determine how best to secure western interests against the communist enemy and *vice versa*.

Now that that conflict is over and it is no longer possible to understand world politics in terms of a supposed conflict between good and evil, the way seems to be open for a resurgence of normative theory. There are several features of the present era which point in this direction.

First, it is now admitted on all sides that we live in an interdependent world. There are ongoing debates about which actors are primary, and about whether the relations between them constitute a system, a society or a community. But that we are involved in at least a minimum system of cooperation is beyond dispute. It is clear that in this context there are choices to be made in international relations which are not dictated by sheer necessity. Many of these involve ethical questions. Rich states, for example, have difficult choices to make with regard to the reconstruction of the former Soviet Union and adjacent territories. In making these choices, normative notions about rights, democracy, self-determination, sovereignty and just distributions, all have a role to play.[7] Governments and citizens of the European Union have decisions to make about economic refugees which turn on ethical theories about the rights of individuals, the rights of states, the duty of hospitality, and so on. With regard to Africa the rich states of the world face decisions about providing aid to victims of famine, civil war, and, in some cases, the genocidal policies of some African governments.

Second, the fact that most states, including the new ones created in the wake of the Cold War, are members of the United Nations (which has a specifically normative charter) also suggests that this should be a period of great flourishing for normative theory. For now most people in the world are joined, through their governments, in allegiance to an explicit set of principles contained in a legal document. It seems plausible to suppose that this would provide a base from which normative theorists could work – focussing their attention on the precise relationships which ought to hold, for example, between self-determination, democracy, and human rights, or, between sovereignty and human rights. Another pressing topic would seem to be that between justice within states and justice between states.

In spite of these developments favourable to the emergence of normative theory as a central concern for the discipline of international relations, normative theory has still not moved centre stage in the discipline. It has failed to do this because, concurrent with the events favourable to normative theory which I have outlined, other things have happened which seem to undermine the likelihood of progress in this direction.

The first of these is the emergence of nationalism which accompanied the end of bipolarity and the dissolution of the USSR. In many cases the nationalist movements which developed are particularly vigorous and often violent too. Second, in the Middle East, Islamic fundamentalism (often violent) continues to burgeon. On the face of the matter both of these present themselves as antipathetic to reasoned moral discourse. In their rhetoric they present themselves as expressivist and irrational. Muslim fundamentalist writers present their creed as rational within its own frame of reference, but quite at odds with the humanistic framework of the dominant Western powers. In their irrationalist forms, nationalist and fundamentalist movements seem to pose a threat to normative theory similar to that once posed by the "communist onslaught". The threat resides in the way that communism, anti-communism, nationalism, and fundamentalism all profess to understand the world in zero-sum terms – that is, as a battle between an insider group in mortal combat with a hostile external foe. Against crusades, ethical discourse appears tame – if not irrelevant.

This impediment to normative theory is not as serious as it might appear at first glance. For these ostensibly "irrational" movements participate in a common practice of international politics with the rest of us. Within this practice they make claims for themselves which refer to well-known principles of political ethics. Nationalist movements refer to the Charter of the United Nations and in particular to the principle of self-determination which is enshrined in it. Islamic states claim their right to sovereignty and appeal for protection to the rule which prohibits intervention in the domestic affairs of sovereign states. They all claim the right to be treated justly in terms of international law. In short there is a distinction between the rhetoric that nationalist and fundamentalist groups use to mobilize their followers and the language that they use when making a case before an international audience. We ought not to let the rhetoric of fundamentalist and nationalist mobilization blind us to the possibility of serious normative argument with such actors.

In summary then I have argued that actors in world politics (including nations, nationalistic states, and fundamentalist states) have to take decisions on normative issues. In closing let me rehearse a short list of the questions which are pressing in our time: How ought we to treat economic refugees? Where several "nations" seeking self-determination in a single territory appeal to us for political, economic and military aid, whom should we assist? Under what circumstances should governments intervene in the sovereign affairs of other states to prevent human rights abuses there? In seeking to protect the international environment would we be justified in interfering in the internal affairs of other states? What are our duties to the victims of famine in states other than our own? What should the rich states of the world do about the poor ones?

If in the daily round of international relations we regularly have to take policy decisions on such normative questions, why is it that the discipline of international relations, by and large, relegates normative theory to the closing chapters of its textbooks, to a few specialized journals, and to "add-on" options at the end of university courses on the subject? The next chapter attempts an answer to this question.

In the first two chapters it will become apparent that there is no single reason for the failure to take normative theory seriously. Instead we find that there is a rather complex set of reasons for this failure. I subject this set of reasons to close scrutiny and find all of them wanting in one way or another. This ground-clearing exercise opens the way for the latter part of the book which is of a more positive nature. Here the aim is to make a start towards the building of a satisfactory theory which will enable us to provide answers to the hard questions of normative theory which confront us all every day. In chapter 3 I list some of the more pressing normative questions in contemporary world politics and suggest that these concerns can be encapsulated in the question: "What in general is a good reason for action by or with regard to states?" This question serves as a useful point of departure in the subsequent quest for a normative theory. But prior to constructing such a theory I consider the contention that the question cannot be answered at all. An attempt is made to counter those who argue that conflicting answers to this question are inevitable, since in seeking an answer one necessarily becomes involved in a conflict of ideologies within which no rational solution is possible. I also consider the natural law/community of humankind approach to the pressing normative questions in international relations and indicate why it is not satisfactory.

In the latter part of chapter 3 I outline a constructive approach to normative theory which will, I argue, enable us to find answers to the difficult normative questions facing us in world politics today. In seeking solutions to these hard cases my point of departure is that, although there is no agreement amongst the actors involved in international relations about how to handle the difficult cases, nevertheless there is a substantial agreement on a whole range of normative matters. For example, there is widespread agreement that the preservation of the system of states is good, that intervention in domestic affairs of a sovereign state is normally wrong, that peace between states is better than war, and so on. I argue that this area of agreement provides a foundation from which we may start reasoning towards a solution of the difficult cases. I introduce a method of argument for doing this which was developed by Ronald Dworkin within the narrower context of jurisprudence. This method of argument involves, first, listing what is settled within the domain of discourse in question; second, constructing a background theory which will justify the list of settled beliefs within that domain; and, third, using this background theory to generate answers to the contentious cases.

In chapter 4 I start by listing what may be taken as the settled norms in international relations today. After that I consider three possible background justifications for the list of settled goods; the justification which stresses the primacy of order, the utilitarian justification and the contractarian rights-based justification. All of these are found to be wanting in specified ways.

In chapter 5 I articulate a background justification which I call the constitutive theory of individuality and give reasons for preferring it to the others. This justification involves us in a strikingly different mode of theorizing from that used in the other three justifications considered. There is, of course, considerable overlap among the different modes of theorizing, but for the sake of the analysis the distinctions between them are drawn as sharply as possible.

Finally, in chapters 6 and 7 I seek to show how the mode of theorizing developed in chapter 5 can be used to answer two sets of pressing questions in world politics. The first has to do with justifying the use of unconventional modes of violence (such as sabotage and international terrorism) in world politics. The second grapples with the problems that arise where groups claim the right to establish new states in disputed territory. I suggest that constitutive theory can be successfully used in seeking answers to other hard cases mentioned in chapter 4, but demonstrating this is beyond the scope of this book.

1 The place of normative theory in international relations

Introduction

Actors in the realm of international relations are regularly faced with normative questions. They are often called upon to decide what, given the specific situation, would be the right thing to do. The problem is not, or not only, the one of deciding upon the best means to an approved end; in other words, the problem is not purely technical. The moral problem is to choose the ends to be pursued and to decide upon what means might legitimately be used in pursuit of those ends.

As I indicated earlier such questions press most heavily on key decision-makers in government, but not all actors in world politics are office bearers in government. Most of us are actors in world politics in one capacity or another. Individuals, whether as ordinary citizens or as members of some non-governmental organization (such as a church, multinational corporation, international agency or welfare organization) also have to make important normative decisions relating to international relations. I mention but three. Citizens called upon by their governments to fight in a war (be it a conventional war or a counter-insurgency war) are often faced with difficult choices regarding their obligations. Ought they to agree to fight, ought they to refuse to fight or ought they to protest against the order to serve in some other way? Shareholders are called upon by certain pressure groups to influence a given company to withdraw its investment from a specific state for moral or political reasons. Voters in democracies have to make decisions about foreign policy questions with a normative dimension in order to cast their vote intelligently at election time. These examples could be multiplied.

Thus far we have been concerned with the ways in which normative questions are important for actors in world politics. But normative issues are important for students of world politics too. Every agent acts upon some understanding of the situation in which he finds himself and since such an understanding requires some study of the situation (however rudimentary it might be) every actor must, perforce, be both a practitioner in, and a student of, international relations. Furthermore, since we are all in one way or another actors in international politics (merely to be a loyal citizen of a state in a time of war or in a time of peace is to be an actor in international politics), all students of international politics are also actors in international politics and are thus likely to be confronted with some of the pressing normative issues which arise in the domain of world politics.

Given the centrality of these normative questions, what is striking is that within the discipline of international relations very little work is done towards answering them; normative theory is generally eschewed. The past decade has seen increased interest in normative theory, but it certainly is not acknowledged as a central component of the discipline. In international relations as a discipline it is generally taken for granted that the aim should be primarily descriptive and/or explanatory. The focus is firmly on explaining what happened in the past, what is happening now, and what is likely to happen in the future. Very little attention is paid to questions about what ought to be done. This has become so much the accepted practice that it is simply taken for granted without any attempt at justification. That a discipline within which normative issues arise so often, should fail to take normative theory seriously is a paradox that calls for critical investigation. I shall contend in this and the following chapter that there are two main types of reason for this dearth of serious argument about values.

First, there is a particular epistemological and methodological bias held by most scholars in the field of international relations in common with scholars in many of the other social sciences. This may be called the bias towards *objective explanation*. On this view explaining the facts is something that can be done prior to deciding on the normative question: What ought to be done? In its strongest form this bias rests on *positivist* ideas about the nature of science. The bias towards objective explanation is premised on a radical distinction between facts and values which gives epistemological priority to factual knowledge. The bias towards explanation in its positivist form has been subjected to rigorous criticism as we shall see below. Positivists in social science are now largely discredited, yet the bias towards objective explanation, understood as an activity quite distinct from normative theory, remains.

Second, there are some prevalent views regarding the characteristic features of moral arguments (such as their alleged non-cognitive status, as well as an amoralist implication which is a supposed consequence of this status, and an alleged status in terms of which such arguments are seen as derivative from naked power relations) which are held to make moral discourse in general, as well as normative arguments within the discipline of international relations, not worthy of serious intellectual consideration. This type of reason may, for the sake of convenience, be caught under the heading *moral scepticism*. I shall be considering this latter type of argument in chapter 2. In this chapter I shall consider only the first type of reason – the widespread bias towards objective explanation in the discipline. This will involve a critical investigation of the methodological and philosophical assumptions underlying the activities of scholars in the field. It is these assumptions which supposedly provide reasons for eschewing normative theory in international relations.

The argument proceeds by looking at some general developments in the philosophy of the social sciences which have a bearing on the role of normative theory in international relations. I start by outlining the strongest form of the bias towards objective explanation, namely the positivist bias. According to this view of social science it is quite possible to explain the social world, in our case international relations, without becoming involved in normative theory. After this I proceed to examine the most important criticisms which have been directed at positivist social science in order to find out whether, and to what extent, they effectively open the way for normative theory within the discipline of international relations. I find that although most of the criticisms against positivism have been accepted, the overall bias in favour of objective explanation (as an activity quite distinct from normative theory) remains in place. Finally, I provide arguments in support of my main conclusion which is that it is not possible to study international relations without becoming involved in substantive normative issues. It is the bias towards objective explanation which has led scholars in international relations to eschew any involvement in substantive normative theory; once this assumption is challenged it will become clear that scholars in international relations must of necessity take normative argument seriously.

The positivist bias against normative theory in international relations

The discipline of international relations, as distinct from the more traditional disciplines of history and law, is a comparatively new one. Like most academic disciplines within the social sciences, international relations is plagued by an ongoing dispute about the proper methods to be employed by its practitioners.[1] Scholars argue about the merits of different methodologies, paradigms and traditions.[2] A common division is made between realist, pluralist and structural approaches to the subject. Martin Wight distinguished between Machiavellian, Grotian and Kantian traditions.[3] More recently Terry Nardin and David Mapel have identified twelve traditions.[4]

For a twenty-year period after the Second World War the major division in the discipline was that between the so-called classical and scientific approaches to the subject.[5] In this era the scientific approach came dramatically to the fore. The dominant approach to science at that time was a "logical-empiricist" one in which the logical techniques of Russell and Whitehead's *Principia Mathematica* were wedded to an empiricist epistemology. In social science the behavioural approach was dominant. A few of the early scholars committed to the scientific approach were Morton Kaplan, Richard Rosecrance, Klaus Knorr, Sydney Verba, Karl Deutsch, James Rosenau, J. W. Burton, Stanley Hoffman, Charles Kindleberger, Charles McCelland and J. D. Singer.[6] Since then there have been major disputes within the scientific tradition as to what precisely constitutes a science.[7] Some of these are mentioned below. But notwithstanding these differences most scholars in international relations (the vast bulk of whom are in the USA) still see themselves as broadly situated within the scientific tradition.[8]

The classical approach is the approach pursued by most British scholars, then and now. The term "classical" is somewhat misleading, suggesting as it does an ancient lineage and a Greek connection. In the debate within the discipline of international relations "classical" (or "traditional") is used to identify a predominantly British group of scholars who combine the methods of the liberal historian, the Oxford philosopher, the international lawyer and the political theorist. Some well-known names include E. H. Carr, Martin Wight, Hedley Bull, D. C. Watt and John Vincent.[9] More recent writers in this tradition are Michael Donelan, Andrew Hurrell, James Mayall, Adam Roberts and Cornelia Navari. Indeed, most British scholars in international relations fall into this category rather than into any strictly defined "scientific" approach. At issue between the scientific and classical approaches to the subject is a question about the proper method for the study of international relations. The classical theorists (then and now) see the subject as akin to history whereas the scientific approach seeks, as the word "scientific" suggests, to make the study of international relations more rigorous. Following the example of many theorists in the other social sciences at the time, and spurred on by a belief in the unity of science, they aimed ultimately to follow the paradigm of the natural sciences as it was then understood. In practice this meant that they stressed the use of clearly formulated hypotheses and the testing of these against observable data using quantitative methods as far as possible. The distinction between classical and scientific approaches to the study of social phenomena is not confined to international relations, but occurs in other areas of social study as well, for example within the disciplines of history, political studies, anthropology, sociology and so on.

There have been important debates within and between both of these approaches to international relations. Furthermore, there have been debates between them and a third, rather underdeveloped branch to the discipline, namely the Marxist one.[10] For our present purposes though, the important thing to notice is that, for the most part, those who see themselves as pursuing the traditional approach belong, broadly speaking, to the empiricist school of thought.[11] The dominance of the empiricist tradition has important implications for the topic in hand, namely, the epistemological bias against normative theories in international relations. These will become apparent later.

In the scientific approach to international relations there is a broad commitment to explanatory and descriptive goals, but little consensus about the precise nature of the method to be pursued. There have been disputes about what ought to be analysed and about the methods to be used in doing the analysis.[12] Scholars in the scientific school thought that international relations should provide explanatory theories firmly based on facts, but ought the aim to be the establishment of general theories or ought the researcher to aim initially at the middle range theories or even "frameworks" for ordering the facts?[13] Ought the focus to be on data collection or on the formation of hypotheses?[14] Within the broad scientific approach to the discipline there are ongoing disputes about which facts should be taken into consideration. We need briefly to consider these disputes.

In the heyday of behavioural approaches to international relations (which is not over yet), a common understanding of what was involved in science, properly so called, was that it involved subsuming observable facts under covering laws which were in turn related to one another in terms of strict relationships of deductive logic. This scientific calculus, it was believed, would make predictions of future events possible. The guiding idea was that underlying the observable data were "laws" or "regularities" which could be made explicit by science and which would facilitate prediction. The guiding epistemology in all this was empiricist. It was thought that the scientist should approach the facts in an unprejudiced frame of mind and that the facts would present themselves to the viewer in an unproblematic way. The business of perceiving the facts was taken to be a theory-free and value-free activity. On this positivist view of science progress was made by verifying theories against the facts. Testing usually required fine measurement and quantification of the data in question.[15]

The challenge offered to this view of the relationship between fact and theory by Thomas Kuhn in the early 1960s is well known, both generally and in the discipline of international relations.[16] He showed that scientists normally work within communities with common sets of premises, assumptions, criteria and techniques. That is, they work in what he called a paradigm. Crucially such a paradigm specifies what are to count as the relevant facts in terms of which a given theory is to be tested. He pointed out that within a stable paradigm (that is, within the practice of normal science) when anomalies arise, they do not immediately falsify the core theory as some positivists had supposed; instead they are normally accommodated by adjusting the paradigm in certain ways. With regard to training, would-be scientists are initiated into the accepted ways of the scientific community by being taught the lore through the use of standard textbooks and by being taken through the well-known experiments. Once the novices have mastered these they then pursue their careers extending the well-known theory in standard ways. Kuhn made a sharp contrast between what he calls *normal science* (which I have described above) and something quite different which he calls *revolutionary science*. The latter occurs from time to time when a well-established paradigm is challenged by an emerging community of scholars who challenge the very bases of the previous one. The revolutionary scientists reject the corpus of accepted premises, theories and techniques of the existing paradigm and suggest new ones instead. When such a challenge is successful a scientific revolution has occurred. In such cases the previous paradigm may wither away. *What Kuhn stressed though, is that there is no neutral observation language – no neutral world – against which rival paradigms may be tested.* There is a very real sense in which paradigms are incomparable in that what each specifies as verifying data is not recognized by the other.

Kuhn developed his account of scientific revolutions while studying the history of the natural sciences. However, his insights have had a major effect on international relations for it is now widely accepted that there is no single scientific paradigm accepted by all scholars in the discipline. In other words there is no normal science in international relations. The early hopes of the logical empiricists that the discipline would soon become a science, *strictu sensu*, accumulating a reliable and widely recognized body of knowledge have been disappointed. The last two decades have been characterized by intense debates between supporters of competing paradigms, each with its own assumptions, foci, theory sets, and its own view as to what is to count as significant evidence.[17] The paradigms in the ring (the metaphor is not really appropriate for there is no agreement on what would count as a knockout) include realism, neo-realism, transnationalism and structuralism.[18] Most theorists in international relations who presently see themselves as falling within the scientific school accept the Kuhnian insight that in some measure their judgement about the facts is a judgement already infused with theoretical presuppositions.

It is not my purpose here to evaluate the merits of Popper's or Kuhn's understanding of scientific method, nor to attempt an evaluation of competing paradigms in international relations. My central purpose in this chapter is to point out certain underlying assumptions common to the classical and the scientific approaches to the discipline. With regard to the scientific approaches I include here both the strict logical empiricists and those who understand their science in terms of the Kuhnian analysis.

There is, despite their differences in orientation, a broad measure of common ground linking the liberal historical approach and the bulk of the scientific approaches. I have decided to label this rather broad common ground as *the bias towards positive explanation.* I use the phrase in a wide sense to include theorists who hold objectivist theories of knowledge (according to which an item will not count as a piece of knowledge unless it corresponds to an item in the world), empiricist theories of science, verificationist theories of science, falsificationist theories of science, *and* value-free approaches to social science. Importantly I also include in this list those scientists who explicitly understand their scientific activity in terms of Kuhn's theory of paradigms. These theories are obviously not always compatible with one another and adherence to one does not indicate an adherence to them all (indeed the contradictions and conflicts between them make this impossible). Nevertheless, they all have this in common: they are all premised upon a strong distinction between facts (theory determined or not) and values.[19] Both the classical and the scientific approaches stress some or all of the following related things: their methods, it is claimed, are (in terms of the standards of their scientific community) in the final instance objective;[20] they seek to verify their conclusions by reference to "the facts," which are in some sense "hard" and there for all in their scientific community to see.[21] They stress that the results of their studies do not derive from subjective, relative or intuitive judgements. Scientific judgements are, on this view, to be understood in sharp contrast to value judgements which are held to be subjective, relative or conventional. In short, common to the dominant approaches in international relations, there is a radical distinction between the status accorded to factual judgements (on which the findings of international relations are to be based) and that accorded to value judgements.[22] Facts are given epistemological priority. This forms the core of the bias towards positive explanation underlying both the traditional and the scientific approaches to the study of international relations.[23]

The core of the positivist assumption is to be found in the distinction between fact and value and the different cognitive status accorded to each. On the positivist view, what distinguishes facts from values is the characteristic which the former have of being intersubjectively verifiable, i.e. accessible to the senses of anyone who would observe them. Moreover, factual statements are informative; they give us knowledge about the world. Some positivists argue that there is a congruence between factual statements and reality.[24] For them, the matching or picturing guarantees (in some way) the objective basis of factual knowledge.

Empiricists and those committed to one of the scientific approaches to international relations may view normative theories in any of a number of different ways. They may adhere to emotivist, expressivist, prescriptivist or some other theory of normative discourse.[25] For example, on one such view, namely, the emotivist one, a value judge-ment may be seen as purely arbitrary, i.e. it may be seen as a judge-ment for which a person simply opts.[26] It is neither right nor wrong, but is simply what the person has chosen. Alternatively, such judge-ments might be looked upon as conventional, i.e. as being in accord-ance with criteria which have been agreed upon within a given com-munity. Here there may be talk of the judgements being right or wrong in terms of the conventions. Yet there is nothing beyond the conventions which can be referred to as final proof of the matter to somebody who rejects the conventions. In the final instance there is no possible verification for value judgements.

I contend that this bias towards explanation in its positivist form is the most basic reason for the persistent neglect of normative questions in international relations. This bias is common to both the scientific and classical schools in the discipline.[27] To demonstrate this conclus-ively is, of course, difficult. Biases tend to be assumed rather than explicitly stated or argued for. But a glance through the literature will suffice to show that such a bias is indeed implicit in the approach of most of the scholars referred to.[28] Often authors do acknowledge that values will inevitably influence their findings in some way. Typically they admit that value orientations might colour the way in which the data are perceived, they might influence the choice of the initial prob-lem to be studied, they might influence the selection of data, and so on. But in each case the intrusion of personal values, at all (or at some) of these points, is seen as something negative, something to be guarded against. Furthermore, the values which intrude are typically seen as personal values, as values subjectively chosen by the actor. On this view, then, values are choices and not true or false in the way that factual judgements are.[29] It is this pervasive view which follows from the bias towards positive explanation. On this view values are choices which threaten to disturb the path of science.

Positivism challenged

I have argued that the dominant approaches to the study of inter-national relations all assume a sharp distinction between facts and values. They all stress that scholars ought to focus their attention on factual data which will support (or fail to support) their theoretical claims. This is true, I claim, even of those scientists who, following

Kuhn, no longer believe in a neutral data-set radically distinct from any theory. For although a Kuhnian paradigm specifies what are to count as salient facts, for the scientists within the paradigm the salient facts are seen as independent of the scientists' values; what the facts are is not a matter of choice.

Positivism has been severely criticized from several different quarters. The criticisms fundamentally challenge the sharp distinction which positivists draw between objective explanation and normative theory. A first criticism has already been hinted at in my brief discussion of Kuhn above. He claimed that there is no realm of objective facts which can be inspected independent of theory and which can be used as a touchstone for evaluating the merits of competing paradigms. A similar point has been made by V. O. Quine (and the core insights have been usefully condensed by Martin Hollis and Steve Smith in *Explaining and Understanding International Relations.*)[30] Quine argued, first, that facts do not present themselves to our senses in a brute way, but have to be interpreted. We determine what is to count as a relevant fact in the light of the concepts we use. Second, it follows that facts cannot confirm or falsify our theories in the way that logical positivism suggests. The "facts" do not stand free and independent of the theories we are seeking to test. As Hollis and Smith put the matter: "Since theory is involved in deciding what the facts are, there is room for choice when deciding whether the theory at stake is consistent with them."[31] Third, Quine argues that in science we do not test each discrete hypothesis against the facts. Hypotheses are bundled together and the whole bundle is evaluated so that it is difficult to know just which hypothesis within the set is falsified by a particular fact. On Quine's view, theories are under-determined by facts. The direction of determination may, indeed, go the other way.

What are the implications of this for normative theory? Baldly put, if it is not possible to provide an objective test against which explanations may be verified (or, following Popper, falsified), then it must be the case that we prefer one theory over another for other *non-factual* reasons. It may well be that theory choice is guided in part by normative considerations. (Another possibility is that we may be swayed by aesthetic considerations.) How scientists treat apparently disconforming facts depends, in part, on the *choices* they make. Here again there is the possibility that such choices may be guided by normative considerations.

The implications of the criticisms of positivism discussed above are drastic indeed. If we accept these criticisms then, as Hollis and Smith put it, "there is no longer a universal test of what is probable or what it is rational to believe on the basis of experience."[32] This conclusion is so disquieting for the authors that they baulk and simply assert: ". . . we must hold on to the basic idea that science discovers the truth of how the world works."[33] In order to "hold on to" science they then put forward an alternate view of a testable science to which I now turn. But in my view this alternative fails to get past the criticisms of positivism outlined above.

Hollis and Smith, following Lakatos and Bhaskar, suggest that we ought to understand scientific theory in terms of models.[34] "A theory is a model whose internal logic we understand together with a claim that reality conforms to the concepts and logic of the model."[35] The model is not a reflection of reality but is an intellectual construct which enables us to predict events. Since the criticisms discussed above have shown that theories cannot be conclusively verified against the facts, Hollis and Smith suggest that we have to treat models *as if* they give us an account of how the world in fact works.

The problem, of course, as Hollis and Smith admit, is that conflicting models are quite capable of being modified to accommodate recalcitrant facts. In international relations three well-known models – the realist, the pluralist and the structuralist – do not seem amenable to being tested against the facts in a way that would produce a clear winner. All three manage to adapt their models in order to accommodate awkward facts, or, alternatively, they treat these facts as anomalies. We are thus left with no objective scientific way of choosing between the three competing models. Yet within the discipline of international relations we find that most theorists opt for the realist model. On what grounds do they do this? Smith and Hollis suggest an answer which I find quite unconvincing, if it is supposed that the test which they are offering is an objective test.

Realism, they claim, has become the preferred model in international relations because of its institutionally entrenched position. But they suggest a further criterion: "Realism is dominant because, despite anomalies, its selection of aspects of events and identification of trends is more enlightening and fertile than those of its rivals."[36] How are we to interpret this claim? What is the measure of enlightenment or fertility? How are we to distinguish between "progressive" and "degenerating" research programs? It is clear that this is no neutral test. They cannot be construed as advocating a return to positivism requiring a matching of theories against objectively given events and trends. For trends are not objectively given. The trends identified by Francis Fukuyama are quite different from those identified by Paul Kennedy.[37] If there is no objective test for such trends then once again it seems plausible to suggest that the choice of what is to count as "progressive" or "degenerating" may be determined by normative considerations.

My suggestion in the previous paragraph that our choice of explanatory model may well be guided by normative considerations is one that is made explicit by McKinlay and Little in their *Global Problems and World Order*.[38] In order to do this they present, in impressive and convincing detail, three models of world order: the liberal, the socialist and the realist. Each is presented as a comprehensive whole, which has within it a normative component. Thus the "organizing goal for the pure liberal is the promotion and protection of negative freedom," for the socialist model the major goal is "the promotion and protection of equality" and for the realist it is "to establish and maintain a society of sovereign states."[39] Each model simultaneously prescribes and explains. On their view, there is no objective way of choosing between the paradigms. We are to suppose that one's final choices will be guided by normative considerations.

Returning for a moment to Hollis and Smith's book we can see that there is in each of the three models discussed (the realist, pluralist and structural models) a clearly discernible normative component. There are, as is well known, different variants of these models (for example, there are Marxist and non-Marxist variants of structuralism) but the built-in "value slope" of each is not difficult to discern. In choosing models, theorists in international relations will pick (we are led to believe) that model with the value slope they prefer.

Conclusion

In brief compass I have examined some radical critiques of positivist science. The thrust of these has been to show that facts do not, as it were, stand outside theories as objective touchstones against which theories may be tested. Theory choice is guided at least in part by other considerations some of which are normative. Thus in international relations we find that liberal explanation is underpinned by a normative commitment to individual freedom, socialist accounts are imbued with a commitment to equality, and realist accounts have embedded in them a commitment to the maintenance of a system of sovereign states. Theorists will choose the model which best suits their own commitments.

What we see then, in the light of this discussion, is that normative theory is not something which enters the picture *after* the explanation has been completed (i.e. after it has been tested against the facts), but that the very choice of explanatory theory is itself partly dependent on normative considerations which enter at an earlier stage of the inquiry. This suggests that argument about the merits of the different normative positions should be taken very seriously indeed. For these will influence the descriptions and explanations we give of the world of international affairs.

Thus far I have focused on criticisms of positivist science which apply generally to both the so-called "natural sciences" and to the "social sciences." I now turn to a completely different criticism which is directed specifically at positivism as it applies to the social sciences.

The *Verstehen* critique and its implications for normative theory

The primary feature of the bias towards positive explanation is, as we have seen, a commitment to testing theory against facts which are in some broad sense independent of the normative preferences of the scientist. These facts are supposed to be objectively given: i.e. they are given to the senses independently of interpretation or theory. Such facts, according to this view of science, provide a touchstone against which the hypotheses and theories of the investigator can be tested. It is of particular significance for our problem that a major challenge to the positivist approach to social science has been posed by what may be called the *Verstehen* school of social science. This approach is also referred to as "interpretative social science" and sometimes as "humanist social science."[40] The origin of the approach is to be found in the work of two independent German social theorists, Max Weber and Wilhelm Dilthey. In 1958 Peter Winch combined the insights of these earlier theorists with some of the implications of the philosophical work done by Ludwig Wittgenstein in his late period. Winch published his conclusions in his seminal work, *The Idea of a Social Science*.[41] This modern version of the *Verstehen* approach involves a rejection of the positivist assumptions about the nature of social reality. Essentially the positivists supposed that social reality was, in principle, knowable in a direct way which need not involve the investigator in any interpretation. Furthermore, the observation of this reality was, in principle, no different from the observation of the natural reality with which the so called "hard" sciences were concerned. Winch denies that this is an adequate account of the nature and status of societal facts. He argues that social science is primarily concerned with the analysis of the *actions* and *interactions* of people and that actions are not givens which are immediately observable in the way that the data of the physical sciences are.[42]

Let us look more closely at this distinction between the data of the physical sciences and the data of the social sciences. The difference is not that human behaviour cannot figure as the object of physical science, or that the latter is exclusively concerned with data other than that of human behaviour. The physical aspects of human behaviour can quite appropriately provide data for physical science as well. But the point is that such data have a different relation to scientific concept formation than do human actions which comprise the data of social science investigations. In investigating some aspects of the physical behaviour of humans, a physical scientist can introduce the appropriate scientific *concepts* relative to the purposes of the investigation. Thus an orthopaedic specialist who seeks to study the various mechanisms involved in running requires an appropriate concept of "running" for his purposes, e.g. he would have to specify what is to be counted as a single unit of running. There may be good reason for him to look at a whole sequence of two strides or more as the unit to be analysed. If he is interested in taking a single stride as the unit to be investigated , he would have to specify exactly what is to count as a "stride" and so on. The important point here, though, is that the investigator has a degree of freedom in concept formation; relative to his scientific research purposes he can specify what items are to count as the data being studied. He cannot be said to be right or wrong in making this decision. A unit of "running" adequate for the purposes of one investigation may be inappropriate for that of another. The movement of the human body in running is not naturally divided into several discrete units. The investigator can divide it up into separate components in any number of ways dependent on his purposes and requirements in various scientific contexts.

Winch, and social scientists in the *Verstehen* tradition, deny that *actions*, which are the basic data of the social sciences, can be individuated in this way. For an event to be individuated as a specific action according to the interpretative approach, it needs to be *understood*.

Let me demonstrate this point by looking at a hypothetical example from the realm of international relations. Before any observer (be she a social scientist or a historian) can recognize a piece of human behaviour as an example of, let us say, a summit meeting between heads of state, she must be able to understand that behaviour from the point of view of the people involved, i.e. from the internal point of view.[43] In order to identify this particular action the investigator needs to have some knowledge of the practice of summit meetings from the point of view of a participant. Let us consider a hypothetical summit meeting between heads of state in more detail. An external observer with no knowledge of the practice of high-level diplomacy with its elaborate rules of protocol, and who is restricted to the observation of the physical aspects of the event, would be able to record the arrival of a large aircraft, which is met by crowds assembled beside a strip of red carpet. She would record that when a man emerged from the aircraft, lights popped and bands played and that the man walked up and down rows of men all uniformly dressed in unusual clothes. The observer might individuate pieces of the observed data in ways that seemed useful or significant to her. For example, she might specify as significant pieces of data the appearance of a person at the door of the aeroplane immediately followed by intense flashing of light sources amongst a certain section of the people on the tarmac. If she observed several such occasions she might find a high correlation between the appearance of figure X and the bursts of light from group Y. But to individuate and correlate events in this external fashion is not to make sense of them. To make sense of the proceedings she would need to understand the practice of international summitry from the internal point of view. She would need some understanding of what a state is, and she would need to know what a head of state is and how states conduct their relations with one another. She would need to know what a guard of honour is, what press photographers are, what red carpets symbolize and so on. Understanding a guard of honour requires some understanding of the role the military play in inter-state relations. To comprehend the presence of the photographers and journalists she would need to know what the press is and something of the relationships which hold between the press, public opinion and the state.[44] In this way, the individuation of all *actions* (and actions are the basic data of all social sciences including international relations) presupposes participant understanding.[45] The concept formation of the social scientist is rooted in the conceptual structure of such participant understanding.

What are the implications of the *Verstehen* approach to social science? There are several interrelated ones worth mentioning. First, *Verstehen* requires that the investigator adopt a participant perspective as the basis of her investigation. This requires that her interpretations be tested against the self-understandings of the investigatees.[46] It precludes the social scientist from remaining an external observer in the way that positivists suppose social scientists ought to be.

Second, this approach stresses the importance of the constitutive *language* of the investigatees. It is patent that any understanding of a social practice must rest upon a detailed understanding of the characteristic language of the practice in question. What is called for is the identification and classification of actions in terms of the participant language. Thus, for example, no worthwhile comparison is possible between modern-day summitry between heads of nation states and the ways of meeting between feudal lords without an appropriate understanding of the languages characteristic of the two different practices. The reference here is not to any particular natural language like English or French. For the language of a given practice (modern inter-state diplomacy or feudalist diplomacy) may be articulated in various natural languages. The point is rather that the social scientist must learn to know what would count as, for example, an "insult" (or any other important term) in the practice of international diplomacy. Whether the term used to designate this action is the English one "insult" or the Afrikaans one "belediging" (or the French, German, Italian, Japanese terms) is neither here nor there. The stress on language is important in the following way: it highlights that what is to count as an "insult" in the practice of international diplomacy cannot be determined by identifying patterns of physical behaviour or by finding out what went on in the mind of any particular actor (this would be the perception-oriented psychological approach), but by the rules implicit in the practice as a whole as best exemplified in its characteristic language.

Third, there is an important *holist* implication of the *Verstehen* approach. As our example of the summit meeting shows, it is not possible to have a proper understanding of the single act of a meeting between heads of state without a knowledge of the whole practice of diplomacy and of inter-state relations and of the ways in which the parts of this practice cohere. This is in sharp contrast to the positivist approach in terms of which particular theory-verifying (or theory-falsifying) facts are supposed to be available to the senses as discrete entities – i.e. individual data that can be identified independently of theory and interpretation.

Fourth, the interpretative approach stresses the permanent possibility of misunderstanding actions. An investigator's understanding of a given act is always *corrigible* or *defeasible*.[47] For example, what she at first took to be a summit meeting might turn out to be a rehearsal for a film of a summit, or a meeting between people claiming to be heads of state who are not in fact that at all. The investigator is faced not merely with the task of recording the immediate events of the summit meeting; she is also faced, if only implicitly, with the problem of determining when a person really is head of state. In many cases (for example, Rhodesia immediately after UDI) this might be a very contentious issue and one which cannot be resolved merely through scrupulous observation of the "facts" of the meeting. Here we find the interpretative school challenging the supposed "hardness" of social facts, which on the positivist view were held to be ascertainable as correct in a direct manner. Of course, positivists acknowledge the possibility of misperception, of being under an illusion and so on. However, for the positivist such cases must be the result of a malfunction in the perceptual apparatus of the observer. Correcting such a malfunction may be likened to refocusing a telescope; it is a matter of adjusting the instrumentation properly. For the *Verstehen* school, clearing up a misunderstanding involves the observer in something quite different. It involves the investigator entering into a discussion with the participants in order to sort out the possible misunderstanding. This discussion will be about the correct interpretation of the action concerned; it will be about the meaning of the act and will refer to the norms, rules, principles and maxims of the practice in which the action took place.

Fifth, *Verstehen* requires that the investigator take notice of the value system of the investigatees. She cannot avoid this, for all actions have an ineluctable normative element. Let me demonstrate this by referring back to the example of the summit meeting. As already noted, to make sense of the summit, the summit watcher needs to know what states are, what heads of states are, what journalists are, and so on. To understand the importance attached by the participants to the summit, she would need to understand the underlying set of values which inform their judgement that such summits are important. This in turn would require at least a rudimentary knowledge of the participants' political philosophy, that is, of how states are supposed to protect certain values. Such a political philosophy would no doubt refer, *inter alia*, to the value of national security, which in turn could be shown to be linked to the value of the security of the individual. It is knowledge of this background value system which makes it possible for the investigator to predict the range of future actions open to people within a practice.

The limits of interpretation

Although the interpretative approach challenges the foundations of positivism in the social sciences by showing that the assumptions on which positivism had been founded were suspect in certain specified ways, this approach does not yet lead to the full establishment of normative social theory as being at the heart of the discipline of international relations. This will become clear if we consider the interpretative approach to participant values more closely. The interpretative approach does not require the social scientist to accept or evaluate the values of the participants. It requires merely that she understands them. In a sense her understanding may still be said to be objective and compatible with the basic dichotomy between facts and values. There is a sense then in which the interpretative approach is descriptivist.

The argument here may be put slightly differently: The *Verstehen* theorists make a valid point when they show that the data of social science are not observable in the way that the data of the natural sciences are; when they show that understanding is required. But this does not undermine the positivist distinction between scientific inquiry and moral judgement. The data of social science, viz. understandings, like the data of the natural sciences, are either right or wrong according to non-subjective criteria. In short, on this view *Ver stehen* leaves the fact/value distinction intact. Ironically, the interpretative approach, itself an attack on positivism, is open to criticisms which show it to be positivist in a different, but related way. It is positivist in that a proper understanding, according to this school, is achieved where the investigator's insight properly matches the rules of the practice being investigated. A correct understanding depends on a positive match between the understandings of the investigator and the self-understandings of the investigatees. This positive match does not require any serious theorizing about matters of value on the part of the theorist. Indeed, the *Verstehen* theorist may charge the positivist with not being value-free enough. The positivist is charged with interpreting the social data through the filter of his own value system rather than through the interpretative criteria provided by the value system of the investigatees.

This criticism of the supposed value-freeness of the interpretative approach can be clarified by means of the following example. Consider a social scientist investigating the behaviour of the Greek government with regard to the newly created state of Macedonia during 1993–4. The Greek government objected to the establishment of the independent state of Macedonia and it objected even more vigorously to the use of the name "Macedonia" by the new state. It pursued a range of antagonistic policies towards the new state; policies which range from political protest in international forums, to the imposition of economic sanctions against the fledgling state. Any scholar seeking to explain these actions would first need to *understand* these actions from the point of view of the Greek government and people: why (i.e. for what reasons) did the Greek government oppose the emergence of a Macedonian state? Clearly part of what has to be understood is the set of values held by members of the Greek cabinet. One possible interpretation would depend on an understanding of Greek nationalism. A clear understanding of this is essential for any proper grasp of events in the region, but this understanding in no way depends on the social scientist herself subscribing to (or even critically evaluating) the value of Greek nationalism. She may personally be highly critical of Greek nationalism, but her own stance is irrelevant to the investigation. It is, on this view, possible to understand values of the investigatees in a value-neutral way.[48]

From the foregoing it is clear that the interpretative approach to social science maintains a strong distinction between doing social science and arguing about normative theory.[49] The fact/value distinction is essentially maintained. It follows that this debate in the philosophy of the social sciences which we have considered in this section has not yet indicated the necessity for (or the unavoidability of) serious normative theory in international relations and the other social sciences. It is only after the next phase of the discussion that the necessity for social scientists, *qua* social scientists, to become involved in debate about normative issues will be demonstrated.

Critical social science: still not normative

The *Verstehen* approach to social science has been severely criticized on numerous counts. Many of these criticisms have come not from positivists seeking to rebut the criticisms levelled at positivism by the interpretative theorists, but from theorists who essentially agree with the main thrust of the anti-positivist attack launched by the *Verstehen* school. This approach seeks to push the anti-positivist attack even further than did the earlier school and we may, for the sake of convenience, call it the *critical* approach.[50] This approach is critical in several different ways: first, it does not accept the self-understandings of the investigatee as being beyond criticism. According to the interpretative approach, once the social scientist has understood an action from the point of view of the actor, that is all there is to be done. The theorists would not be warranted in "finessing" the self-understandings of the investigatee; the agent's self-understandings are incorrigible.[51] In a critical approach the scientist considers it legitimate to examine the self-understandings of the subject in the context of the practice as a whole and in the context of its history. Such an examination might reveal that the subject's self-understandings help uphold a system within which he (the subject) is being disadvantaged in terms of his needs and purposes and thus that his understanding is defective in important ways.[52]

Second, the approach is critical in that it does not presume coherence in the practice within which the subject understands his act. The *Verstehen* approach sought to understand actions within the context of a practice which was presumed by the participants to be a coherent whole. A critical approach takes seriously the possibility of there being deep-seated internal contradictions within a practice. This has profound political implications. Pointing out such contradictions indicates the kind of actions necessary for a changed practice. Interpretative theory is implicitly conservative in so far as it seeks only to understand the existing practice, not change it.

Third, the critical approach rejects the conception implicit in the interpretative approach about the relationship between theory and practice. Because interpretative theory sought to understand a practice from the internal point of view and because it disallowed the "finessing" of the self-understandings of the investigatee, theory had always to be seen as following practice and could not be seen as having any particular role to play in the development of future practices.

Our particular interest is in the way a critical social inquiry rejects the *descriptivism* inherent in the interpretative approach. Interpretative theory is descriptivist in that it portrays the social scientist's task as being the description of the self-understandings of the subject being investigated. The method precludes the social scientist from passing judgements on the self-understandings of the investigatees. Understanding is a method which allows the investigator to arrive at the proper description of an act. But description does not require the social scientist to become involved in any evaluative enterprise. His task is to understand the practice in question and not to judge it. Although part of what the social scientist seeks to understand will include certain value positions held by the subjects under investigation, the *Verstehen* method does not require the social scientist, *qua* social scientist, to enter into normative argument about the values of the investigatees. A critical approach denies that it is possible for social scientists to proceed in such a neutral way. Let us explore this contention more fully.

The core of the critical approach's attack on the descriptivism of interpretative theory lies in the rejection of the rule that the subject's self-understandings may not be finessed. The critical social inquirer asserts that a subject's self-understandings may be wrong in important ways. What the critical approach takes over from the *Verstehen* method is the conviction that no proper understanding of a subject's actions is possible without engaging in a dialogue with the subject. But the critical approach does not accept as sacrosanct the initial self-understandings of the subject, for it may well be the case that, in the course of the dialogue between the investigator and the subject, the latter comes to see that his original self-understanding was wrong in some fundamental way.

Does the critical approach establish the importance of normative theory within the social science, and of particular importance to us, within international relations? I contend that although it moves in the direction of legitimating normative theory, by and large it does not finally arrive at a point where it does so. Critical theorists are, I maintain, blocked from participating in normative debate because they are still victims of the bias towards objective explanation. In order to demonstrate this let me examine in some detail the major insights of critical theory and show how these are still influenced by the bias towards objective explanation.

First, critical theory claims that it is often the case that people's self-understandings are ideological. On this view people often hold sets of beliefs about how international politics works (together with beliefs which specify where they themselves fit into international politics) and these beliefs systematically mask from them the ways in which they are manipulated by power structures which disadvantage them. Critical theorists of this kind seek to reveal the structures of power which lead people to adhere to the ideology in question. As an example of this kind of writing, consider Justin Rosenberg's article "The International Imagination"[53] in which he argues, following C. Wright Mills, that classical social analysis is primarily concerned with just this kind of endeavour. It is concerned to make explicit the structures of power which block the realization of certain key values in society which the theorists take as being fundamental for both themselves and for society at large. In these inquiries the norms that are being frustrated are considered to be freedom and reason. Rosenberg advocates the application of this classical method to international relations. The work of theorists ought to be directed towards *explaining* the history and form of structures of power which block human progress to freedom.

A second insight of critical theorists is that international relations scholars often produce paradigms which, far from being neutral descriptions of what is happening "out there", are in fact instrumental in constituting the world order as we know it. The paradigms which include a normative component (realism, for example, has a built-in bias that the maintenance of a system of sovereign states is a good) play a role in maintaining and promoting that good. The role of critical theory then is to bring into view the norms which the supposedly "objective" explanatory theories uphold in the real world of international affairs. But what we need to notice is that this "unmasking" role of critical theory is itself supposed to be objective and explanatory. It is supposed to explain (objectively) just how realist theory, for example, upholds the status quo, (i.e. our present-day system of sovereign states). Here we see then that for critical theory explanation is still the fundamental goal of theory. Such theories are designed to expose the values which other theories tacitly promote. Being self-reflective, critical theorists would, of course, indicate what values their own theories advance. The focus, though, is still on explanation, and there is little or no attempt to engage in serious ethical argument.

A third strand to critical theory is a variant of the second. Critical theorists are aware that propounding a theory of world politics is itself an action in that domain. Thus they attempt to be open and "above board" about what values they are seeking to promote. Built into their explanations is an explanation of how their *explanans* will affect the *explanadum*. Once again, though, the focus is on explanation.

A fourth feature of critical approaches is that its adherents are committed to doing their research openly and in dialogue with the investigatees. They are opposed to secret research which may be used to give the ruling elite knowledge about how to manipulate the investigatees. Critical theorists espouse a normative commitment to a certain way of doing research, but the aim of the research is to explain in such a way that the explanation unmasks power relations. Such approaches do not call for the theorists to become involved in normative theory.

Escaping the bias: the place of normative theory in the discipline of international relations

There are indeed important differences between positivist social science, on the one hand, and the *Verstehen* and critical theory approaches, on the other. However, as I have outlined above they all seek primarily to explain what is happening in an objective way. Most social scientists, even the most positivistic, are to some extent aware that values may impinge on their inquiries and they diligently try to reveal these. Critical theorists are extremely diligent about indicating the different ways in which normative concerns enter into social research at a number of points. But for all that these theorists acknowledge normative concerns, they do not for the most part engage in serious normative theory. They believe that normative theory is a separate activity which they do not have to practise. It can, on their view, be left to a specialist class of political philosophers.

I wish to argue that there is no way in which social scientists may legitimately avoid becoming involved in normative theory.

Let me use as a starting point the insights of the interpretative approach. What we are dealing with in the first place in international relations are actions in the arena of world politics. These actions are the raw material to which scholars direct their attention. They are the raw material for scholars no matter what level of analysis they choose to work on, whether it be to study the individual citizen protesting American inaction in Bosnia, the State Department protesting the decisions of Congressional foreign affairs committees, or the British government's decision to send further troops to aid UN forces in former Yugoslavia. The analysis must always start with reference to individuals, bureaucracies, states, multinational corporations or international organizations *doing things*. There is no other place to begin doing social science with regard to international affairs. Whatever school, tradition or paradigm the scholar chooses to use after starting with an examination of these actions is irrelevant for my purposes. Realists, pluralists, structuralists (and all the others – empiricists, rationalists, Grotians, transnationalists, interdependence theorists, Marxists, neo-realists, and so on) all have to *start* their inquiries with reference to who is doing what to whom. Realists refer, for example, to states' preparations for, and declarations of, war. They then seek to explain these actions. Pluralists point beyond the state to the actions of other significant players on the world stage, such as transnational corporations and international organizations, and then explain the effects of these in world politics. Structuralists (like psychoanalysts in the realm of personal behaviour) start with the surface phenomena, that is the actions of those they are studying and then proceed to explain these with reference to deeper societal forces. But, come what may, they all start with the given and the given consists of actions.

Let us examine this starting point closely. In order to understand what is being done (or has been done) the investigator must, as was made clear in my discussion of *Verstehen*, understand the language of the actors, and, in order to do this, she must understand as a whole the social practice within which the action takes place. This in turn requires that she learn what would count as a mistake within that practice. Doing this will require of her that she understand the value systems of those active in the practice. *A close examination of this last step will reveal how the analyst cannot but become involved in substantive normative theory.*

The value systems of actors within the practices of international relations are not simply there, as it were, to be "read off" the face of the practice by the international relations scholar. For as often as not the participants in the practice are not themselves sure precisely what values are being realized by their actions taken individually (or what values are being advanced by their practice looked at as a whole). What the values underlying the practice are is often highly contested. The analyst cannot but become involved in this contested terrain.

To repeat, I am claiming that any form of explanation of international relations must start with an understanding of an action (or set of actions) and this requires that the action in question be understood. In order to do this the investigator must become involved in substantive normative theory. Let me show this by means of a hypothetical example.

Imagine an international relations scholar, let us call her Social Scientist, seeking to explain recent events in the former Yugoslavia. In particular she is called upon to focus on the conflict in Bosnia between the Bosnian Muslims, Bosnian Croats and Bosnian Serbs.[54] She has to start with some superficial account of who is doing what to whom in that area. (Where else could she start?) It obviously would not do for her to start with a vague statement to the effect that "Something is going on in Bosnia" and then proceed to give a realist, pluralist or structuralist explanation of that vague "something." "Deep" theories (whether they be systems theories, structural theories, Marxist structural theories, or whatever) always purport to explain some precisely defined set of social actions (e.g. these battles, this war, this incursion, this arms race, this secession) or some precisely defined series or class of actions (wars, incursions, arms races, secessions). But note that even if Social Scientist is concerned to do the latter (i.e. explain wars in general) she has to determine whether or not these acts in Bosnia constitute a war in terms of her general classification.

Whatever is happening in the ex-Yugoslav territories does not present itself to Social Scientist (or anyone else) in an unambiguous way. For what she is examining are actions and, as we have seen, these need to be interpreted. There are a number of possible interpretations. Which one she chooses to regard as the valid one will have a profound effect on whatever it is that she later claims to find beneath the surface in the realm of structures, systems and the like. The surface of an action is not like a bridge which stands unambiguously there with its supporting structure neatly attached underneath, with both clearly observable to the social scientist.

In order to determine who is doing what to whom in the former Yugoslavia, Social Scientist makes her way there and, following good *Verstehen* procedure, she interviews some of the people involved. Here are some of the different answers she might be given (I have included in parentheses after each, some "deep" questions about causes and structures which a social scientist might typically ask):

1. "What we are engaged in in Bosnia is a liberation struggle. We the Bosnian Croats are striving for the self-determination of our people. Our group has a primordial ethnic identity with a long and distinguished history. We have a distinct language, religion and culture of which we are rightfully proud. We are fighting for the rights of our nation." (What are the structural determinants of ethnicity?)

2. "In Bosnia, which is part of what was Yugoslavia, the old state apparatus has crumbled. There is no longer a civil service and the police cannot be relied on to protect us. There is a general condition of lawlessness. Certain strong men, call them 'warlords' if you like, have raised armies under an ethnic banner. They promise and deliver protection of a kind. I can see that they have contributed to the lawlessness, but nevertheless as things now stand they are the only power around which is able to provide me and my family with a modicum of order. So I have joined the Bosnian Croat group under General X and I am fighting to establish some resemblance of order in this chaos." (Why do states crumble and how are they built up again?)

3. "We Croats are fighting for the maintenance of civilized standards against an onslaught by a backward, primitive group led by the Serbs. This is another round of a fight that has been going on for centuries between civilization and barbarism." (What are the causes of the long cycles of violence between civilization and its enemies?)

4. "We the working class (or we women) in Bosnia are once again being dragged into a war not of our making and not in our interests. We are powerless to oppose the roles of soldier and wife that are imposed upon us by the structures of international capitalism and patriarchy." (What are the structures

which can get people to act in these ways which are so patently contrary to their interests?)

What we have here then is warlike action in Bosnia where those directly involved differ in their accounts about what it is they are doing.

Before Social Scientist can tackle any of the deep questions, she has to decide which of these insider accounts of the action immediately to hand is the correct one. She has to decide whether the people in Bosnia are fighting for their self-determination, are fighting for order in circumstances of anarchy, are fighting against barbarism, or are fighting under duress for the side they happen to find themselves on.

Which interpretation ought she to accept? Few social scientists (if any) would accept that an arbitrary choice would be acceptable.[55]

Similarly Social Scientist cannot simply choose/impose an interpretation without reference to what the actors think they are doing. This would be to throw overboard all the insights of the *Verstehen* approach to social investigation. We have seen that there are good reasons for taking the insider point of view seriously. The problem here, of course, is that from the insider point of view (in this case the Bosnian-Croat one) we have not one point of view, but many. How ought Social Scientist to proceed from here?

One insight from critical theory seems to me to be of particular relevance, viz. the insight that agents' self-understandings may be mistaken. Let me demonstrate the relevance of this insight by pursuing the hypothetical example further. Imagine Social Scientist (following the sound practice of the *Verstehen* school) going through an interview with a Croatian warlord. The warlord claims to be fighting for the liberation of the Croatian minority in Bosnia. Social Scientist establishes that the warlord certainly presents himself in this way in private, at public rallies, and through the media. But we can imagine Social Scientist quite plausibly being sceptical of this claim and questioning it. Through further questioning and investigation she might establish the following:

- That for forty years prior to the present events the people the warlord claims to speak for did not agitate for their own state. During this period they got on perfectly well with their Serb and Muslim neighbours, they cross-married, worked happily together in the civil service and in the police force, and voted together in national elections.
- That many people, on being questioned, showed that far from

being fervent nationalists they were puzzled and bemused by the sudden developments of these animosities.

- That the warlord in question started the present stage of hostilities by murdering people from his own nation who sought a compromise deal in the early stages of the dispute.

In the light of these findings Social Scientist might plausibly decide that in spite of what the warlord says he is doing (namely, leading a nationalist struggle) he is in fact better understood as an opportunist engaged in running a protection racket dressed up as a national liberation struggle. It is crucial to my argument to note that *the making of this judgement requires of Social Scientist that she have some idea about what counts as a genuine national liberation struggle. This in turn presupposes that Social Scientist has a rather full (and complex) normative theory which would have to include in it ideas about the link which ought to hold between nations and states, about when it is appropriate for a nation to secede from the state within which it finds itself, about what rights for minorities ought to be constitutionally protected within states, about the conflict between individual and group rights and about the ways in which these might be legitimately resolved (and a notion about identifying those extreme cases in which resort to force would be justified).*

In order to reinforce this point consider Social Scientist interviewing the Croats who make the claim that they are fighting for civilization in a battle against barbarism. Ought Social Scientist to simply accept their self-description to this effect (and reserve for herself the private evaluation that their claim is far fetched)? I contend that she cannot plausibly do this because what the Croats are saying to her is not "We think we are defending civilization and what you think is irrelevant." Rather they are asking Social Scientist (and all who read her work) to believe that what they are saying about the struggle in their country is true; they want Social Scientist (and everybody else who will listen to them) to believe this and to act on this belief in support of their cause. In other words Social Scientist is not simply called upon to listen to an account of how these people interpret their own actions. She is required to judge whether their claim is valid or not. Once again this requires Social Scientist's involvement in a rather sophisticated *normative* exercise which would involve her seeking answers to the following kinds of questions: What is civilization? What kinds of behaviour threaten it? What is the appropriate response of a civilized people to a threat to their civilization? (and so on). These are profoundly normative tasks and very complicated ones, too. They are not "add on" tasks to be taken up by Social Scientist after she has finished describing and explaining "the facts of the matter." The tasks have to be (and are) done (implicitly or explicitly) by Social Scientist at that point where she attempts to answer the question "Who is doing what, to whom, in Bosnia?"

What I have argued is that Social Scientist in this example, and international relations scholars generally, have to take normative positions, not as those blinded by the bias towards objective explanation would have it, *after* explanation has been completed, but *at the very outset* of their inquiries. Deep theories (such as structural analyses) have to be preceded by the giving of some description of the actions which the *subsequent* structural theory is to explain. It is my central assertion that this preliminary description of the actions to be explained requires sophisticated normative judgements. Involvement with normative theory proper (not vague references to freedom and reason) is called for before any structural analysis can take place.

My claim is not that social scientists do not presently do this and ought to start doing it now. It is rather that all social theorists start out with this rather thick normative engagement with the subject under investigation, but almost always the normative position is implicit and does not get spelled out or rationally defended. This, of course, opens up the possibility that the normative stance implicit in the inquiry is often "half baked," incoherent, full of internal contradictions and the like. It is high time that this state of affairs is remedied; that international relations theorists be required to spell out and defend the normative positions implicit in their descriptions of the actions which they seek to explain (be the actors individuals, groups or institutions such as states). International relations theorists for the most part do not do this (and are not required to do so) because they still live in the shadow of what I have called the bias towards objective explanation (especially its positivist form, according to which the facts of the matter can be determined and explained in a value-free way).

Conclusion

In this chapter I have argued that a major reason why normative theory has not been taken seriously in the discipline of international relations has to do with beliefs which theorists have held about what it is that distinguishes the practice of social science from the practice of normative theory. It has been widely believed that science is somehow more firmly grounded than normative theory. This belief is based on what I have called the bias towards positive social explanation in terms of which a good scientific explanation is in the final instance grounded in observable (and measurable) facts in a way that normative theory is not. What I have argued is that there are reasons to doubt this portrayal of the method of science, especially social science, and thus there are reasons to be sceptical about the shadow it casts on any serious engagement with normative theory. The main contention in this chapter is that the material which social scientists study is human actions (either individual or group) and that these actions cannot be simply observed but need to be understood. Doing this requires of the observer a sophisticated engagement with normative theory.

2 Sceptical and realist arguments against normative theory in international relations: a critical appraisal

Introduction

In the previous chapter I discussed in some detail the general positivist bias of much international relations theory as one of the main reasons for the lack of normative political theory in the discipline. I showed how positivism, and the fact/value dichotomy on which it rests, has come under serious attack in the philosophy of the social sciences and I showed how the main thrust of that attack indicates that it is not possible to do social science without to some extent becoming involved in arguments about the substantive issues in normative political theory. But this positivist bias of the discipline is only a partial explanation for the poverty of theory in this field. It is the aim of the present chapter to look at certain other common assumptions held by theorists in international relations which prevent their taking normative theory seriously. In particular I shall examine certain pervasive assumptions regarding the nature, status and use of substantive value judgements and moral theory in international relations.

There can be little doubt that most scholars in the field of international relations do not consider substantive moral arguments and normative theory to be a worthwhile endeavour and consider them to be suspect in certain ways. If asked to give reasons for their scepticism with regard to normative argument and theorizing, the answer would most likely be something akin to the following. Such theories are *soft* in that they fail to take account of the realities of international relations. A main contention of the present chapter will be that when normative theory is thus accused of being "soft" it is often far from clear of what precisely this softness is supposed to consist. I wish to argue that when the charges are isolated and examined they fail to stand up to scrutiny.

The arguments considered in this chapter may all be comprehended under the general rubric of sceptical arguments. Yet they are sceptical in different ways. Some are sceptical about the epistemological status of normative arguments, while others derive their scepticism from other than epistemological considerations. Yet others are sceptical about the applicability and relevance of normative theory irrespective of its epistemological status. It will be the aim of this chapter to consider the underlying problematic and the proper implications of this charge of moral scepticism.

In order to indicate some of the diverse ways in which scepticism about normative theory has been expressed in international relations let us start with a long list of its alleged shortcomings:

1. Value judgements simply express the theorists' own attitudes, whims, emotions, tastes, etc.
2. The propositions of normative theory are not capable of being true or false because there are no normative facts.
3. Normative theories cannot be verified or falsified in the same way that scientific theories, properly so called, can be.
4. Theories about the way the world ought to be are produced by the world as it is. They are epiphenomena of the way the world is. They cannot guide the world, but rather serve as *post hoc* rationalizations.
5. Normative theories are utopian and cannot be realized in practice.
6. In the real world of sovereign states, each state seeks to maximize its power unfettered by considerations of principle. In such a world, normative theory is otiose, for the pursuit of power by states is not governed by norms.
7. So-called normative theories are themselves practices of power which individuals (and states) use to secure their own advantage. Such theories cannot be construed as rational constraints on power.
8. In the actual world there are diverse sovereign states and a multiplicity of moral orders. This in itself rules out the possibility of a universally agreed normative theory of international relations which would in fact require a universal world order maintained by a single all-powerful sovereign.
9. In their relations with one another sovereign states use normative arguments as tools of policy. States will always find some

normative rationalization to suit whatever purposes they have. Thus the only worthwhile investigation to be done concerns the effectiveness of different normative theories as rationalizations. The question of the truth or falsity of the norms invoked is irrelevant.

10. The system of states is one way of organizing relations between groups of people and is different from a moral practice which is a kind of ordering which exists between people as individuals. The ordering principles of a state system are quite incompatible with those involved in a moral order properly so called. Consider the following typical differences:

   a. A typical moral order will sometimes require people to act against their self-interest in specified situations. A morality which *always* coincided with one's own interests would not be recognized as a morality at all. In sharp contrast to such moral constraints, the practice of international relations assumes that governments will generally pursue the self-interest of the state. Governments will generally not sacrifice national interest for the sake of some high principle.

   b. Several moral orders take the well-being of individuals as the ultimate value, whereas the rules of international practice demand that reasons of state take priority over reasons referring to the well-being of individuals. Indeed, in terms of the accepted practice of international relations states are often called upon to sacrifice the well-being of individuals for the good of the state within the system of states.

   c. A further example of the difference between the reason of states and moral reasoning is that a requirement of the latter is that individuals ought to be treated equally. In international relations statesmen are required to benefit their own citizens, often at the expense of others, viz. foreigners. The interests of foreigners are often not considered equally or not brought into the equation at all.

   d. All moralities count honesty as a virtue, but in international relations governments are often called upon to use deceit. This is considered justified if it serves the self-interest of the state.

     e. Moral reasoning typically requires that people be treated as ends and not as means to desired ends. States often act contrary to this principle where this is required by the over-riding interest of the state.

     f. Moral reasoning requires that agents act on principle and not for the sake of expediency. Within the system of states this principle does not make sense.

This list does not claim to be exhaustive, but it is quite sufficient to reveal the diverse ways in which it may be alleged that norma-tive theory in international relations is not worthy of serious con-sideration and of the various forms which scepticism about the status and use of moral discourse can take within this discipline. The arguments in the list can usefully be classified into the follow-ing three broad categories. First, there are the arguments that make philosophical claims about the status of normative assertions (items 1–3 on the list). Second, there are arguments about the relationship between normative theories and political practice (items 4–9). Third, there are arguments about the supposed distinctions between the rules guiding behaviour within the sphere of private morality and the rules guiding behaviour in the sphere of international politics (item 10 on the list). These different kinds of argument against normative theory in international relations are often run into each other and are rarely separated out. Let us now evaluate each of the three broad classes of argument in turn.

Non-cognitivism as the philosophical basis for scepticism about Normative Theory

Objections 1–3 – those regarding the philosophical status of value judgements – are not confined to the discipline of international relations but may be seen as applicable to normative discourse generally. Thus someone who is convinced by sceptical arguments that value judgements cannot be true or false and thus have no cognitive substance will be convinced of the worthlessness of moral arguments generally and not merely as they pertain to international relations.[1] A proper discussion of the issues raised by such value non-cognitivism would involve a major work in meta-ethical theory which is beyond the scope of the present study. Here we shall concentrate on one or two central issues.

Amoralism as a consequence of moral scepticism

The core of all non-cognitivist positions is that about matters of value (in sharp contrast to the position about matters of fact) there can be no truth of the matter. The moral sceptic then proceeds to draw certain implications from this conclusion. I shall evaluate scepticism indirectly by examining this second step first. Let us start by considering one possible implication of non-cognitivism, viz. the amoralist implication. The amoralist implication follows directly from the denial of cognitive status to value judgements: if about matters of value there is no truth or falsity to be had, then an actor is warranted in ignoring traditional moral injunctions and following the dictates of self-interest or prudence or, indeed, any other imperative at all. The core of amoralism, then, is that any reasons are good reasons for action. A person convinced by the amoralist position would deny that an actor ought to be bound by rules of the form "in situation X you ought to do Y." Although the amoral attitude is not often found among individuals, it is often supposed that it is well displayed in international relations. It is often said that in the real world states have no reason to follow rules of the form "In situation X states ought to do Y," except where it is in their national interest to do so. This latter constraint is hardly considered a constraint at all, for states may determine what is to count as the national interest as they will.

Bernard Williams shows that on closer scrutiny a consistent amoralist individual could hardly be considered a sane man, for a consistent amoralist may pursue his own whims but his philosophy precludes him from ever criticizing the behaviour of others on moral grounds.[2] He may not claim to have been wronged on grounds of unfairness, injustice, deceit, cruelty, and so on. All he can say in terms of the logic of his own philosophy is that he likes some of the things which happen to him and dislikes some of the others. Notice that if the amoralist tries to avoid these consequences of his position by saying, "I am not bound by moral rules, but I expect others to be," then his case is lost because he must then be arguing a moral position with special permissions built in it for him. The amoralist might find it in his interests to encourage others to believe themselves bound by moral rules whereas he, himself, is not. However, he cannot make serious moral judgements about others if they, too, would deny that these moral constraints apply to them. It is difficult to conceive of a person who never claimed to have been wronged, unjustly treated and so on, for it is part of our conception of a person that he/she is a being who makes this type of claim for him or herself.

Does the argument applied to the individual case discussed above have the same force when applied to states?[3] Would it also be a contradiction in terms for a state to be consistently amoralist? Try to picture a practising amoralist state. It could, by definition, never level charges of unfair, unjust, deceitful, inhuman (and so on) actions against other states. If it did so it would have to acknowledge that such charges were mere posturing and empty moralizing. Conversely, it would have to deny the validity of any similar charges against itself, not as being wrong, but as pointless. It is patent that states in general are not overtly amoralist in this way. In their dealings with one another they talk the language of right conduct; they abide by the conventional discourse of international relations. For example there are disputes about "hot pursuit" raids. Typically such raids are justified as necessary for the maintenance of national security or condemned as unwarranted violations of the sovereignty of a neighbouring state; they are depicted in terms of justifiable self-defence or as unjustifiable aggression. There is often disagreement between states about what constitutes right conduct in a particular situation or about what the proper standards of right conduct are. But of the fact that all states acknowledge that there are some standards of right conduct there can be no doubt.

Might it not be the case that states are all covertly amoral?[4] This suggestion, although initially plausible, will not stand up to critical inquiry. The charge by state A that it has been wronged by state B (even if it is made hypocritically) will only be meaningful if it is the case that there exists a practice in which the alleged wrong is generally recognized as a wrong and if both A and B are members of that practice in which it is recognized in this way. Consider the rule "States ought not to invade the boundaries of other states except under the following specified conditions . . .". Appeals to this standard, even hypocritical ones, can only be made because, in general, it actually is accepted as a binding norm within the practice of states. Hypocritical appeals to the norm are dependent on a non-hypocritically adhered to practice. In short, the occasional act of covert amoralism is dependent on the existence of a functioning and open moral practice.

Finally, someone arguing for the amoralist position with regard to states might argue that states find the whole practice of right conduct an expedient fiction. Whenever they appeal to moral norms of right and wrong, they are actually merely acting *as if they were moral*. This argument fails because it misunderstands the connection we have been trying to establish between being a state and recognizing rules of right conduct for states. The hypocritical state argument suggests that there are entities called states which can be conceived of as choosing to pretend to play the game of right conduct for a state. My argument is that it is not possible to conceive of something as a state independently of its making and recognizing claims based on some code of right conduct. Recognizing such rules and being recognized in terms of them is what is involved in being a state. Those arguing the case which I have been attacking need to give some plausible account of what the state is, which account does not contain within it any reference to rules of right conduct (such as the right of sovereign control over a given territory, the right to declare war and the right to make treaties, etc.) I do not think that this is possible. In chapter 5 I discuss in some detail the way in which the notion of statehood is situated within the context of a set of rules within which the parties reciprocally recognize one another in specified ways.

We may summarize this section thus: the person or state who acted as a consistent amoralist would not be recognizable as a person or state properly so called. This does not imply that all individuals and all states are at all times moral. It also does not imply that any specific moral stance is the right one. What is being argued is that individuals and states must have *some* moral position, for having such a position is partially constitutive of what being a person or being a state is.

The compatibility of non-cognitivist scepticism and serious moral argument

There is a philosophical position which is non-cognitivist with regard to the epistemological status of moral discourse, but which does not draw an amoralist conclusion from the non-cognitivist premise. An example of this form of moral scepticism is provided by John Mackie in his book *Ethics: Inventing Right and Wrong*.[5] He is concerned to defend the proposition that there are no objective values. His argument is primarily ontological. He states, "Values are not objective, are not part of the fabric of the world."[6] As reasons for this conclusion he appeals to what he calls the argument from diversity (which asserts that since there is such a multiplicity of moralities in the world, it is implausible to suppose that there is a single true morality) and to the argument from queerness (which says that if there were objective values they would have to be entities, qualities or relations in the world which could only be seen by some special "queer" faculty quite out of the ordinary).[7] However, Mackie's scepticism does not preclude the possibility of serious argument about values between people who share certain basic premises. But where disputes about these fundamental premises arise there is no objective base which may be referred to in order to settle the matter. This sceptical position is put forward against Plato, Kant and Sidgwick, amongst others.

Scepticism of this type is perfectly compatible with conventional moral behaviour (where such behaviour includes having serious moral arguments). Indeed, John Mackie in his book reaches certain substantive moral conclusions. It is thus possible to have moral beliefs and to adhere to a moral code based on them while at the same time being sceptical about the ultimate ontological status of moral statements.

A crucial question is what (if any) normative implications follow from a non-cognitivist position like Mackie's? An important implication is hinted at in the subtitle of his book which refers to "inventing right and wrong." If values are not objective, then they must be man-made. It is this implication which is unacceptable to many and leads to the general belief that serious theorizing about values is not worthwhile. Is this scepticism justified?

I have already indicated that it is quite possible to be a sceptic and consider oneself bound by a moral code. Still, non-cognitive scepticism of this kind easily gives rise to the supposition that if there is no ultimate objective standard in terms of which moral propositions may be judged true or false, then ultimately moral judgements must be *subjective*. Scepticism about values then allegedly commits one to a moral subjectivism. Finally and crucially, this is then taken to warrant an "anything goes" approach to life and to the conduct of affairs in international relations as well; it is seen as a warrant for amoralism. What we have here is an unwarranted slide from a non-cognitivist epistemology to an amoralist position.

It is easy to see what dire consequences this belief could have within the discipline of international relations. First, on this view there could be no serious discussions of right and wrong with regard to international conduct. Second, there could be no argument with the view (widely held in international relations) that might makes right.

The link between non-cognitivism and subjectivist amoralism is not warranted. There are ways in which an assertion may not be ultimately traceable to an objective basis, yet may still not be *merely* subjective. We have already seen one way in which this may be so. A value judgement may be validated or invalidated in terms of a set of premises held in common by a group of people. These premises may not be, in any ontological sense, true, but simply be premises to which the people involved are committed. Here I want to argue as I did earlier that what is involved in being a person or being a state cannot be explicated without some reference to a common commitment to some such set of shared normative principles – be it a liberal Western set or a primitive tribal one.[8] We would not recognize as a person someone who did not claim that certain kinds of conduct towards him/her were right whereas others were wrong, and who did not recognize similar claims against him/her in terms of a conventionally shared morality. The same point applies to states. As a matter of fact we find all people and all states making just such judgements about their own and others' conduct. It is in the making of such judgements that moral disputes arise. Subjectivism (amoralism) consistently maintained would have to hold that ordinary moral practice is nonsensical, based on a lie, or some such thing. I have already indicated how any suggestion that individuals and states may be seen as hypocritically moral may be countered.[9]

A sceptic may well be prepared to accept this argument against the subjectivist position, but argue that although his scepticism does not imply subjectivism, it does imply *relativism*. The relativist position is that the moral discussions all take place within and are relative to a specific moral practice. Within such a practice there is a wide base of mutually agreed upon premises. The arguments within such a practice are about the application of those premises to a given situation. Thus some statement of a moral position may be shown to be true or false *relative* to the basic premises held in common by the disputants within the practice. But where inter-practice disputes arise there can be no truth of the matter.[10] Applied to international relations this line of reasoning leads to the following kind of conclusion. We can conceive of moral disputes among liberal politicians and statesmen. Such disputes may be inter-subjectively settled by reference to the conventions to which in fact all liberals are committed. Similarly there may be disputes among messianic statesmen open to inter-subjective tests. But there are no objective standards for settling any disputes between members of the two groups. For the relativists there thus comes a stage in moral argument at which conflicting bedrock positions are reached and that is when the dispute transcends the shared conventions.

Sometimes a normative consequence is drawn from this relativist position, viz. that since there are no objective standards for settling inter-practice disputes we ought to be tolerant of the norms and behaviour of those in practices other than our own.[11] What we have here is a relativist attempt to avoid the amoralist implications of relativism. The problem with this conclusion is that it is a non-relative *moral* prescription made by a relativist. Why should we make the jump from the lack of a standard of truth to the moral requirement of tolerance? The relativist's own premises undercut the conclusion urging tolerance. For when the relativist says that we ought to be tolerant, this "ought" must, on his own premises, be a relative "ought." It cannot apply across practices because the situation as defined excludes inter-practice agreement.

Before considering what conclusions may properly be drawn from the sceptical/relativist thesis, there is one other mistaken conclusion that must be noted. This is the conclusion that because there are so many different moral practices and because there is so little consensus between them, people are justified in withdrawing into a general apathy. Here there is an unwarranted jump from non-cognitivism to a form of amoralism.[12] It does not follow from the sceptical position asserting that there are no ontological moral truths and from the fact that there exist diverse moral practices that there are good reasons for being apathetic. If we take relativism seriously there is just as much reason (viz. no reasons) to be the opposite of apathetic (which presumably involves being fanatical in some way). Neither an injunction to be tolerant nor a permission to be apathetic is a necessary consequence of relativism. What may be correctly drawn from the sceptical/relativist thesis is the conclusion that where there is an inter-practice dispute there is no guarantee that a right answer will, in the fullness of time, be found. There is, by definition, no agreement on the criteria for the right answer. If agreement is to be achieved it will have to be created (made) between the disputants. However, this does not imply, for the reasons already given, that we are obliged to accept subjectivism.[13]

Saying that moralities have to be built does not imply that the building of a morality is not a worthwhile activity, nor that we ought to refrain from morality building and concern ourselves with more important tasks (like the search for truth through scientific method). It is arguable that we have to do *some* morality building if things are not to go badly with us. This is the *constructivist* implication of the sceptical/relativist thesis. In so far as moralities are invented or built they are designed to overcome certain problems which people face in society. For example, any group of people will need some shared morality if they are to cooperate together to achieve those goods which cannot be achieved without cooperation, (maintaining security, upholding property relations, regulating sexual relations and so on). Moralities are answers to predicaments which any society faces. A conflict of moralities is itself such a predicament for which a moral answer must be created.

Let us stand back and look at the argument thus far. We have been evaluating the argument that scepticism about morals undercuts all serious theorizing about values. Without considering the positive arguments for scepticism about values I sought to show that amoralism (which is sometimes taken to be a consequence of non-cognitivism) cannot be coherently maintained in practice. Subsequently I argued that non-cognitivism concerning the ontological status of value judgements does not warrant or imply amoralism, tolerance or apathy. Such scepticism is quite compatible with serious theorizing about questions of value in all disciplines including international relations.

Thus far I have not done any substantive theorizing with regard to the evaluation of different normative theories in international relations. I have merely been concerned to show that scepticism about the existence of objective moral values does not entail that normative theory is pointless or worthless. More positively, two things have emerged from the discussion: first, there are many human predicaments which cannot be solved without the building of a normative order. Human flourishing depends on the creation of such orders. Second, the creation of such orders requires the participation of the people involved in the dispute. In sum, then, non-cognitivism establishes certain ways in which normative arguments are different from arguments about facts. It does not establish that normative argument is not worthwhile.

51

Realist arguments against normative theory in international relations

Realist arguments based on the primacy of the structure of world society

There is a widespread tendency in the discipline of international relations to eschew explicit discussion of normative issues on the ground that such thought is derivative from the structure of social reality and is thus of secondary importance. (Indeed, on this view, normative theory is derivative from the structures of the real world.) Normative theory always presupposes that actors in the practice of international relations do have alternatives and real choices, and can change their conduct. Only if we accept these presuppositions do ought-statements in the context of international relations make sense. Similarly, normative theory in international relations presupposes that the international order itself can be deliberately changed in specified ways. In short then, normative theory presupposes that there is an important sense in which people's normative ideas can shape the order in which they live. It is this presupposition which is often regarded as suspect in the discipline of international relations – for many scholars in the field (be they balance-of-power theorists, inter-dependence theorists or neo-Marxists) see themselves in some broad sense as "hard-headed realists." They are extremely wary of the notion that it is possible in the realm of international relations for people's notions about what is normatively acceptable to shape the order in which they live.[14] Normative theorizing is dismissed as utopian thinking ("soft," "tender-minded").[15]

If it is the case in international relations that people's normative ideas do not play any major part in shaping the international order in which they live, there must be implicit in this general position some other view of the link between political reality and normative ideas. The general assumption implicit in such "realist" view is that the normative ideas people have are determined by the general structure of the social and political reality in which they find themselves. There is an underlying notion that the political structures are "autonomous" in some sense. They are "autonomous" in so far as they are supposed to be independent of the normative ideas held by those in the international practice and not able to be changed by these ideas. This is clearly one pole of opinion in the well-known structure versus agency debate.

The nature of the underlying structures is portrayed differently in different theories. In political realism the fundamental structure is the structure of political power. In interdependence theory it is the international economic system which is presented as the determining basis of world politics. Marxist structuralists have an alternative vision of an underlying economic structure, understood in class terms, which determines all other social phenomena. But in their understandings of what structures are, these approaches are remarkably similar, as we shall see below.

In what way is the structure of the social reality supposed to be independent of normative ideas and in what way does this supposed autonomy have a bearing on the worth of normative theory? The precise nature of this structure is a core problem for all the theories mentioned. Although there is clearly some assumption about the primacy of these structures and although it is assumed that the nature of the structures has a bearing on the worth of normative argument, it is far from clear what the positive content of these assumptions about the autonomous/determining/underlying social "reality" is. Yet it is possible to give an approximation of its general features.

First, society as a whole is conceived of as some sort of social system. A system may be defined as a set of parts which are interdependent in certain specified ways. There are wide variations in the way that different theorists conceive of the social system. Some conceive of it as a whole within which there is a general equilibrium between the parts. According to one such model the modern world is an emergent system of technological and economic interdependence between peoples. Within the context of state-bound economies it is no longer possible to sustain economic growth. Growth can only be sustained where new patterns of cooperation between states develop. This ever more complicated pattern of interdependence will have the effect of making the sovereign states, as we know them, increasingly less sovereign, less independent. There will thus emerge from this process a new form of world polity to replace the system of sovereign states.[16] Other theories each operate with their own different concept of system. Historical materialist theories argue that there is indeed a global system of interrelated parts, but the parts, far from existing in a state of harmonious equilibrium, are pictured as being in a process of change caused by fundamental contradictions within the system.

The reference here is, of course, to Marxist and neo-Marxist accounts of the international order, and to theories of imperialism, neo-colonialism, underdevelopment and the like.[17]

Second, it is supposed that the way in which the system operates is independent of any single person or group of people's wishes.[18]

Third, it is supposed that the actors in the system are, in some sense, determined by it. Both their behaviour and their thoughts (what they tend to do and the prescriptive rules/norms specifying what they ought to do) are in some way determined by the underlying structure. The implications for normative theory now become clear. On this view the system determines the ideas (including the normative/ethical ones) which people have. Normative theorizing can thus not be of any importance; the system operates independently of such theories and itself determines whatever operative normative notions arise. As I said at the outset, normative theory always presupposes that it is possible for actors, guided by their normative ideas, to change the order in which they live in significant ways. If it is the other way about, i.e. if their normative ideas are determined by the underlying structure, clearly normative theory is of little consequence. At best it is enjoyable for its own sake, as an art.

There are many examples of this way of thinking. Let us look at two: one an equilibrium model and one a system-in-conflict model. The equilibrium model is the one presented by Kenneth Waltz in his now classic *Theory of International Politics*.[19] In this work he develops a theme he himself had made famous in an earlier work.[20] There he had stressed the need for different levels of analysis in international relations. A narrow focus on either the individual or on the state – although both are important levels of analysis – would not permit a full explanation of international phenomena, unless it was supplemented with a systems-level analysis. This three-levels-of-analysis approach is widely accepted within the discipline. But for Waltz it is the systems level of analysis which is primary. Without it a proper analysis of the other two levels would not be possible. His *Theory of International Politics* is devoted to further exploration of this fundamental level – the systems level.[21]

A systems theory, Waltz says, is one which explains the interactions between the parts of the system without reference to the specific character of these parts. It would explain war in general without referring to any particular states or state leaders. Crucial to the enterprise is the notion of *structure*. It is the underlying structure of international affairs which, in Waltz's view, is a primary determinant of the actions of states and individuals within states. What is a structure? It is distinct from a *device*, which is something consciously designed to produce a given result. A structure is not a direct cause, but acts as a set of constraining conditions – as a selector.[22] Systems (composed of structures) are thus supposed to emerge from our interactions without our intending them. Once they have emerged they constrain our actions. The market is such a system. The international order between states is another one. Notice that what is crucial for Waltz is that structures not only develop spontaneously and are unintended, but serve as determining constraints on our actions and our intentions. Once developed, structures reward and punish actors according to whether these actors uphold the system or not.[23] It is clear that Waltz envisages the structure of the international system as being, in some sense, the fundamental determinant of world politics – as being in some way independent of the ideas people happen to have. The international order as a structure of this kind is thus assumed as some kind of basic political "reality" and it is, moreover, one which clearly diminishes the possible relevance of normative theory.

Historical materialism, too, is a theory in terms of which there is a determining and in some sense autonomous base which determines the ideas of the participants in international affairs. Although there has been and continues to be an extended debate about the proper definition of historical materialism, there is little doubt that most scholars pursuing the historical materialist method would agree that "world society emerges in this view not as a consequence of 'power' relations or decision-making routines or the rest of the paraphernalia of a traditional approach, but as a function of or reaction to the world economy."[24] As an example of historical materialist method applied to international relations, let us look briefly at Lenin's theory of imperialism.

Lenin sought not merely to explain the First World War, but to provide a general theory of why wars occur in the modern capitalist world. His aim was thus very similar to that which later inspired Waltz to develop his systems-level analysis. Lenin's view sees the capitalist world order as being shot through with fundamental contradictions which will in the long run lead to the demise of that system. In Lenin's classic work on this topic, *Imperialism the Highest Stage of Capitalism*, he argued that capitalism in the modern world has taken on a significant new form. It has left the free-market phase and has entered the monopoly phase. There are four main features of this phase. First, production cartels or monopolies were formed within the major capitalist countries of the world. These monopolies seized control of the most important sources of raw materials within these states. Second, the role of the banks changed significantly. Instead of being modest middle men through which funds could be channelled they became monopolistic controllers of finance capital. Third, as a result of this formation of monopolies in business and banking, there arose a surplus of capital in capitalist states for which new avenues of investment had to be found. Opportunities for investing this surplus were found in the colonies. Fourth, because the major capitalist countries were all seeking outlets for their surplus capital and the available territories for expansion were limited, these countries came into competition with one another in their imperialist project. It is this imperialist competition which explains the outbreak of wars in the modern world. The First World War is shown, according to this theory, to have been a war "for the division of the world, for the partition and repartition of colonies and spheres of influence of finance capital, etc."[25] Lenin referred to empirical data to show that the businesses and banks of the capitalist powers had become increasingly monopolistic during the latter half of the nineteenth century and early twentieth century. The accuracy and details of these contentions need not concern us here. For my purposes it is the way in which he portrayed the link between the underlying processes of capitalism and the political results thereof which is relevant. "The capitalists divide the world not out of any *malice*, but because the degree of concentration which has been reached *forces* them to adopt this method in order to get profits."[26] A few lines later he wrote:

> The epoch of the latest stage of capitalism shows us that certain relations between capitalist associations grow up, *based* on the economic division of the world: while parallel to and in connection with it, certain relations grow up between political alliances, between states, on the basis of the territorial division of the world, of the struggle for colonies, of the "struggle for spheres of influence."[27]

For Lenin the political aspects of imperialism are thus a necessary outcome of the basic economic processes at work. He argued vehemently against those such as Hobson and Kautsky who denied the "inevitability of imperialism."[28] He wrote: "Whatever the political system, the result of these tendencies is everywhere reaction and an extreme intensification of antagonisms in this field. Particularly intensified become the yoke of national oppression and the striving for annexation."[29] The annexations revolutionized the existing social relations in the colonies. At the same time hostility to the annexations was generated, leading to the rise of nationalism in those areas which would become increasingly hostile to domination by the capitalist powers. Here then, we see a contradiction emerging which was predicted to lead to important changes in the future.[30]

The brief outline given here of Lenin's historical materialist account of the international order during the "highest stage of capitalism" is sufficient to indicate how Lenin envisaged the basic capitalist structure of world society as the *primary determinant* of the actions of citizens and states alike. On this view, what happens comes about not through people deciding what morally ought to be done and then setting about doing what morality dictated, but rather through contradictions within the system becoming more and more sharply defined until some form of revolution results. This is not to say that there is within this theoretical perspective no room left for agency. Lenin was a consummate political activist as shown by his famous piece entitled *What is to be Done?*[31] But the "ought" in this title is not indicative of any moral imperatives; rather Lenin's deliberation was of a technical nature, i.e. it was about the best means to be used to achieve agreed ends.

Lenin's is, of course, not the only historical materialist account of the international order. There are other more recent examples of this approach to international affairs.[32] These more recent examples are not all of a piece. There are important and sustained disputes between the different theorists. Yet they are all similar in so far as they assert that it is the basic economic structure of society which in the last instance determines what happens in the political, moral, religious and cultural spheres. A superstructure of religious, moral and political ideas is determined by the economic base. A too crude view of this relationship is nowadays characterized as "vulgar Marxism" and rejected as an erroneous interpretation of Marx. Nevertheless, even the non-vulgar theories hold that in the last instance the relations of production are determining of the super-structural elements of society.[33] A feature of these approaches is that normative ideas are characterized as ideological, which is taken to mean justifying the existing relations of production.[34] On this view, ideology is non-autonomous thought; it is thought which reflects the base structure, or rationalizes it, or which is in some or other way an automatic response to it. In such a vision of the world order there is little room for any autonomous normative theory.

We have been looking at theoretical approaches to international relations, which because they rely on an underlying notion of a determining basic structure, seem to make normative theory otiose. This notion of a pre-normative basic structure is seriously flawed in that it wrongly supposes that the underlying determining structure (base, system, etc.) is independent of norms; i.e. it wrongly supposes that there is a structure (base, system, etc.) which could be identified without reference to the normative ideas of those participating in it. If it can be shown that all, so called, basic structures are themselves largely constituted by sets of normative ideas, then the whole determination thesis must fail. It can be easily shown that normative notions necessarily enter into any description of the supposed determining structure of society; normative theory cannot be avoided in any attempt to identify or articulate such a structure.

Consider Waltz's characterization of the international system. Its primary units are, he says, states. But a state is not a political reality that exists independently of the ideas and norms which people adhere to. In like manner, a system of states does not exist independently of the ideas and norms of the people involved. Amongst other things the existence of a state always implies the existence of a group of people who are in some way bound together, in large part, by a set of normative commitments and obligations. There could be no such thing as a state without people adhering to such obligations. Against this it might be argued that a state is not wholly (or always) a consensual arrangement in which people see themselves as bound together by mutually accepted rules; a state often rests on coercive elements.[35] Although it is true that states are not all based on consensus, this objection misses the point. For us to call a given arrangement a state it must be the case that there exists a practice within which the participants recognize themselves as members of a state and that they recognize certain of these members as forming a government having the authority to make laws which are binding upon them.[36] In order to recognize themselves in these ways the people involved must acknowledge certain rules.[37]

A critic may argue at this point that I am paying insufficient attention to the whole question of *power*. Further, it may be argued that my account ignores (or seriously underplays) the fact that people are often *forced* to obey the rules (laws) of a practice (be it a game or a political arrangement like the state or the system of states) and that this oversight on my part allows me to present norms as more important than they are. Now, of course, I would not deny that people are often forced into social practices of one kind of another. For example, the Romans forced slaves to participate in gladiatorial contests, i.e., forced them to participate in this rule-governed practice. Indeed, this would be a second coercive act following the first in which free people were forced to become slaves (which is itself a rule-governed mode of participation in a social practice). But the point to notice is that these acts of coercion were done by a powerful practice (namely the Roman state) which cannot be understood without some insight into the rules in terms of which the Romans constituted themselves into this powerful social form. It may well subsequently turn out to be the case that people relating to one another in terms of the constitutive rules of a given practice (like a state or a market economy) might produce certain systematic unintended results which constrain what they can do, i.e. their behaviour in terms of the rules may have certain structural effects on their future conduct, but such structural effects are consequences of the initial norm-bound behaviour, not the other way about.

In order to make this point most forcefully, my critic might ask us to consider the following imaginary case in which a very powerful group of people *forces* a less powerful group to participate in the practice (game) of gladiator fighting. This "game" is played by putting a gladiator in a ring with a hungry lion. The rules are: if the gladiator stays alive for five minutes he is rewarded by being given a club as a weapon. If he then kills the lion straight away (thus depriving the audience of a good fight) the club is taken away and a fresh lion is brought in. But if instead of killing the lion straight off, he manages to keep the fight going for half an hour before killing it, the gladiator is set free. The "game" thus depends on the players recognizing and abiding by the rules. My critic concedes that there is a sense in which this game is constituted by the ideas which the participants (gladiators and spectators) have of it, but he/she stresses that this game (this set of ideas) was *forced* upon the gladiators by the stronger group.

To recapitulate I do not wish to suggest that all practices (including the one we call the state) are voluntarily entered into or based on consensus. Nor is it my aim to make the notion of power obsolete. My point is that wherever reference is made to a *structure* (or base, or system) which is said to force people to act and think in certain ways, this structure itself cannot be identified without reference to some social practice which consists of people bound together by some set of constitutive ideas which guides the actions of those participating in it. Thus Waltz cannot give an account of the structure of a system of sovereign states without (if only implicitly) referring to the ideas whereby the people involved come to see themselves as members of sovereign states within a system of sovereign states. Similarly, neo-Marxist theory cannot give an account of a determining economic base of society without referring to the normative ideas in terms of which the people involved constitute themselves as participants in a market, which in turn involves them recognizing one another as occupying various positions within a given set of property relations. Relevant here are notions of private property, contract, and so on.

The central point, then, is that participating in a practice (be it a game or a political arrangement) requires that the participants recognize themselves as bound by a set of rules; that is, as bound by certain norms. Thus where a state exists there must be a group of people who see themselves as constituting a state through their mutual recognition of a specified set of rules. In this sense, then a state consists of a group of people recognizing one another as bound by a specified formation of rules. Thus (and here I return to the main point of the present argument) a state is not a political reality which exists independently of the ideas (including normative ones) to which people adhere.

I am arguing that states are constituted by people mutually recognizing one another as reciprocally bound by a certain set of rules. The argument is that no coherent account of the structure of the state can be given without referring to this practice of mutual recognition: the set of ideas and rules constituting the civil and political relationships between them. If the argument is sound then the evaluation of these rules – which activity I have called normative theory – is clearly of cardinal importance.

The argument above must not be taken as suggesting that the current state of the world is an intentional product of some person or group. Nor is it being argued that *any* arrangement people might wish to see in the world can necessarily be brought about. Similarly it is not being denied that the unintended consequences of multiple past actions will influence people's future thought. What is being asserted is that a highly relevant and indeed constitutive feature of social wholes is the set of norms to which the participants adhere. Thus it follows that normative argument and theory must be of central importance in social (and *a fortiori* in international) life.

A critic may retort that all I have established is the centrality of ideas in social wholes, but that this is not the same as establishing the need for normative *argument*, for propaganda can weld a society together just as well. A partial answer to this is that propaganda is parasitic on proper argument.[38] The "arguments" of the propagandist "piggy back," as it were, on practices of sound argument, just as the distorted uses which advertisers make of certain words derive their power from ordinary sound usages. The other part of the answer will be found within the following section in which a different kind of realist argument against normative theory is considered.

Realist arguments from the primacy of power

At its most general, the conventional doctrine of *political realism* asserts the primacy of power over reason. The political realist is not primarily concerned with the logical or epistemological status of normative propositions; he is not concerned whether such propositions may be said to be true or false. The political realist asserts that even if normative theories are in some ontological/objective sense true, normative theorizing is not worthwhile, because what the theories prescribe can and will always be overridden by those with the power to do so. Consider international relations. The realist argument is that even if it were possible to establish how states ought to behave towards one another, the problem of getting states to behave in that way would still remain. The statement of a reasonable position does not bring about a reasonable order. What is needed, the political realist argues, is the power to implement that order. But, the argument continues, power is not a neutral instrument which can be attained and put to use for good or for evil. Power has its own imperatives which those seeking to gain or maintain power must follow. A power seeker who ignores these and sets out to implement some or other desired normative order does so at his peril, for the imperatives of power are given and he who disobeys these "realities" will either fail to gain power or lose the power he has.

It is easy to see how this line of argument leads to the conclusion that normative theory in international relations is not a worthwhile activity. For on this view, power is required for the implementation of *any* desired order in international affairs, but what is required for the *maintenance* of power is not dependent on the truth or falsity of a particular normative theory. Indeed, the requirements of power often run counter to what is considered an acceptable normative code. The imperatives of power make normative theory otiose.

Modern political realism in international relations may be seen as a reaction to earlier "utopian" or "idealist" ways of thinking about international affairs. The modern realist rejection of normative theory stems largely from the disappointed hopes of the inter-war generation of scholars in the discipline. After the First World War there had been a widespread hope that a new order based on the notion of collective security would introduce an era of lasting peace. Fundamental to this movement was the belief that it would be supported by public opinion which, by the light of reason, would see the wisdom of a collective security arrangement as self-evident. That generation of scholars failed to predict fascism, the breakdown of the League of Nations and the outbreak of the Second World War. Political realists in following generations thus came to blame the earlier thinkers for failing to take note of the irrational aspects of human nature (nationalism, fascism) and the realities of power.[39] The conventional wisdom of such political realism came to be that it is the "realities of power", not any normative views or theories, which are decisive in international affairs.

What are we to make of this seemingly plausible claim that in the final instance might is more fundamental than right? The realist position is an untenable one because might and right (power and values, reality and ideal) are not conceptually and practically distinct in the way they need to be to maintain this position. Evidently this argument is very similar to the one made in the previous section. But let us expand it somewhat by looking closely at the link between political power, on the one hand, and human aims, values, norms, morals, principles and so on, on the other.

The core of the political realist position is that the structure of power determines the appropriate course of conduct for actors in the realm of international relations in a way that is not dependent on the truth or falsity of the values (norms, etc.) which people happen to have. On this view actors in world politics are, at any given time, constrained by the *structures of power* existing in the world. What is crucial for the realist is that the imperatives of power are in some sense objectively given in a way that is not dependent on people's theories about right and wrong. My argument against the realist is that power is always intimately linked to specific sets of ideas which constrain what that

power may be used for. An example will illustrate this. The late Ayatollah Khomeini of Iran had power over his followers because he was
seen by them as their religious leader within the context of that whole
set of ideas which comprises the Muslim religion. Within that context
he had power to execute certain decisions. But the range of possible
decisions was also limited by the theological context. The Ayatollah
was not able to pursue the policies of, for example, an Israeli prime
minister (to take an extreme case) for this would have been in breach
of the principles adhered to by the Ayatollah's followers from which
his power, in part, derived. Similarly, the power of leaders in the erstwhile Soviet Union were situated in and constrained by the ideas of
Marxism–Leninism as manifested in the constitutional and party
arrangements within that country. It was these constraints which
made it so difficult for reformers such as Mikhail Gorbachev to turn
to liberal economic policies without losing the support of his followers. These two examples refer to the ideas which bind a leader to
his followers and which constrain his power. Power always exists
within a practice which is partially constituted by certain normative
ideas. Far from it being the case that the leader has the power to
choose what value system (ideology) to implement, he is, himself, constrained by the value system in terms of which he holds power.

Against the argument outlined above a critic may want to argue
that this may apply to the leader and his followers, but does not apply
to the relationship between a power wielder and his victims. Thus,
the critic might argue, the US President is constrained *vis-à-vis* his
followers (i.e. the citizens of the USA) by certain democratic/capitalist
ideas, but deny that this applies to the relationship between the USA
and the citizens of certain Third World client states. This criticism fails
because even in dealing with third parties these ideas bind the power
holder. When dealing with the Third World states (who often refer to
themselves as "victims"), the US President is obligated to follow policies which are justifiable in a certain kind of way – the liberal/capital-
ist way – rather than in some other way. His is not a power to use
according to whim. Indeed, most of the criticisms levelled at the USA
by Third World states are in terms of the principles which the USA
itself professes to uphold. To repeat the point bluntly, the President's
action is subject to moral criticism and his power may ebb and flow
as a result of such criticism. Contrary to the political realist thesis,
power analysed in this way accentuates the importance of normative
theory.

The critic may not be satisfied with this response. He may claim that all I have shown is that the power of the wielder is vulnerable to moral criticism in terms of the principles of the wielder's own practice. Thus the power of the US President is constrained by broad liberal/democratic principles as embodied in the US constitution. The critic may then proceed to point out that from the point of view of the "victim," for example a Third World state, the role of normative theory in the constitution of the power of the oppressor is of no particular interest. Similarly the normative theory which binds the leader of the "victim" state to his followers is of no particular interest to the "oppressor" state. My response to this critic is that it is not possible to characterize a power relationship at all without reference to the ideas (norms, morals, principles, etc.) which the wielder holds *and* to the ideas (norms, morals, principles, etc.) which the subject holds, even though these may be antipathetic to those held by the former. Consider the example mentioned earlier, viz. the claim made by many Third World states that the great Western powers exert unwarranted economic and political power against them. The political power of the Western statesmen depends on their being office holders within the context of their particular respective states. Their political power depends on a whole set of ideas, held in common by the citizens of those states, regulating the relationship between governors and the governed. Similarly, their economic power depends on a set of beliefs, held in common by the same group of people, concerning what is right and wrong with regard to property relationships at home and abroad. Such a power relationship depends, too, on certain sets of political and economic ideas held by those in the subject states. Those in the subject states aspire to be citizens of a state of a certain kind (an independent, democratic one, for instance) and they aspire to participate in a certain set of property relationships (be it capitalist, socialist or communist). If those in the subject states were not bound together in terms of these commonly held notions, then it could well be the case that the power relations which exist between them and the developed states would cease to be (or turn into something different). Let me make this point by means of an extreme example. Were the people in a given region which is now identified as a subject state to convert to an extremely ascetic and other worldly oriented religion (i.e. they ceased to believe in the values of statehood, modernization, democracy and ceased to believe in the value of private property) then the great powers, such as the USA, would no longer have the same power over them. The powerlessness of the subject, too, thus cannot be portrayed without reference to the ideas (norms, etc.) that bind those in the subject state together as a community of a certain kind. Thus these states, too, are vulnerable to critical normative theory. Normative criticism may, at least in principle, significantly affect the so called "realities of power."

Once again it will not do to respond to the argument above that although it establishes an important link between power and normative ideas it does not yet establish the importance of serious normative *argument*, that all it establishes is the importance for power wielders of legitimating propaganda. It is important that we consider this response, for it is implicit in many theories of power held by scholars in international relations. These theorists admit that what people think or believe is an important element in determining the power of a state, but they see this as only one element in the overall power structure. This element of power is customarily referred to in such theories as the element of public opinion.[40] On this view governments that want to maintain power must take good care of domestic and international public opinion. This is done through the media, by propaganda. Other elements of power often mentioned are: economic resources, industrial capacity, military strength and so on. If the link between power and ideas is conceived of in this way, i.e. where ideas are merely synonymous with opinions (without any particular link to the other elements of power such as the military and the economic ones) and where opinion is only one of the elements of power, then no clear case is made for the importance of reasoned normative argument at all. Establishing the power of public opinion does not establish the importance of normative debate. The link which I have been seeking to establish between power and ideas is not this one; it seems rather to undermine it.

The public opinion view of the connection between power and ideas once again assumes the position which I have repeatedly tried to refute, viz. it assumes that power can exist independently of ideas. On the propaganda view of power, the wielder of power "has" power which he may then use to make propaganda in order to increase his power. On the view for which I have been arguing, the political power of a power wielder consists in part of a norm-constituted relationship between him and his audience/followers. If they did not adhere to these ideas he would not be a leader. Furthermore this is not a point which relates to only one of the "elements" of power. All the so called "elements" of power are partially constituted by people cooperating one with another in terms of some specified set of norms. Thus, in a capitalist country economic strength derives from the members of the country cooperating according to the constitutive rules of capitalism. The same applies to industrial and military power. Power is thus based on cooperation according to norms.[41] Power wielders cannot be indifferent to how those norms are evaluated, and must therefore take normative thinking seriously. If the ideas in terms of which they hold power are eroded, then their power is eroded. Criticism is the acid which corrodes ideas. However, critical scrutiny may also reinforce a given set of ideas and thus reinforce power. So we see that all power holders have an interest in justifying their position and refuting their critics. This is not a peripheral interest as is sometimes suggested by the use of the words "rationalization" and "legitimation." It is crucial, and we thus come to see the normative theorist as a player in the game of power.[42]

It might be thought that I have been blurring crucial distinctions between such notions as power, authority and influence. Although the distinctions between these notions are important for some purposes, they are not crucial to the argument here. The argument is that for any group of people to exercise power over another group, both groups have to be constituted as groups, in terms of some set of ideas (which will include normative ones). No doubt, the members of the power-wielding group will see these constitutive rules as legitimate and as conferring authority on the rulers to rule, whereas those subject to the group's power may see the rules as illegitimate (and thus as not conferring authority on that government to do what it does). Settling the controversy about whether the rules are legitimate or not is a matter for moral argument. The details of this argument are not my concern here. I am concerned merely to establish the general point that power relations cannot be characterized without reference to the ideas binding people together.

The super realists: post-modern impediments to normative theory

The final realist argument against normative theory in international relations is to be found, ironically, in the post-modern approach to the discipline – an approach which has burgeoned during the past decade.[43] Implicit in this approach is a super realism which suggests that normative theory is not a worthwhile activity. That post-modernism turns out to be super realist is ironic, for theorists in this school direct their attack at the realist school.

Post-modern writers in international relations take their cue from developments in fields outside, such as literary and social studies. Key influences have been Derrida, Foucault and Lyotard.[44] The central insights of the post-modern approach are that theory is not something which may be understood as representing a world that is given "out there." Nor are there neutral free-standing facts against which theory may be tested. The post-modernists insist that theory must be understood as practice. Theories as practices establish and maintain power relations between people. Such practices work to the advantage of some people and to the disadvantage of others. Thus, for example, realism in international relations portrays a world of nation states, relating to one another in terms of their national interests, by means of the balance of power, and through the use of warfare. The concepts of realist theory determine what are to be taken as the core facts of the discipline (viz. states and interstate relations conceived in a certain way) and rules that certain other phenomena are to be understood as secondary (viz. corporations, voluntary associations, and social movements). The realist theory taken as a whole plays a part in upholding the practice of present-day international relations and within this practice some people make gains at the expense of others. Realist theory itself helps maintain this pattern of gains and losses.

Post-modern theorists stress that human practices are not *natural* but *made*. It follows from this that practices (like the one described and upheld by realism) could be other than they are. Thus we need not live in a world which is as the realist theory describes it to be. People (including you and me) can and do set up new practices to replace old. Post-modern theory exposes the way in which some theories, like realism in international relations, may present a practice as natural and eternal when, in fact, it is a human product and changeable. Post-modernism, then, seeks to show that what we take to be the natural order of things is in fact changeable and falls within the realm of the political.

A further insight of this approach is that the multiplicity of practices in the world do not form a coherent whole. In particular they do not form a coherent whole inexorably developing towards some known final goal. The diverse practices develop in different ways and at dif-

ferent paces. It follows from this that social power (which is constituted by and exists within practices) is dispersed and fluid and that
accordingly it is not possible to construct a plausible meta-narrative
which can elucidate the development of the whole. The relationships
between the different practices are contingent. In short, power is, on
this view, de-centered. Applying this insight to international relations
it follows that world politics is not evolving towards a single coherent
end which might be termed "The End of History," instead it must be
seen as being in a state of permanent flux.

On this view since people are members of a diverse range of practices which do not necessarily cohere, there is a sense in which people
themselves are de-centered. They are de-centered in that they are constituted in diverse practices which change in different ways and at
different paces in the course of time. There is thus, according to post-
modern theory no essential human nature.

When the post-modern approach is applied in international
relations it indicates a certain method of inquiry. If power is de-
centered and if the myriad practices do not develop according to some
coherent *telos* then social scientists must perforce focus on the past,
i.e. on the study of history. What the post-modern investigator finds
are layers of practices – new practices replacing the old. The activity
of post-modern scholars exploring the layers of social practices in history is often referred to as "genealogy" or "archaeology." As we have
seen, such scholars reject at the outset any suggestion that their task
is to describe some natural order of things in world politics. What
they seek to make explicit are the practices of power in modern world
politics. Their inquiry has revealed, not surprisingly, that the dominant discourse in world politics today is realist. They show how realist
theory upholds/constitutes an order which advantages some at the
cost of others. This is done with a view to suggesting that some other
order could be put in its place.

In terms of their own premises post-modern scholars are not able
to claim that they are giving a neutral description of the way the international world is and always will be. For they stress there is no solid
foundation or Archimedean point from which to give such an objective account. On their own premises post-modern analysts concede
that their own theorizing is a practice which like all practices creates
power relations.

Ironically, post-modern analyses which have primarily directed
their efforts at criticizing the realist approach to international relations

may, themselves, justifiably be called super realist. Although they reject the realist commitment to the *state*, they remain firmly committed to the realist canon that the primary focus in all social analysis must be on *power*. A central question for one of the post-modern theorists, Richard Ashley, is "how, by way of what practices, are structures of history produced, differentiated, reified and transformed?"[45] Throughout, the aim is on bringing to light *structures of power* which were previously hidden by, for example, the silences created by other theories. We can clearly see here a distinct link between the post-modern approach and the realist arguments for the primacy of power discussed in the previous section.

The effect of post-modern analysis for normative theory is to entrench scepticism about the worth of normative theory. Any particular normative theory (liberal, equalitarian, communitarian, state centric) must on post-modern terms be itself seen as a practice upholding or seeking to uphold a set of power relations. The claims made for any one of these theories must be a claim to the superiority (sovereignty) of this theory *vis-à-vis* the others. But, as the post-modern theorists have shown, there are no firm grounds on which this claim could rest. So we are driven to be sceptical about the possibility of a substantive normative theory. This conclusion follows from the super realism inherent in post-modern theory. What has to be analysed, on this view, are relations of power for that is all there is.

This sceptical conclusion is not eroded by the professions of some post-modernists that although they reject foundationalist ethics they wish to advance a "second order ethicality" which seems to involve a permanent attitude of questioning our ethical concepts and an ongoing openness to the ethical concepts of others.[46] This does not erode the sceptical conclusion of their argument for no matter how tentative open and tolerant we (or they) are, any ethical order (second order, or third, or fourth) at some point has to ground our decisions about what to do. On post-modern premises such a grounding is not possible, thus our ethical theories can in the end be nothing other than practices of power. This is the super realist conclusion of post-modern thought.

What are we to make of the super realism of the post-modern theorists? Does it invalidate the practice of normative theory? I shall argue that it does not. The post-modern approach is quite correct in stressing that we live in social practices within which power relations are embedded. It is also correct in stressing that international relations theories (with an ethical component embedded in them) play a role in upholding particular practices. Realist theory does help maintain our present international system. But it does not follow from this that normative argument between theorists from different schools of thought is not possible or important. Consider liberal, socialist and realist scholars in international relations. Each school of thought has its own theories about how world politics works and its own ethical approach to questions about what ought to be done in international relations. Liberals stress individual freedom, socialists equality, and realists international order. Although each of these three approaches may be understood as a separate theoretical practice, it is not the case that they have no language in common between them. Quite the contrary – we find that the proponents of the three schools of thought share a large moral vocabulary which includes concepts such as liberty, equality, justice, rights, the rule of law, democracy, self-determination, non-intervention and the like. They have among them enough in common to start a serious conversation about ethical questions.

In the light of advances in the philosophy of language and the philosophy of the social sciences we have to admit that we have failed to find the kind of foundations for knowledge which philosophers once thought possible when they were strongly empiricist and positivist. But this philosophical failure does not imply that we cannot reach conclusions about ethical matters through argument from the premises which we hold in common. Argument may show, for example, that if I hold certain positions with regard to liberty then I cannot coherently continue to hold certain other beliefs I previously held about the rights of the majority in a democracy. Similarly it is perfectly possible for me to enter into argument with the post-modern theorists about the rights which they claim for themselves (the rights for example, of citizenship in more-or-less just states like Canada and the USA, the rights of freedom of speech and freedom of conscience, the right not to be assaulted at conferences, and other rights which they enjoy). In such an argument my interlocutors (the post-modern theorists) might demand that what is tacit (the "silences" in post-modern jargon) in my position be made explicit, that hidden assumptions be brought out in the open, and so on. But pointing to these tacit assumptions does not indicate the impossibility of serious ethical argument.

In summary then, the absence of the kind of foundations of which philosophers once dreamed does not require of us that we desist from arguing the merits of particular ethical positions. The common ground which allows the post-modern writers to put their argument in a way which others can read and appreciate is also ground enough for worthwhile and far-reaching arguments about what is right and wrong in international affairs.

What can be achieved by working from the common ground which holds among many actors throughout the world in their international dealings is worked out in much greater detail in subsequent chapters.

Morality and the imperatives of world politics

I here come to consider a final argument against taking seriously theories about how the world ought to be organized. At its most general the argument goes as follows: in whatever way the world is organized it will always be a *political* arrangement and political arrangements are always non-moral in important respects. There is, on this view, an irresolvable tension between politics and morality. In the popular mind Machiavelli is the chief proponent of this view. It derives most of its plausibility from the belief that politicians and state leaders are often required to act in ways which breach the rules of private morality. Thus state leaders are often called upon to act in non-altruistic ways – not to tell the truth, not to adhere to the principle of equality, and so on. In short, politics requires of its practitioners that they act in ways contrary to the fundamental requirements of private morality. On this view, politics is necessarily a dirty business.[47]

What are we to make of this position? It is, of course, possible to define "moral" in such an individualistic way that it applies to widely accepted private codes of conduct, but not to codes of conduct governing public office. But stipulating that a word be used in a certain way does not tell us anything about actual moral practice. Such definitional *fiat* is positively harmful if it obscures important similarities between the members of the arbitrarily distinguished classes. It is true that in practice we do consider that the standards for evaluating the conduct of public office holders are significantly different from those used to evaluate our own private conduct. But it is not true that we consider the conduct of public office holders to be governed by a general "anything goes" rule or that the standards of private morality have no application to the public sphere at all. On the contrary, in public debate about the proper standards applicable to the conduct of international relations the traditional vocabulary of private morality is much to the fore. For example, in the North–South dialogue a central concept is that of a just distribution. Reference is also often made to notions such as equality, fairness and desert. Also, there is constant reference to one or other concept of individual rights. Furthermore, we find in international debate that there are references to concepts such as promise-keeping and integrity.

Once again it is not an answer to say that the public office holders merely pretend to be governed by the standards referred to. As I have mentioned several times before, pretending is always a parasitic activity.[48] One can only pretend to be a just statesman because there is a real (not pretended) practice of just statesmanship. Thus there might be one or two politicians who can pretend to be just, but it is incoherent thinking to suppose that all politicians could pretend all the time. There could be no plays were there no real life.

The argument thus far must not be taken as suggesting that a private morality and a political morality of international affairs must be identical. It would be odd if they were. For it would be most implausible to think that a satisfactory moral code for an individual could be the same as a satisfactory moral code for a public office holder. We generally consider the former to be responsible only for himself, whereas the latter is responsible in a collective and public context. A single example will demonstrate the difference I am trying to illustrate here. An individual may properly decide whether to act courageously in a given situation and to put his well-being at risk by so doing. In contrast we do not think that political leaders have the right to commit a state to a risky action in the same way, for politicians not only put their own welfare at risk, but also that of the citizens of the state. By acting on behalf of the citizens, politicians have moral constraints placed upon them.

Delineating the precise distinctions between the standards by which private conduct ought to be regulated and those applicable to holders of public office is an important task, but one that I cannot deal with here. For the present I am concerned merely to establish that the standards applicable to the two spheres are different, but related. It is not the case that the standards governing the public sphere are either amoral or immoral. That there is a common vocabulary in discussions about both private and public morality seems *prima facie* a good reason for supposing that the two spheres share a common concern and are interrelated in some way.

Conclusion and recapitulation

In this and the previous chapter I have raised and argued many points. Let us now take stock of the argument as a whole. The main thrust of the argument so far has been to show that normative argument cannot be avoided in the study of world politics. In chapter 1 I argued that social scientists seeking to explain international affairs could not but get themselves embroiled in arguments of a normative nature. They become thus embroiled when in the course of their inquiry they characterize what happened as an act of this or that kind. Characterizing what happened as acts of this or that kind is a requirement of *any* explanation of social phenomena. This identification of an act requires of the social scientists that they understand the act in terms of the practice within which it takes place. However, we saw that even in the context of a given practice, what is to count as the proper understanding is often hotly contested. Deciding upon a proper interpretation requires that the investigating social scientist become involved in debate about the most fundamental normative issues within the practice being investigated. In our attempts to understand what the actors in Bosnia are doing we found that a social scientist has to decide in the light of *normative criteria* whether a given act was an act in pursuit of national self-determination or not.

In the present chapter we have considered a variety of different reasons which have been given for not taking the study of normative theories in international relations seriously and found them all to be flawed. Our major findings in this chapter are that:

1. Amoralism is not a position which can be coherently argued by a person or a state, for to be a (sane) person or a state implies the making of moral claims for oneself.
2. The arguments (such as Mackie's) against objectivist theories of morality, even if they succeed, do not lead to (or imply) amoralism or a general scepticism about the worth of moral argument. Anti-objectivist arguments are designed to demon-

strate that moral assertions lack a *certain kind* of cognitive status, not that they have no cognitive status at all.

3. Certain realist contentions about normative issues being derivative from power relations and thus being of secondary importance were shown to be wrong in that they are based on a misunderstanding of the relationship between power, norms and normative theory.

4. Although public morality may be different from private morality there is no reason to construe public morality as not a morality properly so called.

These chapters have been directed at dispelling the main reasons which have prevented normative theory being taken seriously in international relations. We have seen that involvement in normative theory is unavoidable.

3 Normative issues in international relations: the domain of discourse and the method of argument

In the previous two chapters I sought to clear the way for substantive normative theory in international relations. I sought to do so by showing that the reasons often advanced (or assumed) for avoiding substantive normative theorizing within the discipline of international relations are not sound. Indeed, in the course of the discussion it became apparent that scholars in the discipline cannot but become involved in issues of a normative nature. Having completed this preliminary stage of the argument let us now begin the more positive task of constructing a substantive normative theory. A first step will be to identify some of the pressing normative issues facing actors and theorists in the sphere of international affairs. This immediately raises the question of how these may best be settled. Finally we shall have to face the general question: "What is to count as a satisfactory normative theory?" I shall tackle these problems by arguing that the very statement of the list of difficult issues implicitly indicates the existence of an area of agreement between people – a domain of discourse – which gives us a basis from which we might construct an argument towards a substantive normative theory. I shall introduce and use, for this purpose, a method of argument first used in the context of jurisprudence.

But before going on to attempt the construction of such an argument we must first consider two objections to my contention that there actually is an area of agreement (domain of discourse) in international relations on the basis of which the difficult cases can be settled. After considering these two objections we shall proceed to outline a method of argument which I believe will facilitate a solution to the list of issues mentioned.

The normative issues in international relations and the central question for normative theory

What are the pressing normative issues in international politics today? Here is a list of some of them.

1. Questions relating to the causes and conduct of war. When may states justifiably go to war? Once at war, what are the normative constraints on the belligerents? What are the rights and duties of those states not directly involved in the war *vis-à-vis* other states?

2. Questions relating to nuclear armaments. When should nuclear arms be used? How ought they to be deployed? Is a deterrence policy justified? Who should be allowed to have nuclear weapons? What institutions ought to control their proliferation? What controls should there be on the technological research leading to the development of new nuclear weapons?

3. When may and ought individuals to agree (or refuse) to participate in the use of force against other states or other political groupings?

4. How ought states to respond to unconventional forms of violence like international terrorism? Who ought to do what about those who hijack aeroplanes, take hostages, etc., for political purposes?

5. When is intervention by one state in the domestic affairs of another state justified? What means may justifiably be employed in such interventions?

6. How should those fighting wars of national liberation (self-determination) be treated by states not directly involved in the conflict? Ought they to treat the conflict as a war? Or should they treat it as a domestic matter within the state concerned? Are the captives in such a conflict to be regarded as prisoners of war, political prisoners or criminals?

7. How should refugees from one state be treated by other states? Who is responsible for them? Should they be allowed to choose a new home state or are they obligated eventually to return to their state of origin?

8. How should those not fighting for secession of a particular territory treat those who are engaged in such a conflict?

9. When may a state divide itself into several smaller states? (When is secession justified?)

10. Questions relating to the international use and distribution of the resources of the world. Who ought to get what, when, how? Ought a distribution to be achieved by the operation of a capitalist free-market in which multinationals are allowed to operate? Or should the distribution be governed by a worldwide democratic body of some kind?
11. Who would be justified in doing what in order to preserve the global ecology?
12. What kind of international organizations ought to be established? What authority should they have *vis-à-vis* states?
13. What human rights are there and how ought they to be protected? Ought states to protect them? If a state fails to protect such rights, ought other states to intervene? Should there be international institutions to secure these rights? If so, what are states and individuals justified in doing in order to bring about the establishment of such alternative institutions?

These questions are posed in a general form, but in each case it is easy to think of specific cases to which the question could be applied. For example, questions about the right of states to manufacture and deploy nuclear weapons arise for the international community with regard to North Korea, Iraq and Israel. Another example of one of the general questions being given a specific application concerns the proper action to be taken by surrounding states in response to drives towards national self-determination by nationalist groups in the area of Eastern Europe.

It is likely that others may want to add further questions to the list of pressing issues in international affairs. But most people would agree that the normative problems mentioned on the list are crucial ones. It is highly unlikely that anybody would want to argue that these problems are not important problems at all. Such agreement on the statement of the main issues is of fundamental significance, for by implication it indicates a common basis from which argument towards a solution of these key problems might proceed. This contention needs further elucidation. What kind of agreement does agreement on the list of problems reveal? How and why is this agreement (if it exists) relevant to finding possible solutions to the key issues mentioned?

Let us consider this latter question first. A problem cannot be formulated as a normative issue except within the context of a given practice of normative argument. Normative issues only arise as such within the context of certain shared understandings. This is, of course, a very general point indeed. A similar point can be made by means of an example from sport. The issue of whether or not a given move in a game of rugby is a foul or not can only arise amongst the initiates of the game. It could not arise as an issue at all between people not familiar with the game. In a similar way moral issues do not arise among psychotics because, amongst other things, psychotics have no understanding of the practice of morality as it exists amongst normal people; they lack any concept of moral wrongness. Moreover this point – that normative issues can only arise within the context of a wider area of agreement – has a further significance as well: it indicates to us where we ought to start looking for a solution to such issues, namely within the area of agreement in which the issue arose. Thus someone seeking to determine whether a given kind of event in rugby is a foul or not must start by acquainting herself as fully as possible with the rules and underlying principles of the game as a whole. Similarly, we who are seeking answers to pressing normative issues in international relations, must start by seeking an understanding of the area of normative agreement implied by our agreed list of pressing issues. Our task is to outline the relevant *domain of discourse*. A domain of discourse is an area of discussion within which the participants generally recognize (and recognize others as recognizing) many rules as settled. Thus an outline of the domain of discourse pertaining to rugby would involve indicating that range of rules which speakers in the domain regard as settled, such as the rules which determine what is to count as a scrum, a tackle, a pass, a conversion and so on. In our case we are called upon to outline what is considered normal in the domain of discourse relating to the interstate practice.

This initial step of outlining the domain of discourse within which the issues arise is not, of course, the same as answering the specific questions or constructing a general theory. Theory building is an attempt to pass beyond what participants within a given domain of discourse normally do, which is to answer the pressing questions that arise in an *ad hoc* way. Theory building is a subsequent stage where an attempt is made to show how all the diverse things accepted by initiates within a given domain of discourse form a coherent and orderly whole which indicates how difficult cases might be solved. Thus within the sphere of morality, what participants normally do is make individual moral judgements on an *ad hoc* basis. They judge, for example, that killing people, torturing people and so on is bad, and that helping the needy and preventing harm is a good. A moral theory would then be a theory which "introduces order and system into our considered judgements over a wide range of positions."[1]

Let us return to the initial step. Within the context of what area of agreement (i.e. within the context of what domain of discourse) do the pressing questions we have identified arise as issues? Imagine a specific application of any (or all) of the thirteen questions on our list. Whatever specific application is thought of for each of the questions on the list (which is far from being exhaustive), it is certain that it will arise in a context where reference is made to one, some or all of the following: states, inter-state relations and citizens of states. Even those questions which point towards the creation of a new order in the world (one which might not consist of states) must prescribe what states and citizens ought to do now in order to move towards a new world order later. Similarly, some questions which on the face of the matter do not appear to apply to states, for example questions about the proper role of multinational corporations, may, on closer consideration, be shown to be concerned with states. Thus many normative questions about multinationals may be better formulated as: "What ought states to do about multinationals?"

I contend that all normative issues in world politics today refer, either directly or indirectly, to the state, inter-state relations and the role of individuals as citizens of states. If this is correct it is then possible to encapsulate all the several normative questions in the one central question: "What in general is a good reason for action by or with regard to states?" This question clearly covers questions as diverse as: "What ought John to do when called upon to take up arms against another state? When ought a state to support another state in a war with a third state? How ought states to deal with international terrorism?" And so on.

The domain of discourse: modern state ordinary language and its alternatives

The domain of discourse within which the listed issues must be settled has been identified as what might be termed the *modern state domain*.[2] Any argument regarding these questions will be within the modern state centric practice.

However, before proceeding I must first consider two objections which might be raised against my argument so far. The first is that there is no such area of agreement within which the difficult issues may be situated. On this view the most conspicuous feature of the domain of international affairs is the lack of any such core consensus to serve as a base from which to solve the more difficult cases, since the difficult normative issues typically arise between peoples with radically opposed ideologies. On this view, opposing ideologies are taken to rule out any common area of agreement. This argument has already been considered in relation to scepticism, so I shall not go into it in great detail.

The second objection to my approach is not that I am wrong in identifying an area of agreement from which to argue to a solution of the hard cases, but that I have identified the wrong area of agreement. According to this view – the modern natural law view – there is an area of agreement which can give us a base from which to argue. However, it is not situated in the state centric practice, but in a more fundamental community, namely, the community of humankind. Let us consider each of these objections in turn.

The "conflict of ideologies" objection

One way of portraying the modern world is to depict it as a world in which there is little or no moral consensus. Hans Morgenthau, for example, wrote of the dissolution of the European international society. In this society, from the Treaty of Westphalia until the beginning of the First World War, an elite consensus about the fundamental rules of right conduct in international affairs had existed.[3] However, on Morgenthau's view the consensus has been eroded since the end of the First World War. In its place there has arisen a diversity of nationalisms which are no longer based upon any set of common norms:

> Thus carrying their idols before them, the nationalist masses of our time meet in the international arena, each group convinced that it executes the mandate of history, that it does for humanity what it seems to do for itself, and that it fulfils a sacred mission ordained by providence, however defined. Little do they know that they meet under an empty sky from which the gods have departed.[4]

On this view, then, far from it being the case that there is an underlying consensus, there has in fact been a retrograde movement to tribalism, irrational nationalisms and fanatical religious zealotry. Writing in a completely different tradition, Michael Walzer makes a similar point. He argues that in the modern world there is no political consensus; that in the modern world people do not experience a sense of political being within a single frame of reference. Instead people have divided political allegiances. His argument is against the applicability of the state centric view according to which a person's political being is conceived within a single state centric frame of reference.[5] Writing in yet another tradition, Barrie Paskins and Michael Dockrill argue that "The contemporary world is living with the aftermath of what Nietzsche termed 'the death of god,' that is, the collapse of all consensus on an authoritative political, social, moral and religious order."[6] The outbreak, in recent times, of wars of a fundamentalist religious nature has served to reinforce the position of those arguing that the modern world is best characterized in terms of the absence of any overarching consensus. Although there may still be some minimal "raft of consensus" between, say, the precarious democracies in Latin America and developed liberal democratic states, there is, so the argument goes, surely very little consensus at all between liberal democratic states and the deeply religious states like Iran and Libya. Similarly, the emergence since the Second World War and, more recently, since the end of the Cold War, of many new states, the populations of which are not steeped in Western political and cultural traditions, reinforces the view of those scholars in international relations who stress the fundamental absence of consensus in the modern world. This influential perspective on world politics is what Ralph Pettman has referred to as the "pluralist perspective."[7] It is also akin to, though not identical with, what has become known as "communitarianism."[8]

According to this view, disputes do arise, but they are best seen as being of an *ideological* nature. The disputes are such that the justifications produced by the parties to the disputes pertain to domains of discourse which are in some sense hermetically sealed off from one another. In such ideological conflicts any real argument is not possible because of the lack of any basic consensus between the parties and because of the closed nature of each party's belief system. Thus there were disputes, for example, between states and groups committed to a liberal democratic view of world politics and those which held a

Marxist–Leninist view, and there are ongoing disputes between states committed to a humanist/Christian point of view and those which adhere to a Muslim one. The parties to such disputes typically justify their positions in terms of frames of reference which are fundamentally opposed to (or incomprehensible to) those held by the opposing states. What I have called the "ideological" aspect of such disputes is sometimes referred to as "nationalistic universalism."[9] Each side of the dispute comes to see its own value-set as a universalist frame of reference to be applied to all other groups. The alternative value systems invoked by others are rejected as wrong and pernicious *in toto*. It is this aspect of such conflicts which is so graphically described in the quotation from Morgenthau given above. This approach to normative disputes in international relations was manifested most starkly during the years of the so-called "Cold War" when democratic and communist ideologies confronted each other on the stage of world politics.

This view of the international domain of discourse often leads its adherents to conclude that there are insuperable difficulties in the way of finding any rational solution to normative problems. This position may be restated in the following way: because there is no common ground, or because the two sides (Marxist/non-Marxist, Christian/ Muslim) have such different points of departure and such different basic commitments, the matter cannot be settled by argument. If it is to be settled at all, it will have to be settled by power. As C. Wright Mills put it: "In the end, if the end comes, we just have to beat those who disagree with us over the head."[10]

My argument against this "conflict of ideologies" approach is that parties to disputes in international affairs do not normally confront one another in this mutually uncomprehending way. They rather tend to confront one another within the context of a well-established practice. Their disputes are situated within a common state centric domain of discourse, and the participants (usually representatives of states, or of non-state groupings confronting a state or states) share an understanding of the multiple different actions which can be undertaken within this context. More specifically, the very nature of their conflicts presupposes that they all understand what it is to make an incursion over a national border, what it is to threaten war, what is involved in starting a war, what is involved in staying neutral during a war, what is involved in forming alliances, what it is for one state to act as honest broker between two warring states, what is involved in a cease-fire, in signing an accord, in inter-state diplomacy, summitry and so on. Without such a shared understanding of the basic rules of the game, no inter-state conflict would be conceivable. Thus, although it is true that in conflicts between states (or between non-state actors, like liberation movements, and states) the opponent is often *portrayed* (by the opponent) as one with whom argument is not possible, this is, quite paradoxically, only possible if the conflict is taking place within a context of a core of agreed rules within a given practice. Just as within a rugby league certain teams may regard one another in a more than usually antagonistic light, nevertheless to the extent that they still *play* rugby together they show a mutual commitment to the rules of the game. Thus, although the emergence of nationalism (with its attendant ideological trappings) has introduced a new element in the international practice of states, it is beyond doubt that such a practice still does exist.

I argue, then, that it is not the case that normative disputes in international relations today can properly be seen as confrontations between members of one ideology with members of another incomprehensible foreign ideology. The Marxist or fundamentalist confronting the representative of the Western liberal tradition is not in the position as the Western anthropologist confronting the Trobriand Islanders (or a group of Martians) for the first time. All the debates about normative issues in international relations take place *within* a common tradition of political theory – within what I have called the modern state domain of discourse. Thus it could be shown, for example, that the debate between Marxists and non-Marxists (such as state-centrist or interdependence theorists) is, amongst other things, about how the state system can best be understood. Part of the Marxist argument against capitalist democracies is that they purport to be protecting democratic values while in fact such capitalist democracies entrench certain very undemocratic dependency relationships based on the exploitation of one class by another.[11] The details of the argument need not concern us here, but I must point out that the whole debate is rooted in the common ground of the state-centric and modernizing domain of discourse.[12] If there were no such common ground there could be no debate. Some of the central terms of this domain of discourse are: states, citizens, representative democracy, the separation of powers, the rule of law, and that set of terms referring to the creation and distribution of wealth.[13] My argument is not that within this shared language (or, as James Mayall calls it, this "cognitive ethic")[14] there is absolute consensus on all things. Patently there is not. I simply wish to point to the existence of this worldwide domain of the discourse as a basic given. There are no significant groupings of people who fall totally outside it.[15] Previously there were such outside groupings. In earlier times it was plausible to characterize the world as consisting of the civilized groups and the barbarians.[16] The assertion that normative disputes are best seen as confrontations between mutually uncomprehending ideologies would have been far more plausible then than it is now.

Some may question whether democracy is part of this general consensus. Surely, it may be suggested, only a minority of all states are democracies. But this is to miss the point which is that, whether or not most states are in fact democracies, most states claim to be committed to democratic values. Those that are not in fact democracies justify their non-democratic form of government by reference to the abnormal circumstances which pertain in their case. The promise is usually made that a democracy will be established as soon as possible. Furthermore there is also widespread agreement on what might be broadly termed the goal of modernization. This includes the goals of technical advance, industrialization and the education of the populace which is necessary to support the former two goals. James Mayall has spelled out some of the components of what he terms the modernization myth. First, modernization is used as a central justification for the exercise of power. Second, it involves a commitment to nationalist ideology which is used to destroy traditional forms of power and authority and to advance modernist aims. Third, there is a commitment to the traditional diplomatic forms which provide avenues to be used in the pursuit of the modernization goals. Fourth, the language of modernizing development and redistribution is the language of the Western developed world not that of traditional cultures.[17]

In summary, in this section I have tried to counter the claim that normative argument about pressing issues in international relations is not possible because the basic consensus (which is a precondition for *any* argument) is lacking in international relations. I have outlined, in a very introductory way, the domain of discourse within which argument towards a solution of the listed issues may proceed.

The natural law/community-of-humankind approach

Let us now consider the second objection to my contention that there is a modernizing state centric domain of discourse within which we may seek solutions to the pressing normative questions listed at the outset. This is the objection offered by those who adopt a natural law or community-of-humankind approach to normative issues in international relations. For those in this tradition, the normative evaluation of issues pertaining to the practice of states presupposes that there exists a moral community of humankind. If we are to avoid cultural imperialism (i.e. imposing our values on others to whom they do not apply) and if we are to avoid relativism (which would commit us to maintaining that there are no common standards for evaluating the system of states), then, the argument goes, we must assume the existence of a moral community of humankind.[18] The existence of such a community of humankind is supposed to give us a moral perspective from which the system of states can be judged. Michael Donelan talks of a "primordial community of mankind."[19] The underlying logic of this approach is similar to the one I have adopted in that it stresses (as I have) that no argument is possible in the absence of some underlying community of values between the disputants. However, this approach differs profoundly from mine in the portrayal it gives of the basic community from which argument must proceed. It claims that there is a moral community of humankind which it conceives to be in some way independent of the modernizing inter-state practice, whereas I consider just that modernizing state system as providing the idiom within which normative argument takes place.

The crucial question with regard to this approach is, of course: "In what sense, if any, does such a moral community of humankind exist?" A related question is: "What kind of investigation is called for to establish the existence of that community? Could it be established by an empirical investigation (if not that, what then)? All would agree that there is in the world today a large number of states. But is there a community of humankind? There are over 5.4 billion people, but is it right to call this a community? Would it not be better to say that there are many diverse communities?

The natural law response to this challenge is to argue that there are certain self-evident principles or goods common to all the diverse groupings of people. It is the fact that these are held by everyone, so allowing us to talk of a community of humankind. One natural law theorist, John Finnis, lists seven such basic self-evident goods: life, knowledge, play, aesthetic experience, sociability, practical reasonableness and religion.[20] He admits that these values are pursued in many diverse ways and that they take a great variety of forms, but he insists that they are common to all societies. His claim is not merely the empirical one that these goods are considered goods by everyone. It is the much stronger claim that it is *self-evident* that the goods are good for everyone. "Self-evident" does not mean, says Finnis "accessible to some weird extra sense which people have".[21] Rather they are self-evident in the sense that they are bound to be implicit in the thinking of anyone, even (and especially) within the thinking of the sceptic who seeks to deny the good in question. According to Finnis, the sceptic who argues that knowledge is not a good is "operationally self defeating" in that his asserting that knowledge is not a good undercuts the content of his assertion.[22] Elsewhere, Finnis says the principles are self-evident in that they are necessarily presupposed in the way people act and talk.[23] Thus presumably he would argue that one cannot pursue knowledge without presupposing that it is good to do so. Similarly one cannot play games without presupposing that game playing is a good, and so on through the list of goods.

This way of arguing to the conclusion that there is a moral community of humankind with certain natural (objective) basic values will not do. In the first place, Finnis' empirical claim that "anthropologists have shown strikingly similar lists of concerns across cultures" (such as the concern for life, for placing some restriction on sexual practices, for friendship, and for knowledge), while probably true, does not establish that a moral community exists. Consider two cultures (or two individuals) which have strikingly different notions of when life might justifiably be terminated (imagine an argument between a Roman Catholic and a Japanese believer in the *hara-kiri* ritual). Even if we could show that they both value life in some way, this would not provide proof of any fundamental consensus from which moral argument can proceed. Pointing out that people in different societies face (and have faced throughout history) similar issues does not establish the existence of a primordial moral community of humankind.[24]

In the second place the argument for the self-evidence of such basic values will not do what it is supposed to do. Consider Finnis' argument about knowledge, which says everyone values knowledge in that even the sceptic's assertion that knowledge cannot be had is (if anything) a piece of knowledge, so that the sceptic, by making his assertion, shows himself to be valuing knowledge. Donelan reaches a similar conclusion via a different route. He argues that although throughout history there has been an ongoing polemic about the nature of knowledge, nevertheless this polemic itself is "throughout a process of reasoning."[25] He says, "we change our minds from time to time over the centuries about the nature of reason, about how we know and how we criticize: but that we know and that we criticize is confirmed to us in the very procedure itself."[26] Thus both Finnis' and Donelan's arguments get their force from the allegation that the very process of reasoning demonstrates a commitment to knowledge which is constant over time. But it is by no means certain that the scholastics of medieval times arguing with one another and the Oxford ordinary-language philosophers in the time of John Austin were all committed to the *same* underlying conception of knowledge. It would be interesting to explore this matter. But notice that in order to do so, an investigator would have to understand the scholastic practice of disputation from the internal point of view. Then he would likewise have to understand the practice of the ordinary language philosophers. Only then could he attempt to extrapolate from each practice what the underlying (or presupposed) notion of knowledge was in each case. These notions might turn out to be radically different from each other. Whether or not they would in fact be so different is not important here. I am simply concerned to point out that we cannot infer from the fact that most people in most cultures throughout history have engaged in argument that there is a common commitment to the same value: knowledge. What we can properly infer is that wherever people reason with one another those engaged in this activity must presuppose *some* point or purpose to it. But whether it is the same in each case is a matter for research. In short, the fact that reasoning is ubiquitous does not warrant the conclusion that there is a community of humankind which naturally has this good in common.

Similar arguments may be brought to bear against all the other goods which the natural law theorists identify as objectively given for humankind as a whole, viz. friendship, sociability, religion, practical reasonableness and so on. Consider play. It is no doubt true that something analogous to play (in a very broad sense of the word) might be found in all societies. But on closer scrutiny it might turn out that what was initially identified by the investigator as examples of "play" in different societies were really not very similar at all. The difference may be more radical than that which exists between two different kinds of game (e.g. cricket and bull fighting). It may be the case that within one society the activity initially identified as a game is considered play in that it is an essentially light-hearted pastime. In another society the game in question may be understood as a far more serious activity; success at it is considered an indication of a man's stature as a "real man," as indicating that he is a genuine member of the society to which he belongs. Finding out such differences involves gaining a participant and holist perspective on the societies being investigated. The investigator will have to face up to all the problems of interpretation which I mentioned in chapter 1.

To summarize: the natural law theorists' case rests on their being able to assert that play (or knowledge, sociability, etc) are the *same* across all cultures in some quite profound sense. It also involves the claim that they have been the same throughout history. My argument is that it is not possible to assert this simply on the basis of a super-ficial glance at the apparent similarities between the different peoples of this world. Finding out whether these actually are similar or not requires extensive research which is fraught with both practical and philosophical difficulties. In sharp contrast my assertion (which is more minimalist than the extensive claims of the natural lawyers) that a state centric domain of discourse exists can be established with com-parative ease. It simply is the case that most actors in world affairs would formulate the list of core problems much as I have done and in formulating the list they would necessarily rely on several key common concepts such as state, citizen and community of states.

The objection that issues arising in the modern state domain of discourse can only be settled from a wider moral point of view

I must briefly consider an objection which is closely related to the one which we have just discussed, viz. the objection that the serious moral issues which arise in international affairs can only be solved from a wider moral perspective. This objection is raised against my conten-tion that the major issues can be solved within the modern state cen-tric domain of discourse. Against this it is argued that in normative theory we require some wider moral perspective which would enable us to evaluate the modern state domain of discourse as a whole. Michael Donelan articulates this objection in his article "The Political Theorists and International Theory," where he argues that *only* if we accept that there is a moral community of humankind is it possible to morally evaluate the state system itself.[27] On his view there are only two possibilities: either the state system (together with its associated domain of discourse) is the primordial given (in which case that state system cannot itself be morally evaluated because there is no wider, more inclusive perspective from which it can be judged) or there is a primordial community of humankind (which gives us the necessary perspective from which the state system can be judged). I have already considered the difficulties involved in the notion of a community of humankind in the previous section. In this section my argument is that Donelan's dichotomy is wrong in so far as it suggests that unless our domain of discourse is based on the assumption that there is a moral community of humankind, it would not be possible to evaluate the major issues which arise in the state centric domain of discourse itself.

Donelan purports to explain why there has been so little normative theory in the discipline of international relations. This is due to the fact that most political theorists have taken it for granted that a human is fundamentally a being who "lives and always will live in a separate state."[28] For Donelan doing this is a paltry business, not worthy of those interested in serious moral theory. I dispute this. We are not condemned to critical impotence if we accept that the answer to the pressing normative issues in international relations must necessarily be found within the modern state domain of discourse. Neither does it commit us to the maintenance of the status quo. Accepting the centrality of this domain of discourse does not imply that there can be no normative political theory of world politics. That there has been little normative theorizing in international relations is true enough, but the reasons for this lack are not because working out the "implications of the theory of the state" is a trivial thing to do. The reasons for the lack of normative theorizing have already been covered in chapters 1 and 2. In this section I want to argue that seeking answers within the state centric domain of discourse to the list of pressing questions is a worth-while activity and that far from being a trivial residue of state theory it is of primary importance. What I take to be involved in this endeavour will be elucidated in some detail in the following two chapters. It involves constructing a coherent background theory justifying the settled norms in the modern state domain of discourse.

It is necessary to be quite clear about what is, and what is not involved in having recourse to the modern state domain of discourse. The language of this domain is the ordinary language of international relations. This language is a functioning whole – not a completely coherent one – which includes within it a mix of the following terms:

state, sovereignty, self-determination, citizen, democracy, human rights (individual rights and group rights), and a set of terms connected to the notion of modernization. Asserting the primacy of the modern state domain of discourse for my purposes does *not* commit me to holding that people will always live in states as we know them or that life in states, as we know them, is the only proper life for human beings, or that the way states are organized at present is the best way of organizing them. I simply contend that any discussion about what ought to be done in world politics (be the proposed action a small one or a large one such as, for example, the wholesale reorganization of the global political system) must be conducted in the language of the modern state system. No other suitable language is available. Viewed in this way, it will become clear that the various objections against the modern state domain of discourse as the ground of normative theory in international relations fall away as misconceived. There are several such objections which must be confronted.

A first objection which seems inherent in Donelan's approach is that utilizing the modern state domain of discourse in effect sanctifies the state: it assumes that people will always live in states and that it is not possible within such a language to consider alternatives to the system. This objection is not well founded. By having recourse to the ordinary language of international relations I am not thereby committed to argue that the state system as it exists is the best mode of human political organization or that people ought always to live in states as we know them. As I have said, my argument is that whatever proposals for piecemeal or large-scale reform of the state system are made, they must of necessity be made in the language of the modern state. Whatever proposals are made, whether in justification or in criticism of the state system, will have to make use of concepts which are at present part and parcel of the theory of states. Thus, for example, any proposal for a new global institutional arrangement superseding the state system will itself have to be justified, and that justification will have to include within it reference to a new and good form of individual citizenship, reference to a new legislative machinery equipped with satisfactory checks and balances, reference to satisfactory law enforcement procedures, reference to a satisfactory arrangement for distributing the goods produced in the world, and so on. All of these notions are notions which have been developed and finely honed within the theory of the modern state. It is not possible to imagine a justification of a new world order succeeding which used, for example, feudal, or traditional/tribal, discourse. More generally there is no worldwide language of political morality which is not completely shot through with state-related notions such as citizenship, rights under law, representative government and so on.

A related objection might be that accepting the primacy of the modern state domain of discourse implies that serious normative theory about inter-state relations is not possible. The reasoning which leads to this conclusion is roughly as follows: if the language of the modern state is taken as primary, this involves taking the notion of state sovereignty as primary, for sovereignty is one of the key terms in the ordinary language of international relations. A sovereign body almost by definition is not bound by any higher norms, thus any normative theory about how sovereign states ought to treat their citizens or how they ought to conduct their affairs with one another would be otiose. This line of reasoning is based on some muddled thinking about the notion of sovereignty. The central problem is easily demonstrated without our having to get involved in the interstices of theories of sovereignty.[29] The muddle arises from conflating two assertions about sovereignty, the first true and the second false. It is true that a sovereign state is subject to no higher law making and law enforcing authority. But it is false that the notion of sovereignty implies "not subject to any higher norms *at all*." To say that a state is sovereign does not commit us to saying that it is wrong or pointless to discuss what norms it ought to follow in its dealings with other states. Any suggestion that it is probably rests on some confusion about the relationship between power and moral theory akin to that which was discussed in chapter 2. We often do criticize sovereign states for immoral or unjust conduct.

This confusion about the nature and implications of sovereignty may be further clarified if we attend to the distinction between sovereignty and power. To say that a state is sovereign is to say nought about the power relations which may hold between states. A sovereign state may well exist in the sphere of influence of a more powerful state. The realities of such power relations between states are widely recognized, but this is not held to invalidate their status as sovereign states. Where a system of sovereign states exists, there is a practice in which states are held to make their own autonomous decisions; a practice in which states may be held responsible for such decisions of their own irrespective of the unequal power relations involved. But if a sovereign state is held to make autonomous decisions on the right thing to do in a given situation, it does not follow that whatever it decides to do is therefore right. The state may well have made a bad decision. My contention then is that it is wrong to assert that where states are considered to be sovereign there is nothing more to be said about the right conduct of states. What has to be determined is: what are the standards of right conduct for sovereign states? More importantly how, within the modern state centric domain of discourse, do we find out what these standards are?

There are further arguments against the approach I am advocating (the approach which stresses the primacy of the modern state domain of discourse), but I must postpone dealing with these until I have developed the method of argument more fully. I shall return to these objections at the end of this chapter.

I have argued that a discussion of normative issues in international relations must take place in terms of the modern state domain of discourse. This view runs directly contrary to the conventional wisdom of the discipline which may be summarized in the following terms:

> It is, indeed, the case that there actually is a system of states, and it is true that the existence of such a system of states indicates that there is some minimal agreement on the ground rules of international relations. However this in no way establishes the feasibility of settling disputes by finding the right answer by means of argument. The most contested issues (which are also potentially the most dangerous) are those for which there are no agreed rules in terms of which they could be settled. Historically there once was a community of European powers led by an aristocracy who subscribed to a common set of religious, political and legal ideas. This provided a wide area of agreement and enabled disputes to be settled by reference to agreed standards.[30] However, this consensus has now disappeared. There exists nowadays a multiplicity of world views. Since the underlying consensus which is necessary for the rational settlement of international disputes is lacking, there are only two possible ways remaining for resolving such issues: either the parties may strike a bargain or they might resort to force.[31] This account quite closely accords with what happens in international relations.[32]

I accept that the modern state domain of discourse offers us no clear-cut rules which dictate solutions to those pressing problems of international relations identified in the list. But I wish to argue that there is a way of overcoming the impasse in which the conventional wisdom finds itself when confronted by contentious normative issues. The way out of the impasse has been brilliantly expounded in the context of law by Ronald Dworkin.[33] His theory has a specifically legal focus, but I believe that it can be generalized to have a much wider application. In particular, a wider interpretation of his theory will be invaluable to our concern with normative argument in international relations.

A method for settling contested issues by argument: Dworkin and the example of hard cases in law

A general outline of Dworkin's method

Dworkin developed his theory of legal argument in order to cope with the problem posed by *hard cases* in law. These are typically cases which come up for decision before a judge and which are not clearly covered by any settled rule of law or precedent. Dworkin developed his position against the orthodoxy of the positivist jurisprudents who argued that where the facts of a particular case did not fall under a settled rule of law, the judge had to *make* new law to cover the case in hand.[34] In such cases, the positivists argued, judges are constrained by the principles and maxims of the law, but nevertheless they use their discretion and *make* the law. In such cases there can, on the positivist view, be no talk of a uniquely right decision. Against this, Dworkin argues that even in hard cases there is a method of judicial argument which can lead to the right decision. It is his portrayal of this method, I suggest, that can be of use to us in seeking solutions to the hard cases of international relations.

Arguably the best way to introduce Dworkin's theory of argument is to outline his discussion of the kind of reasoning a referee in chess might follow in trying to decide a hard case that comes up for decision. Chess is, of course, a game with a well-developed set of unambiguous rules governing every possible move on the board and with established conventions regarding the context of play. Still, contentious issues may arise where no settled rules seem to apply.

Imagine that a dispute arises between two players because one claims that the other annoyed him unreasonably by smiling at him (the Russian grand master Tal once smiled thus at Fischer). The referee is called upon to interpret the rule which stipulates that a player who unreasonably annoys his opponent shall forfeit the game. We are to suppose that no identical case has previously been decided. Evidently there is no mechanical decision possible, yet the referee is also not called on to make an arbitrary decision favouring one or other player according to his discretion. He is to settle the issue in terms of the "unreasonable annoyance" rule. How ought the referee to go about reaching the correct decision? Or to phrase the question differently: what would count as a good reason justifying a decision in favour of one of the players rather than the other? Dworkin holds that, even though in hard cases like this the conventions of chess do not provide ready-made solutions, they still allow a right decision to be reached by argument. It is this aspect of his analysis which is of particular relevance for our purposes.

Dworkin first points out that what the referee is called on to decide in finding for one of the players rather than the other is to confirm or deny an *institutional right*.[35] If a player has been unreasonably annoyed by his opponent then he has a right to be awarded the game. It is institutional in that the player holds it in virtue of his involvement in the institution. In this case the institution is the game of chess. But for his involvement in that institution the player would not have the right in question. The referee is called upon to make his decision in terms of this institution and its constitutive rights. In this hard case the referee faces a situation in which there is no rule which clearly stipulates whether smiling constitutes unreasonable behaviour or not, and yet where the institution still imposes definite constraints on what the referee may or may not decide. He is not entitled to decide on principles taken from outside the institution, for example from general morality. He may not, for example, decide in favour of a player on the grounds that the one player needs the prize money more than the other player does. We would, says Dworkin, reject a decision which was made for reasons of general morality because such a decision is not in accordance with the *character* of the game. The correct decision of the referee would be a decision which protects the character of the game. But what is the character of a chess game?

In arriving at a correct decision the referee is thus to be guided by the character of the game. How is he to determine what this is? Dworkin says, "He (the referee) may well start with what everyone knows. Every institution is placed by its participants in some very rough category of institution; it is taken to be a game rather than a religious ceremony or a form of exercise or a political process."[36] Reasoning thus, it will be clear to the referee that chess is generally held to be an intellectual game. In establishing this, we already rule out several potential solutions to the case in hand (for example, it would clearly not accord with the character of an intellectual game were the referee to decide the issue by spinning a coin). But establishing the character of chess as an intellectual game does not yet uniquely dictate a correct decision. The concept of an "intellectual game" is what Dworkin, following Gallie, calls an essentially contested concept, i.e. a concept which admits of several conceptions.[37] The concept in question (chess is an intellectual game) is not univocal, but is capable of supporting different conceptions. In order to decide the matter in hand the referee must choose the correct one. But which one? How is he to choose?

Dworkin argues that the referee must *construct* the game's character (in so far as it has a bearing on this particular case) by putting to himself different sets of questions. Given that chess is an intellectual game, is it, like poker, intellectual in a sense that includes ability at psychological intimidation? Or is it, like mathematics, intellectual in a sense that does not include that ability? In each case, different implications would follow concerning whether the opponent's smile would count as unreasonable annoyance or not. Such questions thus force him, on the one hand, to look more closely at the game, to determine whether its features provide support for one rather than the other of these conceptions of an intellectual game in its bearing on the contentious issue. But, on the other hand, he must also ask a further set of questions. Given that chess is an intellectual game of some sort, what follows about reasonable behaviour in a chess game? Is ability at psychological intimidation or ability to resist such intimidation really an intellectual quality? These questions ask him to look more closely at the concept of intellect itself.[38]

In looking more closely at the concept of intellect itself the referee will find that some conceptions of intelligence do not achieve a fit with the institutional rules of chess. For example, physical grace may be seen by some as embodying a possible conception of intelligence, but it clearly does not fit the practice of chess. However, the referee may find in the end that two different conceptions of intellect seem to fit the settled rules of the game equally well. In this position he is called upon to decide which of the two accounts provides a "deeper or more successful account of what intellect is." Even so, though such abstract problems are relevant, this does not require the referee to enter the domain of the philosophy of mind for its own sake. He has to determine what institutional rights the players have, and these more abstract arguments are only relevant in so far as they have a bearing on a correct decision regarding the rights at stake. In the last analysis the referee thus has to come to a reasoned decision regarding a specific institutional problem. The context of his decision is the basic fact that once an institution is set up, such that the "participants have institutional rights under distinct rules belonging to that institution then hard cases may arise that must in the nature of the case, be supposed to have an answer."[39] In this case it must be supposed that either the man who objected to his opponent smiling has a right that the smiler forfeit the game to him, or he does not, in which case the smiler has a right that the game continue. It is not the case that the players have a right to whatever decision the referee sees fit to make, i.e. a right to a decision. They are entitled to the right decision about their rights.

What is at stake is a general grasp of the institution as a rule-following practice including the relevant kinds of justification for settling disputes. If the referee is called upon to decide what rights the disputants have, he must "bring to his decision a general theory of why, in the case of this institution, the rules create any rights at all."[40] Obviously in chess this general theory must refer to the consent which the parties playing chess may be presupposed to have given to the rules of the game. Thus, Dworkin concludes:

> the hard case puts, we might say, a question of political theory. It asks what it is fair to suppose the players have done in consenting to the forfeiture rule. The concept of a game's character is a conceptual device for framing that question. It is a contested concept that internalizes the general justification of the institution so as to make it available for discriminations within the institution itself. It supposes that a player consents not simply to a set of rules, but to an enterprise that may be said to have a character of its own; so that when the question is put – To what did we consent in consenting to that? – the answer may study the enterprise as a whole and not just the rules.[41]

How is this account of Dworkin's discussion of the referee's struggle with a hard case in chess pertinent to normative theory in international relations? At the end of the previous section I mentioned the conventional view in terms of which it is not possible to settle contentious issues in the modern state domain of discourse. According to this conventional view in hard cases there are no agreed upon rules for deciding the issues. In the absence of these (so the argument holds) it is not possible to rule that one decision is right and another wrong. With regard to this objection Dworkin's chess example demonstrates several things: first, that where a difficult case arises within an institution, the person called upon to make a decision is not free to make any decision he sees fit, even though in such cases (by definition) there is no clear rule dictating the correct solution. Rather he is constrained by a set of standards (other than rules) which are, we may say, inherent in the institution taken as a whole.

Second, Dworkin's example indicates the kind of procedure that someone called upon to decide such cases may follow in order to bring the inherent standards to light. The crucial features of this procedure are:

1. The requirement that the decision-maker start by inquiring into the *background justification* for the *institution* as a whole.
2. In seeking an answer to 1 he must start with *"what everyone knows"* as the point or purpose of the institution. This inquiry will reveal certain guiding concepts capable of diverse conceptions. Thus, we saw that all chess players would agree that chess is an intellectual game, but there is scope for diverse conceptions of just what this implies.
3. He must seek out that conception of the institution's point or character which best accords with the settled rules of the institution.
4. In the event of his being left (after completing step 3) with two or more conceptions which seem to fit the institution's settled practice equally well, he must decide which gives the deepest and most satisfying account of the concept. This may involve him in more fundamental philosophical questions about the nature of the basic commitments of the participants in the practice. But these are only of interest to him in so far as they reveal to him the character of the institution to which the participants have consented.

Third, the chess example shows how a background theory which must necessarily be quite general can be used to generate a determinant solution to a difficult case. It is this background theory which allows a correct decision in hard cases.

The last point is at the heart of Dworkin's ongoing dispute with positivist theories of law and with our refutation of the conventional wisdom outlined at the beginning of this section. Both the legal positivist and conventional wisdom in international relations hold that we can only talk of a "right answer" to a case where there is a determinate rule specifying what the answer is. On this view, where there is no rule there can be no correct answer, but only a choice among several equally reasonable answers. In such cases, reasonable folk are not called upon to seek agreement. Against this Dworkin argues that the positivist model of argument, with its heavy stress on mechanical rules, cannot account for the fact that arguments do take place where mechanical rules are not readily available. In the chess example, in hard cases in law and, I want to suggest, in the knotty issues in international relations, people do argue in the belief that what they are arguing for is correct and that the view which they are opposing is wrong. In the chess example Dworkin shows that it is possible to arrive at a correct decision about the rights of the players although there is no clear rule covering the case.[42]

For my purposes the question of whether or not there are right answers to hard cases is of interest in its own right, but it also has considerable further significance. According to Dworkin's model, it is possible to settle hard cases (concerning law, chess, and international relations), but not without getting involved in "deep" discussions about the basic justifications for the institutions within which these issues arise. Thus judges in hard legal cases are called upon to get involved in political theory, concerning themselves with such questions as: "What is the underlying justification for the settled rules of the law? Why and when are legislatures justified in creating new rights?" Once the pertinence of such questions is admitted, it is no longer possible to maintain the positivist separation between law and morals. Positivists want to maintain this distinction because it makes plausible their contention that the law can be investigated objectively, without the investigators becoming involved in normative theorizing themselves. In this respect legal positivists are like the positivist social scientists discussed in chapter 1.[43] They are also akin to the realist school of scholars in international relations discussed in chapter 2. All these approaches seek to give a factual account of the practices under investigation which does not require any involvement in normative theory. Dworkin shows how an adequate account of an institution must explain what happens when hard cases arise, and that in order to do this the investigator must become involved in fundamental normative theorizing.

Building coherent background justifications

We have seen, then, that the core of Dworkin's method of argument involves the construction of a background theory for the institution within which the hard case in question arises. Before attempting to apply his method to the hard cases of international relations there is one other device he employs which we need to take note of – the procedure of *reflective equilibrium* which was first used by John Rawls.[44] It will be recalled that according to Dworkin's method of argument a judge seeking a solution to a hard case must start with what everyone knows to be the settled rules of the institution and then proceed to construct that background theory which best accords with these settled rules.[45] The technique of reflective equilibrium is designed to overcome an incompatibility (a lack of fit) between the body of settled rules and the background theory which might arise at this point. To demonstrate the use of the technique let us imagine a judge facing a hard case in law.

The judge must be pictured as seeking a fit (or match) between a whole body of settled law and the justificatory background theory. However, there are several reasons for supposing that it will not be possible to achieve a complete coherence. First, the settled law is extremely complex and was created by diverse judges, legislators and jurists who may well have had divergent educations, abilities and outlooks. It seems plausible to suppose that the law laid down by such a varied group might not easily be subsumed under a coherent theory. Second, the body of settled law was arrived at over a long span of time and, once again, it seems plausible to suppose that earlier rules may not cohere with later ones. Third, the world changes over time and some of the early rules were laid down in a world quite different from that confronting subsequent judges. The rules made for one setting might not easily cohere with those made for another.

Faced with a possibly not fully coherent body of settled law for which he is to provide an adequate background theory, the technique of reflective equilibrium involves a back-and-forth procedure somewhat as follows: in seeking to construct a coherent background theory to justify the whole body of settled rules, the judge finds that it challenges (calls into question) some bits of the settled corpus of law. He now faces a dilemma: either he must return to the background theory and modify it in some way so that it can encompass these awkward pieces of the settled law, or he must simply accept that the settled body of law is not fully coherent and that these recalcitrant pieces cannot be fitted into the best background theory he can construct. If he chooses to modify the background theory to accommodate these pieces it is likely that other bits of the settled body will in a like manner refuse to fit the new background theory. Thus it is probable that in any piece of legal reasoning the judge will end up with some bits and pieces of the settled law which do not fit the proposed justificatory background theory. In this way bits of settled law will become suspect and may well with time fall into disuse. This back-and-forth procedure is the procedure of reflective equilibrium. By moving back and forth between the settled rules and the background theory the judge seeks an equilibrium. After achieving a reflective equilibrium, the final step is to use the background theory to generate a solution to the hard case in hand.

It is important to notice that recalcitrant pieces of settled law are *not* akin to the bits of evidence which a natural scientist cannot accommodate in his theory. For a scientist such evidence poses a potential threat to the scientific theory; it forms part of the data which either confirm or refute his theory. A good scientist is not entitled to push such evidence aside on the grounds that it does not achieve a nice "fit" with his theory. In the face of such pieces of counter-evidence the scientist might decide to wait and see whether more data of the same kind are forthcoming in the future. But he may not disregard it altogether. The judge's position is quite different. The bits of settled law which he confronts are not data for which he seeks a satisfactory explanation. Rather they are pieces of settled law for which he has to try and seek a single coherent justification. The bits which do not fit even the best justification constructible must be deemed to be suspect although previously considered as settled.[46]

I have discussed this procedure of argument in detail for two reasons: first, it indicates in a general way how we might set about solving the hard cases facing normative theorists in international relations, some of which we mentioned at the beginning of this chapter. Second, it enables us to counter several objections which have been raised against theories of intra-practice argument (like Dworkin's and the one I am about to develop). I mentioned some of them in chapter 2. Before ending this chapter let us look at some of the others.

Refutation of the critique of intra-practice argument

In the light of the exposition of the Dworkinian model of normative argument it is now possible to deal with some criticisms which have been made of the notion of intra-practice argument. The method which has been outlined is intra-practice in that the context in which disputes about hard cases are considered to take place is one in which the disputants are pictured as being initiates of a given practice; they are agreed upon the settled rules which constitute the practice in question. Their dispute is about hard cases *within* the practice.

Critics of intra-practice argument, like Ernest Gellner, have argued against approaches such as the one I have been advocating which relies upon the modern state domain of discourse. Gellner labels approaches such as this one, "reindorsement theories."[47] Elsewhere he says that such theories force us into "uncritical acceptance" of traditional language.[48] Against such criticism I would argue that intra-practice argument as outlined above is not inevitably an endorsement of the status quo. As we have seen, argument and reasoning within the practice can lead to the practice changing in significant ways over time. In his major attack on this type of approach, in his book *Words and Things*, Gellner says it commits us to "conceptual conservatism"[49] which in turn, he says, leads to political conservatism.[50] These charges all contain an element of truth in them together with some falsity. The element of truth is that the procedure of argument outlined above is conservative in that it starts from, and is tested against, the settled rules of the particular domain of discourse within which it takes place. What is false is the contention that the method involves an *uncritical* reindorsement of the practice concerned. As we said in the discussion of the procedure of reflective equilibrium, there is a critical dimension to this process. In seeking an equilibrium parts of the settled corpus come to be challenged and thus over time the practice changes and develops. Everything is not left as it was.[51] However it is true that on this view criticism cannot but be piecemeal.

Against this it might be argued that Gellner's major concern is not with validating a single decision within a legal system, but with the problem of validating one domain of discourse, *vis-à-vis* others. In particular Gellner is concerned to validate the scientific mode of discourse *vis-à-vis* other non-scientific ones, such as Marxist ones. This is true as a statement of what Gellner wants to do, but it in no way undermines the relevance for my purposes of the method of argument outlined above. My contention is that argument about the validity of a domain of discourse (e.g. the scientific one), just like argument about the validity of a decision for a hard case in law, will only be possible within an established mode of discourse which has a large component of settled premises from which the argument can proceed. There are two things which reindorsement philosophers (as Gellner calls them) are concerned to deny here. The first is that there is some special philosophical method which can show whether a given domain of discourse is valid or not.[52] The second is that within a domain of discourse it is not possible to doubt *all* the usages ordinarily accepted as valid (unless, of course, the investigator retreats to a higher domain of discourse within which the original domain is seen as but a sub-category). However, it is quite possible to come to doubt some of the settled usages.

A related but different objection to the method of intra-practice argument, which we hope to have countered by portraying the Dworkinian method of legal argument, is the objection that theories of intrapractice argument cannot cope with "creativity," "thought," "game change," or "improvement."[53] On Gellner's view, reindorsement philosophies (ordinary language philosophies) cannot account for conceptual changes (which undoubtedly do take place in all societies in the course of history) because they are committed to the premise that ordinary usage is correct as it is. Once again, this objection contains some element of truth. It is true that reindorsement philosophies deny that philosophy can discover criteria which will show *all* ordinary discourse to be wrong. But we have seen how it is possible via the method of reflective equilibrium to show that some of our settled usages are wrong. In response to new situations new usages will emerge. These may be tested via the method of reflective equilibrium (the method of intra-practice critique) and thus, gradually, the ordinary language will change and grow.

Finally, the description of the procedure of legal argument has shown how it is that the user of the language in a given domain (in this case the judge) may make a mistake. It was shown that endorsing an intra-practice theory of argument does not involve a commitment to the view that those within a practice can do no wrong, can make no mistakes. What the Dworkinian model of legal argument gives us is an account of what is involved in making a mistake in hard case decisions. A judge may make a mistake in any of the stages of argument which were identified: in the identification and articulation of the settled law, in the construction of a justifying background theory, in bringing this into equilibrium with the settled law, and in the generation of a new rule from the background theory to cover the case in hand.

In this chapter I have outlined a method of argument which promises to solve some of the pressing normative issues which face us in contemporary international relations. It starts by pointing out that normative disputes arise only within the context of some shared premises, within the contest of some settled rules. I showed, following Dworkin, how this body of settled rules may be used, in a step-by-step procedure, to generate answers to the hard cases which arise within a given practice.

Let us now attempt to apply this method of argument to some of those hard cases in international ethics identified at the beginning of this long chapter. As a first step we must identify the settled norms of international relations and then we must proceed to construct the best possible background theory which will justify them.

4 Towards the construction of a normative theory of international relations

The task of the present chapter, if done properly, would be a task for Hercules. As was shown in the previous chapter, what we are called upon to do in constructing a normative theory of international relations must involve at least the following steps. First, we must list all those norms in international relations that are considered settled in terms of the modern state domain of discourse. Second, we must attempt to construct the best possible background justification for this settled body of norms. Third, following through on step two, we must apply the procedure of reflective equilibrium. Fourth, with the aid of the background theory we must generate answers to some of the hard cases facing international relations theorists. Since none of us has the capacities of a Hercules we must rest content with something less, something altogether more schematic.

Before proceeding with the work at hand it is worth noticing how the end of the Cold War has decisively eradicated what was once taken to be a major objection to this project. During the period of bipolar world politics the suggestion that there existed a set of settled norms which could be distilled out from the modern state domain of discourse was often greeted with scepticism by critics who would point out that communist states merely *pretended* to accept these norms, but were in fact committed to the transformation (and indeed the complete abolition) of the system of sovereign states. In support of this objection the critics would refer to the canon of Marxist writings in terms of which communist states legitimated their authority. It portrayed the state as an instrument of the capitalist class and showed how this class used it to maintain its exploitative relationship to the working class. The canon then predicted the withering away of states after the revolution. The breakup of the Soviet Union and its satellites has dealt this line of criticism several blows. First, the theories embedded in the canon were revealed to be suspect in that history was clearly not unfolding in the ways they had predicted. Second, the people in the communist states revealed in what they subsequently did and said, a firm commitment to the norms of the state centric domain of discourse. What we have witnessed in the wake of the collapse of communism is an overt scramble for statehood by millions of people in dozens of nations. The people of the ex-communist bloc countries have been (and still are) striving to establish themselves in independent democratic states. They explicitly justify their actions with reference to the settled norms of the modern state domain of discourse which I shall now articulate.

The settled body of norms in international relations

It is not possible to give a conclusive or very detailed account of what is the settled body of norms within the domain of normative international theory. At this stage a very rough and preliminary list will have to suffice. Since we are listing the parts of what is a settled whole, we must also expect that there will be some overlap among the listed items. The items are not clearly discrete.

I shall regard a norm as settled where it is generally recognized that any argument denying the norm (or which appears to override the norm) requires special justification. Where I claim that a norm is settled I am not claiming that most people (or states) do in fact obey that norm. In other words, the claim that a given norm is settled cannot be disputed by pointing out instances where people (or states) have not in actual fact acted according to the norm. For example, that many states infringe the norm prohibiting one state from interfering in the domestic affairs of another state does not undermine my contention that non-interference is a settled norm of the modern state domain of discourse. It would undermine my assertion if it could be shown that states do not even attempt to provide special justifications for their interferences in the domestic affairs of other states. What people say in support of their actions thus gives us an indication of whether a given item is settled within a specified domain of discourse.

Another indicator of whether a given norm is settled within the modern state domain of discourse or not is provided by the way in which acts which infringe the norm are undertaken. Where acts which infringe a given norm are often (normally) undertaken clandestinely, this is *prima facie* proof that the norm in question is a settled one. For the most part states do not openly undertake and publicly defend actions aimed at destabilizing neighbouring states. This is *prima facie* evidence that there is a settled norm prohibiting such actions. Finally, it must be remembered in the case of each settled norm that it is the concept of that norm which is regarded as settled within the modern state domain of discourse, and not any particular conception of the concept.[1]

Let us now consider what is settled, at least in the sense outlined above, within the modern state domain of discourse. I shall start by setting out a rather long list of settled norms. My aim in doing this is to indicate that what is being put forward here is not a "thin" raft of consensus, but is a set of commitments which is altogether more substantial. I present the settled norms under different headings which serve to highlight the scope and range of international agreement on normative matters. At the outset I need to point out that this list is not exhaustive, that the norms are closely related to one another and that it is often difficult to maintain clear distinctions between them.

The sovereignty (S) norms

S1. Within the modern state system it is a settled norm that the *preservation of the society of sovereign states* is itself a good. The claim here is not that everybody actively promotes this as a goal, but that no significant group of actors in world politics acts contrary to this in the conduct of international affairs without invoking special justifications.[2] Those (such as many Third World states) who argue that the present arrangement of the system of states is unfair do not so much call for the abandonment of the system of states (requiring that it be replaced by a world government, for example), but argue for certain modifications to the system.[3] In particular, they demand a new system for the distribution of wealth between states.

S2. For the purposes of the modern state domain of discourse it is settled that it is a good for states in the system to be accounted as *sovereign*, where sovereignty refers to an autonomous state ruling over a specified territory. What is involved here is best brought out by contrasting it with the political organization in a very different kind of system such as the feudal one. In the feudal system the relationships between people consisted in sets of mutual and personal obligations of certain conventional kinds. Typically a set of obligations would be established between a nobleman and a group of serfs, in terms of which he would protect them in time of war in return for a portion of the harvest. The nobleman would himself be bound by mutual obligations with other noblemen and so on. Thus, in a given territory the web of obligation might be quite complicated and also fluid – with no clear and single centre of government having ultimate authority over all the people – and is rather a cross-cutting web of personal obligations.[4] In the modern system of states, assumptions regarding authority relations are quite different. Here all the people within the territory of a sovereign state are supposed to fall under its exclusive authority. This authority is assumed to be binding on them for as long as they remain in its territory. A South African cannot be regarded as bound by the law of Russia while living in Johannesburg. Also a South African cannot be regarded as under the concurrent rule of two or more states. Where a person moves out of the territory of one sovereign state, he moves into that of another and thereby *ipso facto* falls under its authority. A further point to notice is that, unlike the personal nature of feudal authority, sovereign states are considered to be in a sense immortal in that the authority of a state over its citizens is not connected to any particular person's lifespan, but inheres in the enduring political order itself.

S3. It is settled that any attempt by one sovereign state to extend its sovereignty by subjugating other states by force is bad and that action to avoid any such imperial drive towards preponderant power is considered good.

S4. The preservation by sovereign states of the *balance of power* is a settled norm and acts aimed at furthering this end need no special justification, while those tending to upset it typically do. Thus a state that strengthens its internal economy, morale, army and so on will publicly avow that this is required to maintain the balance of power, but it will not acknowledge the contrary aim (i.e. it will not publicly avow an imperialist goal). It might seek to stall the drive towards dominance of another state in one or all of several different ways – for example, by forming defensive alliances with other states, by seeking to influence world public opinion against the expanding power, or by seeking to undermine the internal stability of the threatening state. All of these will be justified as seeking to maintain a balance of power in the face of an imperialist threat.

S5. It is settled that *patriotism* is a good thing where the term is understood as referring to a feeling by the citizens of loyalty to, and love for, their state. That this is a good is explained by reference to the need for internal strength required to meet the threats mentioned in S4. In order to defend itself against a would-be imperial power, a state's economic and military power depends on the cooperation of its citizens. A state without such a patriotic feeling amongst its citizens would be weak. It is important that this should not be confused with the quite different issue of nationalism. Certainly no point about a mystical entity called the nation is being made here. Nationalism is a recent and controversial historical development whereas patriotism is essentially contained in the old adage that unity is strength. There is agreement in the world today that such strength of civic feeling between people living within the territory of a state is a good.

S6. For the purposes of the modern state domain of discourse it is settled that the government of a sovereign state's first duty is to protect the interests of its own citizens. The well-being of its own citizens must be considered more important than the well-being of people elsewhere in the world.

S7. The rule of *non-intervention* in the domestic affairs of other states is a well-settled norm. It precludes direct military involvement against other states except where such action is in self-defence or in terms of a defensive alliance. Military action in self-defence may be undertaken unilaterally by the attacked state or there may be a multilateral engagement authorized by a collective security arrangement such as the United Nations.

S8. It is agreed that within certain parameters the self-determination of peoples is a good. This is understood as indicating that a nation is entitled to be self-determining within a sovereign state.

International law (L) norms

L1. It is settled that in the relations between states, the lack of agreed upon and authoritative rules guiding conduct in specified spheres of activity would be bad. Thus the body of *international law* which is designed to overcome this problem is considered a good. The problem of the status of such law (compared to the status of law within states), and the criticisms levelled at various aspects of it, should not prevent us from recognizing that the idea of international law is a settled norm. As the complexity and scope of the interactions between states have grown, so has the body of settled international law. There are multiple and persistent disputes about diverse aspects of international law, but the modern state domain of discourse assumes agreement on some core body of international law. Underlying this is a deeper agreement on the need for international law.[5]

L2. In their normal dealings with each other states clearly proceed on the assumption that war requires a special justification in a way that peaceful relations do not, thus indicating that *peace* is regarded as a settled norm. This norm is built into international law in the *ius ad bellum* which narrowly restricts the circumstances under which states may resort to war. This norm is also a bedrock norm underpinning the United Nations charter. In setting up the United Nations Organization the founding states made the maintenance of international peace a primary goal. The argument is not that acts of war are never considered justified – they often are – but rather that war is considered to be in need of justification in a way that peace is not. All states going to war take pains to justify their case before the international community, whereas states remaining at peace with other states do not generally go out of their way to justify their peaceful relationship.

L3. It is settled that in the conduct of war, once it has broken out, certain rules ought to be obeyed, i.e. that subset of the rules of international law usually referred to as the *ius in bello*.

L4. When a state acts so as to threaten international peace and security as defined by international law it is agreed that it is a good thing for states to establish a *collective security* arrangement for the purpose of maintaining international peace and security. It is settled that attempts to set up such arrangements are good. Thus there is agreement on the worth of international institutions such as the United Nations Organization and its associated organizations. The agreement on this norm remains whatever criticisms might be levelled against the actual performance of the United Nations.

L5. In general it is agreed that it is permitted for states, in order to support collective security measures, to use *economic sanctions* against the offending state. But note that the use of such sanctions for other purposes is normally considered an unwarranted interference in the domestic affairs of another state.

L6. In order to secure the standing of states, maintain the balance of power and to achieve the other goals mentioned thus far, what is required is a sophisticated means of international communication. The *institution of diplomacy* is designed to achieve this and it is settled that this is a good. A successful diplomatic apparatus requires legal measures for the protection of the persons of diplomats, the protection of their channels of communication, and so on.

Modernization (M) norms

M1. Within the modern state domain of discourse it is settled that *modernization* is an approved goal for states. Modernization is regarded as an approved goal in itself (in that a modernized society is preferable to a primitive one) and it is also invoked as a justification for advancing some of the other settled norms which we have mentioned. For example, a state, in order not to fall under the domination of another state, must, amongst other things, strengthen itself internally. In the world as it is presently constituted this requires that the state replace primitive methods of production with modern industrial techniques. This requires a new division of labour, the accumulation of capital, the acquisition of the necessary technology, the building of advanced infrastructure, the finding and gaining of access to the necessary raw materials, and so on. It is generally recognized that states which fail to modernize successfully make themselves vulnerable to domination by other states.[6]

M2. It is agreed that some kind of system of *economic cooperation* between states is a good.

Domestic (D) norms

D1. It is a settled international norm that *democratic institutions* within states are preferable to non-democratic ones. This implies that states without such institutions are called upon to justify their not being democracies. Defences of this kind might refer to economic necessity (for example, that temporary autocratic rule is necessary to get the economy on its feet), external threat (for example, that autocratic rule is needed to enable the state to cope with an immediate external threat), and so on. That the democratic norm is settled, of course, does not imply that most, or even many, states are, in fact, democracies.

D2. It is settled that *human rights* are a good and that they need to be protected by states and by the international system. Where an infringement of human rights is claimed, the accused state is called upon to deny the charge or produce an excuse for its conduct. Once again we are not claiming that there is an international agreement on what precisely these rights are or on how they ought to be protected. But there is agreement on a core of such rights which ought to be upheld.

To summarize, it is settled that the following are goods:
S1. The preservation of the society of states.
S2. State sovereignty.
S3. Anti-imperialism.
S4. The balance of power.
S5. Patriotism.
S6. Protecting the interests of a state's citizens.
S7. Non intervention.

S8. Self-determination.
L1. International law.
L2. *Ius ad bellum*.
L3. *Ius in bello*.
L4. Collective security.
L5. Economic sanctions (under specified circumstances).
L6. The diplomatic system.
M1. Modernization.
M2. Economic cooperation.
D1. Democratic institutions within states.
D2. Human rights.

Justificatory background theories for the settled core of agreed norms: a critical appraisal

On reflection, what is striking about the foregoing list is the primacy of the first two items on the list. Most of the other settled goods are in some way derivatives of them. Combining the first two items, it appears that the preservation of a system of sovereign states is the primary good. The majority of the other goods mentioned imply a prior acceptance of this good. Thus any satisfactory background theory will have to justify the settled belief that the preservation of a system of sovereign states is such a good. Any acceptable background theory will have to answer this key question: "Why is it a good thing to preserve a system of sovereign states?" An alternative formulation of the question is: "What is the best justification for the preservation of a system of sovereign states?"[7]

What then *is* the best justification for the system of sovereign states? There are current in the discipline three main answers which we must look at. I am not suggesting that these three are the only possible answers to the question; there may be many more. But it does seem a good idea to start with answers which are already current in the debate.

Justifications invoking order

Many theorists in international relations have justified the preservation of a system of sovereign states on the ground that it promotes *order*. This justification has traditionally been given by those theorists preoccupied with theories of balance of power.[8] Such theorists were primarily concerned with explicating and applying the notoriously difficult notion of the balance of power and they were only incidentally concerned with the question of the justification of the system of sovereign states. Their aims were primarily descriptive and explanatory. In so far as they were concerned with justifying the preservation of a system of sovereign states, the problem which they saw themselves called upon to answer was: "Is the system of sovereign states operating according to the balance of power principle justified even though its members are by definition subject to no common law?"

In one way or another the answer to this question was always that the states in the balance formed some kind of ordered society and that the balance of power was justified in so far as it worked towards preserving that society of states. Originally it was argued that this society of states was a Christian one.[9] Let me give a few examples of this type of argument.

Giovanni Botero, writing in the sixteenth century, says that "to effect a balance in politics is simply to prevent others from disturbing the peace and endangering the society of states."[10] In the next century we find Fenelon arguing:

> Neighbouring states are not obliged to observe towards each other the rules of justice and public faith; but they are under a necessity, from the security of each, and the common interest of all, to maintain together a kind of society and general republic, for the most powerful will certainly at length prevail and overthrow the rest, unless they unite together to make a counterweight.[11]

He also wrote, "Nor is this injustice; 'tis to preserve itself and its neighbours from servitude; 'tis to contend for the liberty, tranquillity and happiness of all in general."[12] Daniel Defoe, writing about Europe in the late sixteenth century and early seventeenth century, says, "the safety of the whole consists in a due distribution of power . . . that no one may be able to oppress and destroy the rest."[13] In the eighteenth century, Vattel articulated most eloquently the justification we are considering when he wrote:

> Europe forms a political system . . . not a confused heap of detached parts, each of which had little concern for the lot of others . . . The constant attention of sovereigns to all that goes on, the custom of resident ministers, the continual negotiations that take place, make of modern Europe a sort of Republic whose members each independent, but bound by a common interest unite for the maintenance of order and preservation of liberty.[14]

More recently, Hedley Bull defended the society of states on the grounds that it promoted the goal of order. In the *Anarchical Society* Bull sets out to examine certain institutions such as the balance of power, international law, diplomacy and war. He says: "it is their functions in relation to order that I seek to explain."[15] In spite of the term "function" it is clear that for Bull the system of states may be said to promote order and to that extent it is justified. Bull is careful to state that order is only one value amongst others which the institutions in the society of states may be said to promote. Order is, for example, distinct from the goals of justice. Although Bull makes some confusing remarks about order not being a primary or overriding goal, it is clear from a reading of his book as a whole that in his view the satisfaction of other goals, like justice and welfare, presuppose that the prior goal of order be already satisfied.[16]

The balance-of-power authors I have referred to thus defend the system of states operating on the balance-of-power principle on the grounds that it preserves some kind of ordered society ("the society of states," "a kind of society and general Republic," "the safety of the whole," and "a sort of Republic"). My argument will be that this defence of the system of sovereign states is a weak one. It is weak in that it is either circular, *or* it is a natural law justification masquerading as something else.

Let us look at the first of these criticisms, viz. that this type of justification is circular. Common to the writers we have mentioned we find the following form of argument: "The system of sovereign states operating according to the balance-of-power principle is justified in that it preserves a kind of society." We are entitled to ask of this justification: "What kind of society does it preserve?" The answer to this often appears to be: "It preserves a system of states operating according to the balance-of-power principle."[17] This answer is clearly circular in that the argument now becomes: "The system of states operating according to the balance-of-power principle is justified in that it preserves the system of states operating according to the balance-of-power principle." Of course none of the writers mentioned makes this argument quite so explicitly. It would be self-defeating to do so. That their argument is a circular one is often obscured by the vagueness of the terms employed.

Hedley Bull on order

An influential modern version of this position, open to the same critical charges, is that provided by Hedley Bull. Bull's position on this point is more difficult in that he discusses three different kinds of order, viz. order, international order and world order. However, after making these distinctions in the Introduction to his *Anarchical Society* he reverts in much of the book to talking of order *simpliciter* so that it is often far from clear which kind of order is being talked about. Let us look at his three notions of order.

Order.

Bull defines order as a pattern preserving three primary goals:
1. The preservation of life.
2. That promises should be kept.
3. That the possession of things will remain stable to some degree.[18]

International order.

He defines this as the pattern of activity that sustains the following primary goals of the society of states:
1. The preservation of the system and society of states itself.
2. The goal of maintaining the independence or external sovereignty of individual states.
3. The goal of peace among the member states of society as the normal condition of their relationship.
4. The common goals of all social life.[19]

World order.

Bull defines world order as those patterns of human activity that "sustain the primary goals of social life among mankind as a whole."[20]

A glance at the above mentioned definitions shows that if Bull wishes to argue that the society of states preserves *international order* (as he defines it) then his justification is of the same circular kind as that used by the traditional authors discussed. Primary goals of international order 1, 2 and 3 all simply refer to the maintenance of the society of states. Thus the justification becomes: "The society of states is justified because it maintains the society of states." At first glance item 4 seems to refer to some other kind of order. But this is not so. For Bull makes it clear that he is referring to the common goals of all social life *as they apply to inter-state relations*. Thus he says states limit violence by maintaining a monopoly of violence in their territories, by respecting one another's messengers, by trying to limit wars to certain "just wars" and by waging wars within certain constraints.

The common social goal is served by states generally adhering to treaties. The property goal is embodied in states' mutual respect for one another's sovereignty over a certain area of territory.[21] Thus even with regard to item 4 in the definition of international order we find that order consists in nothing other than the continued existence of the system of sovereign states. On this view international order would only cease to exist where the situation arose in which only one state existed, or where no states existed. The system of states on this view is justified because it preserves itself. No independent reason is given for the creation, maintenance or preservation of the system of sovereign states.

However, there is another way of reading Bull's justification of the system of states. He may be read as arguing that the system of states preserves *order* (as opposed to *international order*) where this notion involves certain higher level norms as spelled out in his list of primary goals. According to his basic definition of order, as distinguished from the more specific notion of international order, order is that pattern of activity which preserves the primary goals of all social life: the preservation of life, that promises should be kept, and that the possession of things remain stable to some degree. If we read Bull in this way then his justification is clearly not open to the circularity charge. He cannot be interpreted as saying the system of states is justified because it preserves itself. Rather, it is justified because it furthers these more primary goals of order in general. However, this alternative reading of Bull is open to a different objection, which is that order (which involves the preservation of the aforementioned primary goals) is not a criterion which a basic social arrangement can satisfy or fail to satisfy. Order in this sense is, rather, a constitutive feature of all and any basic social arrangement. This constitutive notion of order needs to be explained in more detail.

Consider the following different types of basic political arrangements: a nomadic tribe, a dynasty, a republic, a kingdom, an empire, a federation, a confederation, a communist society, a socialist state. (This list could easily be extended.) Any of the above mentioned social orders, if it is to be an order at all, must satisfy the primary "goals" mentioned in Bull's definition of order. They must all provide ways of coping with violence, contract and property. The precise way in which the different social arrangements deal with these common concerns will obviously vary, but what is not open to doubt is that they must provide *some* solution to the problems mentioned. A traditional tribal order deals with property in a different way to that adopted in a communist society, or a capitalist one, or a feudal one, and so on. It is clear, then, that any of the listed basic social arrangements *in order to be a basic social arrangement or order* must provide ways of coping with violence, contract and property. Where the "primary goals" of order are not achieved, what we have is not an unjustifiable type of order, but no basic social order at all. Where these "goals" are not met, we have social breakdown, chaos, disorder.

The force of my contention that order is a constitutive feature of any and all basic social arrangements now becomes clear. *Whatever* arrangement is advocated for world politics, whether it be world government, a confederation of states, a collective security arrangement, a system of sovereign states or some other arrangement, it will as a form of order have to be some arrangement which provides for the basic goals mentioned by Bull. If it does not provide for these, there will be the absence of order, viz. disorder, chaos, etc. In other words, order does not provide a criterion in terms of which it is possible to evaluate the system of sovereign states as a specific arrangement *vis-à-vis* some alternative arrangement. Rather, order provides a criterion for what is to count as a basic arrangement. If any proposal is to count as a proposal for a basic social arrangement then it must satisfy the criterion of order. Once the proposal has satisfied this criterion, an attempt may be made to go on to the next step, which is to make a comparative evaluation of the merits of the alternatives proposed. In this second step questions will arise about the comparative merits of different ways of coping with the problems of violence, contract and property. What emerges from the foregoing discussion, then, is that order is a defining feature of any basic social arrangement, rather than a goal which such an arrangement might realize.

There is another important point to be made here. I have argued that order is preserved in feudal orders, republics, communes, federations and so on, in that each (if it is to be viable) must provide some way of coping with the three core problems. It is important to notice, though, that it is not possible to answer the question: "Which arrangement best preserves order?" because order in the feudal kingdom is something quite different from the order of the communist state. Order here is not a measure against which the different arrangements can be tested (it is not akin to speed, which provides a standard against which different kinds of motor cars can be tested), but is a criterion for recognizing certain social arrangements as such. Order, to repeat, enables us to distinguish between basic social arrangements on the one hand, and, for example, social breakdown and chaos on the other.

We have seen in this section that order is not a primary goal of basic social arrangements, but a constitutive characteristic of all of them. Thus it cannot be used, as Bull wants to use it, as a standard by which one way of arranging world politics (for example, the system of states way) can be compared with another proposed arrangement (for example, a system of world government).

There is a third way in which Bull's justification of the system of sovereign states in terms of order may be interpreted. Bull may be interpreted as arguing that the system of sovereign states protects order where "order" refers to a further set of values which he has not explicitly articulated. Here "order" might be seen as a shorthand expression for some fuller normative theory which is, however, not fully articulated and difficult to reconstruct.

Consider Bull's discussion of *world order*. He argues that *world order* is more fundamental than *international order*. It is more fundamental because:

> the ultimate units of the great society of all mankind are not states (or nations, tribes, empires, classes or parties), but individual human beings which are permanent and indestructible in a sense which groupings of them of this or that sort, are not. This is the moment of international relations, but the question of world order arises what-ever the political and social structure of the globe.

He says too that if "international order has value, this can only be because it is instrumental to the goal of order in human society as a whole."[22] In these rather obscure passages Bull's argument is that world order is more fundamental than international order *because* individuals are "permanent and indestructible." Clearly individuals are not permanent and indestructible in any literal sense of the phrase. Bull must be read as meaning that individuals are to be valued more highly than "groupings of this or that sort." What else could his point be here? Presumably he is arguing against those who would see the well-being of some collectivity, for example a class, as more important than the well-being of the individuals within it. If this interpretation of Bull is correct then there is implicit in Bull's theory a substantive normative theory in which the good of individuals is more important than the good of social wholes (like states, classes, etc). However, what precisely the nature and implications of this normative theory are is not clear. It could be a theory of human rights (albeit a minimalist one) or it could be a utilitarian theory. The former seems unlikely, since Bull has elsewhere argued explicitly against theories of human rights in international relations.[23] That still leaves us with the latter option. Support for this is to be found in the last chapter of *The Anarchical Society*, where Bull argues against utopian, Marxist and interdependence theories of international relations, which all advocate an end to the system of sovereign states and the creation of a new order. His argument against all of these approaches is that there is no guarantee that the new orders will achieve what their advocates claim; that there is no reason to suppose that a suitably modified system of states could not achieve the desired result just as well; and that the costs of bringing about a new order (rather than modifying the old one) would be exorbitant. The reference to the costs of change suggests that he may be thinking along utilitarian lines.

Let us recapitulate the argument so far. We are seeking to evaluate the contention that the system of sovereign states is justified because it promotes *order*. This kind of justification is implicit in many balance-of-power theories. In order to evaluate this contention we looked at Hedley Bull's *Anarchical Society* where this thesis is explicitly argued. There we found that the justification, on one interpretation proves to be circular. On a second interpretation, it fails because order is a constitutive feature of *all* basic social arrangements and not a criterion in terms of which some basic social arrangements can be judged better (more justifiable) than others. On a third interpretation, the order justification is found to be a veiled reference to some deeper normative theory. In Bull's case the deeper theory involves some notion of conferring primary value on individuals. This deeper theory cannot be explicated in terms of order alone. If we seek a justification for the system of sovereign states, we must seek a satisfactory deep theory which goes beyond order.

What we have found is that the order justification fails to justify the first item on the list of settled beliefs. Not surprisingly, it will be found to fail with regard to all the other items on our list as well. In particular it fails to provide a background theory justifying our settled beliefs that the following are good: modernization, democratic institutions within states, and human rights. What alternative justification is there for our belief that the system of sovereign states is a good?

The utilitarian justification

Kenneth Waltz in his *Theory of International Politics*[24] argues in defence of the present system of sovereign states and against those who wish to see some or other form of world government. He rests his case on arguments such as the following. A world government would need a massive force to police the world. The cost of such a force would be exorbitant. A world government would be a prize of great value and the struggle to gain control of this prize would in all probability be ferocious. The cost of such conflict would be the price to be paid for whatever benefits accrued from world government. The conflicts which would arise in a system of world government would in all probability be between rival nationalist groups. Such conflicts are likely to be particularly difficult to stop. There is thus a high price to pay for the loss of state freedom.[25] All of these arguments are clearly cost/benefit type arguments typical of utilitarian justifications. What we have here, in embryo, is an attempt to justify the system of sovereign states on utilitarian grounds.[26] For our purposes this leads to the more general question: "Is it possible to construct a utilitarian background theory which will justify all (or most) of the items which were listed as being settled within the modern state domain of discourse?"

I think not. There are sound reasons to doubt the utilitarian enterprise as a whole, as will appear from some of the arguments mentioned below. But more specifically there are a whole host of reasons which, taken together, make a formidable case against a utilitarian justification as a background theory in support of the list of settled norms. In the present context it is not possible to go into all the difficulties inherent in any attempt to construct a utilitarian background theory to justify the list of settled norms in the modern state domain of discourse. I shall briefly indicate a few of the main ones.

A utilitarian justification for the norm that the preservation of the society of sovereign states is a good would be of the form: "This norm is justified because adherence to it will achieve a greater aggregate utility than would adherence to any other alternative basic norm such as a norm prescribing, for example, a system of world government." "Aggregate utility" here refers to the sum of wants of the individuals in the world. Presumably this would include the whole adult population. In order to arrive at this aggregate, each person's wants would have to be taken into account without some people's wants being given greater weight than those of others.

There are several major problems facing any such project. A first problem concerns the nature of the wants which have to be taken into account in the calculus of utility. A utilitarian trying to determine whether this norm would maximize utility or not would first have to determine what people's wants were. A problem arises, though, when it is realized that the people whose wants are to be put into the calculus are citizens of sovereign states in the system of sovereign states. What wants these people have will be partially determined by their being citizens of states in a system of states. But wants are not independent variables; they are not unmediated givens. Rather they are socially, historically and institutionally mediated. Thus, for example, a Frenchman's wants will be in part determined by his feeling himself to be a citizen of the French state. This will lead him to favour French interests over, say, Egyptian ones. What follows from this is the implausibility of evaluating two institutions, let us call them A and B, in terms of their want-satisfying capabilities in situations where the wants being measured are in part the creation of the institutions being evaluated. Doing this would be like evaluating the practice of bull-fighting by determining whether it satisfies the wants of bull-fighting fans. Wants thus provide no independent criterion for evaluating institutions of this kind. Utility calculations make best sense with regard to individual actions, like choosing which car to buy. Here we compare models with regard to price, speed, reliability, economy and so on. Our reasoning may quite closely resemble a utility calculus here. However, the notion of a utility calculus makes very little sense with regard to evaluating social and political *institutions* like the family and the state, because wants are themselves socially and historically mediated by such institutions.

A second major problem besetting utilitarian justifications is that an arrangement is deemed to be justified which maximizes the *aggregate* utility without regard to the distribution among individuals. The only distributive criterion built into the utilitarian procedure is the one which stipulates that in the utility calculus each person's wants must be included and that no weighting of wants is to take place; each is to count for one and only one. This aspect of fairness in the procedure does not, however, alleviate the problem caused by the aggregative nature of the enterprise which insists that if X maximizes utility it is to be preferred to Y, even if X involves a very inequitable distribution. Thus if the system of sovereign states maximizes utility it would be justified *even if* it causes extreme misery and deprivation to those living in the poor states. This conclusion offends our basic intuitions about fairness and about social justice.[27] More importantly, this conclusion is incompatible with that settled norm on the list which refers to individual rights. Utilitarian reasoning also justifies arrangements which make some marginally better off, whilst making others very much worse off. On this view, if it could be shown that aggregate utility would be maximized by arrangements making advanced countries marginally better off while keeping Third World countries poor, then this strategy would be justified. It is clear that this line of thinking, pursued to its extreme, is unable to accommodate any satisfactory notion concerning the value of the individual. The fact is that according to this way of thinking the individual is important only as a location for measuring utility. Once the measurement has been made, that person is no longer of any great importance. If what he or she wants does not accord with what the aggregate justifies, then that person is expendable.[28] Once again this conclusion offends our basic intuitions about justice and it is incompatible with the settled norm referring to human rights.

A third problem with the utilitarian justification is that it fails to cope with the fact that people's wants are of differing intensities. John in the USA might want an arrangement which improves his leisure time opportunities, but not as intensely as Tseguy from Ethiopia wants an arrangement which will prevent him starving. Or, because Tseguy from Ethiopia has been reduced by hopelessness to apathy, the intensities of the wants may be reversed. In this latter case we feel John's intensity of want ought to be ignored, while in the former case we feel Tseguy's intense want ought to be taken note of. Utilitarian thought starts out by stressing the primacy of what people *in fact* want. In many cases we feel (on moral grounds) that discriminations need to be made between the different wants that people have. Utilitarian thought does not allow us to make such discriminations.

A fourth problem is closely related to the third, and concerns our strong conviction that some kinds of wants just ought not to be counted in the calculus at all. For example, few would wish people's wants for a fascist political order, for a slave-owning order, for a sexually perverted order and so on, to be counted in a utilitarian calculus. The conviction that these wants ought not to be counted is reflected in some of the items on our list of settled norms, for example in the item referring to human rights. The objection against counting these wants cannot be fobbed off on the ground that such "weirdo wants" are always likely to be minority wants and thus outweighed by the sane majority. Most people would agree that even if, in a given group, a majority wished to enslave a minority it would be wrong to do so. Here, as with the previous problem, the crux of the matter is that when we think about moral issues we want to discriminate between legitimate wants and illegitimate ones. Utilitarian thinking with its narrow focus on *de facto* wants cannot help us make such discriminations. Whatever criteria are introduced to help us make such discriminations, it is clear that they will not be (and cannot be) utilitarian ones.

A fifth problem presented by a utilitarian's justification for the settled norms in the modern state domain of discourse is this. A utilitarian's background theory must argue that the norms on our list are justifiable on utilitarian grounds. His argument must be that by adhering to these norms actors in world politics maximize aggregate utility. His argument must not be taken to be that states ought to stick to these norms *except* where rejecting them (i.e. adopting some other norms) would maximize utility. For adhering to a norm with an exception like this attached to it is not to adhere to a norm at all. Consider the norm on the list which asserts that the protection of human rights is a good. If we understand it as asserting "Actors in international politics ought to adhere to the norms protecting human rights (*a* to *z*) except where doing so does not maximize aggregate utility" we would be loath to consider them human rights norms at all. A right of prisoners-of-war not to be executed out of hand which had attached to it the exception "save where doing so would maximize aggregate utility" would hardly be considered a right at all. For we often assert we have a right in just those situations where denying us the right might, indeed, have the effect of maximizing utility. Indeed, we value rights because they protect us from such decisions. Thus we must take the utilitarian to be asserting that actors adhering to the norms listed (without any utility maximizing exceptions attached to them) will have the effect of maximizing aggregate utility. The utilitarian must be arguing that the utilitarian consequence (i.e. the maximization of aggregate utility) which is supposed to follow from adherence to these norms will come about without any of those bound by the norms making his obedience to the norm dependent on a utility calculus in that particular instance. This is another way of saying that the justification must be a rule utilitarian justification; i.e. it is supposed that utility will be maximized by the parties involved following rules and not basing each of their actions on independent utility calculi.[29] The first few norms on our list call upon states to seek the preservation of the society of sovereign states. The rule utilitarian argument is that out of all the sovereignty preserving actions of states, utility will be maximized, without any state actively pursuing global utility maximization. On the rule utilitarian view the good consequences flow from the actors following the rule, not from the actors following the rule only where doing so will maximize utility. The problem here is that we have a utilitarian justification for a set of norms in which no participant may seek to maximize utility. What is rather weird about this position is that we are here presented with a justification for an agreement, which justification cannot ever provide any guide to the parties involved. The actors involved (in our case, everybody involved in world politics) could never appeal to this background justification to back up any proposed change in the settled norms. Because if they did appeal to this utilitarian background justification, they would not be blindly following the norms which it is supposed (by rule utilitarians) would bring about the utility maximizing result in some automatic way (i.e. in a way that does not involve the participants deliberately seeking the maximizing result).

Our conclusion must be that if we want a background theory which justifies the first few settled norms on the list and which can be used to generate solutions to hard cases, the utilitarian option must be rejected. It could only be of use to an other-worldly non-participant, perhaps a god.

A background theory like the utilitarian one which fails to justify the first item on our list of settled beliefs in international relations is not likely to succeed in justifying the other items on the list. It is worth noticing that it fails to justify item D1, which asserts that it is settled that democratic institutions within the states of the system of sovereign states are a good. No convincing utilitarian justification for democratic institutions has yet been given. It is true that students of politics often talk of the "interest aggregating" function of representative institutions and this language suggests that democratic institutions are engaged in a utility advancing task. Others argue that democratic institutions, by making leaders stand accountable at periodic elections, ensure that the interests of the governors and the interests of the governed coincide. This too shows democratic institutions to be utility-maximizing mechanisms.[30] However, utilitarian justifications for democratic institutions fail because, first, a utilitarian has to provide a plausible account of an independent utility calculus which would show that democratic institutions maximize utility in a way that rule by autocratic technocrats, for example, would not. The many problems which arise in trying to portray what such a calculus would involve have already been hinted at above. Second, a utilitarian justification of democratic institutions justifies these as a means to an end. On this view democratic institutions are justified because they maximize utility. If and when they fail to do so democratic institutions ought to be abandoned in favour of non-democratic arrangements. Most people who support democracy do not see democratic institutions in this way. Democrats are committed to democracy as an end in itself.[31] The utilitarian justification for democracy fails to justify our settled beliefs about democracy.

Finally, it is difficult to see how a utilitarian background justification could be constructed which would both justify the first few norms on our list (which refer to the preservation of the society of sovereign states) and which would justify the item referring to human rights as well as the item which refers to the *ius in bello* (which includes the norm protecting non-combatants in time of war). These latter norms are for the protection of individuals even in those cases where harming a few individuals might well result in an overall increase in aggregate utility. Utilitarian thinking always opens up the possibility of trading off the rights of individuals against a gain in global utility.

Rights-based justifications

In the present state of international relations theory, the last main contender as a possible background justification for the list of settled normative beliefs is a theory of individual human rights.[32] A major problem here is that there are several quite different possible theories of individual rights which could be used as background justifications for the settled list. I shall come to consider some of these shortly, but for the present let us, in a very general way, consider whether a rights-based theory holds any promise at all as a justifying background theory for the list of settled norms.

If we look at the list of settled norms it is immediately apparent that a theory of individual rights is not obviously plausible as a justification for the norms relating to the preservation of the system of sovereign states (items S1 and S2 on our list of settled norms) and those items immediately connected with these (items S3 and S4). By way of a contrast it is easy to see how the beliefs in the goodness of democratic institutions (item D1), international law (item L1), human rights (item D2) and the laws of non-combatant immunity (item L3) could be justified by some or other rights-based theory. This is in sharp contrast to the other two background theories which we have considered (viz. the order justification and the utilitarian justification), which were most plausible when used to justify norms concerning the preservation of the system of sovereign states (and related items) and were least plausible as justifications for our settled norms relating to democratic institutions, international law, human rights and non-combatant immunity. What we are now called upon to do is to see whether it is possible to justify norms S1 and S2 by means of a theory of individual human rights; whether it is possible to construct a rights-based justification which reconciles in a coherent way the norms referring to the preservation of the system of sovereign states and those norms more obviously related to rights.

At first glance there seem to be many obvious reasons why the first two settled norms referring to the preservation of the system of states and to sovereignty cannot be justified by a theory of individual human rights. First, it is generally recognized that sovereign states may and do give overriding primacy to the protection of their national security and to the pursuit of their national interests. In doing this states often act in ways that seem to show callous disregard for the rights of individuals. Thus, for example, the security principle sometimes seems to justify the killing of the innocent. On this view the civilians killed by Israeli action in Lebanon are victims of state action which may be justified by the national security principle. In short, the suggestion here is that reasons of state are often used to justify what are, on the face of the matter, serious infringements of individual human rights. This suggests that it would be difficult to show that reasons of state (which are reasons closely related to the notion of sovereignty) are ultimately justifiable by arguments referring to individual rights.

Second, to many people, the very notion of state sovereignty seems to be opposed to any notion of individual human rights. On this view sovereignty refers *inter alia* to the right of a sovereign to decide what basic rights the people under his or her jurisdiction have. Indeed, there is a basic tension between a theory which accords sovereignty to the state and theories of individual human rights which accord primacy to the individual. It is, on this view, not logically plausible that the norm of state sovereignty could be compatible with a human rights justification.

Third, even a casual student of history would know that, as a matter of fact, states were not in the first instance devised to protect individual rights. There were sovereign states before there were theories of human rights. For this reason historically minded people would be inclined to think any suggestion that the system of sovereign states could be justified on the grounds that it protects human rights is unhistorical.

Fourth, many people would agree that as an institution the state may be well suited to protect human rights within the state and yet they would deny that the *system of sovereign states* is at all suitable for the protection of rights. Domestically the state can protect rights because it has the necessary resources and instrumentalities. It has a law-making power which it can use to this end. It has a judicial power with which it can adjudicate disputes about rights when they arise. It has a police power with which it can enforce judicial decisions about rights. In some states, such as the USA, the basic rights are entrenched in the constitution. However, all of these devices for protecting rights within states are singularly absent within the system of states viewed as a whole. There is no supreme legislature, no supreme judiciary before which all disputes must be settled and there is no coordinated police power which can protect and enforce individual rights worldwide. On this view the system of sovereign states viewed as a political institution seems particularly ill-suited as a means for protecting individual rights.

Fifth, a characteristic way of justifying particular arrangements in rights-based theories seems particularly inapplicable with regard to the system of sovereign states. I refer, of course, to the notion of *contract*. Many theories of human rights justify the authority of the state by postulating a contract (or an agreement based on tacit consent) amongst rights holders. This contract (or tacit agreement) involves the individual rights holders agreeing to transfer some of their rights to the state in return for certain services from the state. Writers as diverse as Hobbes, Locke, Rousseau, Rawls and Nozick all use the device of a contract among the rights holders to legitimize the authority of the state and to set limits to it.[33] These authors vary greatly in the scope of the authority established in this way. There are notorious difficulties involved in the systematic and coherent development of this line of argument which we shall return to later. But for our present purposes the point is that the notion of contract does at least provide a plausible link between individual rights holders and the sovereign state. For it is at least *prima facie* plausible to envisage those within a state as engaged in a joint enterprise which might presuppose some actual or tacit contract. However, the device of such a contract appears to be quite patently not suited to provide a possible link between individual rights holders and the institution of the system of states as a whole. It is not plausible to suppose that the system of sovereign states was or could be the result of a real or tacit contract between individuals. Thus the traditional way of justifying institutions by arguing from rights, *via* a contract to an institution seems closed to us in our search for a justification of the system of sovereign states as a whole.

Sixth, in the world as a whole, although there is a broad agreement that rights are important, there is little agreement about what specific rights people have. In the face of such widespread disagreement it seems implausible to argue that the system of sovereign states is justified because it advances human rights.

It appears, then, that there are many general reasons for supposing that a rights based justification for the two primary norms on the list is not feasible.[34] Thus it would seem that my endeavour to find a background justification which will encompass the items referring to the preservation of the society of states and sovereignty on the one hand, with the items protecting individual human rights on the other hand, must fail. Yet it is clearly of critical importance for my project to find some background justificatory theory that will be able to reconcile and encompass these different kinds of settled norms. For that reason I need to consider more closely the contractarian approach as the standard way in which rights-based theorists have attempted to reconcile the settled norms relating to the system of sovereign states and the settled norms pertaining to individual rights.[35] I shall argue that the contractarian approach does fail in this task, but it will provide a helpful background to our own alternative background justification which also seeks to reconcile both sets of norms.

Contractarian rights-based justifications

Rights-based theories often seek to reconcile the principle of state sovereignty with the principles referring to individual rights by making use of such notions as contract, consent and tacit consent. They seek to show through the use of these notions that a sovereign power need not be destructive of rights, but indeed may be derived from rights holders freely exercising their rights. In order to make the relationship between state sovereignty and individual rights clear we are customarily told a story about how rights are transferred from individual rights holders to a sovereign. The story starts off by asking us to picture an initial situation in which there are rights holders, but in which there is no sovereign.[36] Locke, for example, portrays this original situation as a state of nature in which individuals had what we would today term a set of liberal rights.[37] In this state of nature, though, such individuals faced certain difficulties. One such difficulty was that they lacked the power to enforce their rights against others (individuals or groups of people) who might have sought to infringe those rights. In order to overcome this difficulty, the story continues, the rights holders contracted to create a sovereign power who would be able to enforce their rights. In the contract the parties agreed to cede certain of their rights to the sovereign who would then exercise these rights on their behalf. Where each individual on his own had previously been too weak to enforce his rights against those who infringed them, now the sovereign would (through the concentration of powers in himself as a result of the contract) be able to protect the rights of those who agreed to create him sovereign. According to this story there is thus no basic tension between the notion of sovereign (with the power to rule over his subjects) and the notion of individual rights holders (who are in some sense envisaged as autonomous). There is no tension because the power vested in the sovereign is seen to be derived from the contract freely entered into between the sovereign and his subjects. The power of the sovereign over the subjects is one the subjects themselves have created. The sovereign power is thus a form of self-rule. Of course, rights theorists realize that it is hardly plausible to contend that all the citizens of modern states have in fact explicitly contracted with the sovereign power in their respective states that he exercise power over them. For clearly most people have never made any such contract. This poses a problem for contract theorists, for if most people have never actually made any such contract, what right has the sovereign state to rule over the rights holders living within the state?

In order to get out of this difficulty some rights theorists have turned to the notion of *tacit* consent. According to this notion there are situations in which we may suppose that people have agreed to the transfer of rights (from themselves to the sovereign) even though the people in question have never expressly consented to the transfer. The idea is that people, merely by acting in certain ways (for example, by participating in the democratic institutions of a state, or by generally being law abiding) tacitly signify their consent to the authority of the sovereign. But there are serious problems facing theorists who want to argue the case for tacit consent. For it is crucial to their case that they be able to specify which actions will count as expressing tacit consent and which ones will not. It is important for their case to be able to distinguish between those situations in which the citizens of a state may be said to have tacitly consented to the authority of the sovereign and those situations in which they have not. Clearly we cannot argue that *wherever* people obey the laws of a state they may be taken to have tacitly consented to do so. There are many states in the world where there is general obedience to the laws, but where tacit consent theorists would be loath to say that the people had tacitly consented to the authority of the sovereign, since such compliance is coercively induced. They would not want to allow that the theory of tacit consent may be used in this way in the authoritarian, oligarchical and totalitarian states. They would not accept that the theory of tacit consent may be used to justify the authority of *any state whatsoever*. For consent theorists want to use their theory to distinguish those states whose authority is legitimate from those states whose authority is not. Being law abiding under a junta surely does not indicate the same kind of tacit consent as being law abiding in a liberal democracy. Does the mere fact of obedience signify a similar conferring of legitimacy in both cases? Those living under a junta may obey the law even though they fundamentally oppose the legal system, whereas the citizens in a liberal democracy probably obey the law because they accept it as basically just. The notion of tacit consent itself does not help us distinguish between these two cases. We cannot, as it were, read the tacit consent (or lack of it) from the outward behaviour of the people involved.

I conclude that it is not possible to achieve the reconciliation between rights and sovereignty via the device of a contract (explicit or tacit) for most people have never made a contract and the theory of tacit consent is fraught with difficulties.[38]

I have been considering the difficulties which rights based theories (which reason *via* the contract) have in accounting for the sovereignty of states. Essentially similar problems arise when contract theories are applied to the system of sovereign states as a whole. These fail to deal satisfactorily with the tension between sovereignty and individual rights with which we are concerned. This may be nicely illustrated by glancing at the liberal theory of international relations expounded by Michael Walzer in *Just and Unjust Wars*.[39] That Walzer's theory is in the contract/consent tradition is demonstrated in several places. Let us look at some of these.

In his discussion of the morality of war he says that it is wrong to simply classify all wars as hell. For some kinds of war are not hell; there are those, like feuds and tournaments, to which the participants have *consented*. He writes, "when . . . consent . . . fails . . . 'acts of force' . . . become the constant object of moral condemnation."[40] Even surrender is, for Walzer, a form of consent. Where a soldier surrenders, he promises to stop fighting in return for certain rights. Walzer's contractarian thinking comes out too where he discusses the basis of political sovereignty which, he says, rests on "the right of men and women to build a common life and to risk their individual lives only when they freely choose to do so."[41] In a similar vein he says, "We want to live in an international society where communities of men and women freely shape their separate destinies."[42] Further on he writes, "no one can be threatened with war or warred against, unless through some act of his own he has surrendered or lost his rights."[43] Finally he puts his position in a nutshell where he writes, "States exist to defend the rights of their members."[44]

The string of quotations given above clearly illustrates Walzer's belief that the state's authority is derived from the consent of the governed and that the state's sovereign right to engage in war is thus based, finally, on individual rights. On this view individuals have rights which may be forfeited or transferred only with their consent. The problem with this view, once again, is that it does not reconcile the norms relating to sovereignty with those pertaining to the protection of individual rights. Let us attempt to make the nature of this problem more explicit.

The cornerstone of Walzer's thinking about the moral problems which are posed by war is his notion of the *legalist paradigm* which he uses in developing his theory of aggression. The legalist paradigm is, he says, "the fundamental structure for the moral comprehension of war."[45] He expresses the fundamentals of this paradigm in six propositions:

1. There exists an international society of independent states.
2. This international society has a law that establishes the rights of its members – above all, the rights of territorial integrity and political sovereignty.
3. Any use of force or imminent threat of force by one state against the political sovereignty or territorial integrity of another constitutes aggression and is a criminal act.
4. Aggression justifies two kinds of violent response: a war of self-defence by the victim and a war of law enforcement by the victim and any other member of international society.
5. Nothing but aggression can justify war.
6. Once the aggressor state has been militarily repulsed, it can also be punished.[46]

It is clear that Walzer is thinking of states in the international society as in some ways analogous to individuals within that society we call the state. Indeed, Walzer sometimes refers to the legalist paradigm as the "domestic paradigm." The fundamental feature of this analogy is that we are to conceive of states as having rights in much the same way as we think of individuals within states as having rights. Within states our rights are for the most part protected by law and are enforced by the police. In the international society of states there is no police force so the rights holders (viz. states) have to enforce their rights in other ways, for example by themselves or with the aid of allies.

Now we do indeed find that the international polity in which we live does exhibit the characteristics mentioned in Walzer's legalist paradigm. It is populated with sovereign states who do act as rights holders, who do look upon infringements of those rights as unwarranted acts of aggression, and who do seek to counter aggressive acts of other states in the ways specified in the paradigm. Several of the items on our list of settled norms bear witness to this, especially those pertaining to sovereignty and the preservation of the system of sovereign states. The key point in all of this is that there is a settled norm in international society that infringements of the territorial and political sovereignty of a state are *prima facie* wrong. Any state attempting such an act is taken to be guilty of a wrong unless some special justification can be provided.

Walzer attempts to combine this legalist paradigm with the contractarian theory of human rights. On his view the rights of states which are articulated in the legalist paradigm are, in the final instance, derivable from individual human rights through some or other form of contract. He makes this point explicitly where, referring to the states' rights of territorial integrity and political sovereignty, he says, "the[se] two belong to states, but they derive ultimately from the rights of individuals, and from them they take their force."[47] Later, writing of the same two rights, he says, in a sentence I have already quoted that they "rest ultimately on the right of men and women to build a common life and to risk their individual lives only when they freely choose to do so."[48] On this view, then, there ought to be no incompatibility between states' rights and individual human rights, for in the final instance the one set of rights is derived from the other. However, in *Just and Unjust Wars*, looked at as a whole, there clearly is a tension between the two. This tension shows itself in several ways.

First, consider one of the exceptions which Walzer allows against the strict legalist paradigm (according to which the only legitimate acts of violence by a state are acts of self defence and acts punishing an aggressor). He says that humanitarian interventions are justified in those cases where "massive violations of human rights" are taking place, violations which "shock the moral conscience of mankind."[49] He counts the Indian invasion of East Pakistan in 1971 as an intervention which was justified on humanitarian grounds. What is odd about Walzer's argument with regard to humanitarian intervention is that he restricts it to these extreme cases. For, if the right of states to non intervention is derived ultimately from individual human rights, then surely whenever a state fails to protect the rights of individuals within it that state's right to non intervention is eroded accordingly. Walzer carefully maintains that only gross infringements of human rights warrant armed intervention in another state. This suggests that there is some inner conflict between the claims which can justifiably be made on behalf of states and those claims which can justifiably be made on behalf of individuals.

Second, in discussing the Finnish war with Russia in 1940, Walzer reveals a commitment to the rights of states which seems clearly to conflict with a commitment to individual human rights. Prior to that war Russia felt threatened by the closeness of the Finnish border to Leningrad. Russia offered a land exchange deal to Finland which was less than just. The Finns were faced with the option of accepting this offer or of going to war. They chose the latter option. They were defeated and forced to accept a settlement worse than the one originally offered them. Walzer argues that their decision to go to war was morally to be preferred to any form of appeasement. What is of interest to us is the argument which he offers for his conclusion. "The 'Munich principle' [an appeasement principle] would concede the loss or erosion of independence *for the sake of the survival of individual men and women*."[50] Further on he writes, "I don't want to argue that appeasement can never be justified, only to point to the great importance we collectively attach to the values the aggressor attacks. These values are summed up in the *existence of states like Finland* – indeed, of many such states."[51] Here there is a conflict between the importance attached to the right of the state to survive and the importance attached to the right of individuals to survive. There is no doubt that in this context Walzer grants priority to the former. If it were the case, as Walzer contends it is, that the right of the state to survive is ultimately derivable from the rights of individuals, then this type of conflict ought not to occur.

Third, the tension between states' rights and individual rights emerges nicely in Walzer's discussion of the Israeli pre-emptive strike against Egypt in the so called "Six Day War" in June 1967. This kind of war is not justified on the strict legalist paradigm, but Walzer seeks to show that there are moral grounds for allowing this kind of exception to the paradigm. His general formula for this exception is: "states may use military force in the face of threats of war, whenever the failure to do so would seriously risk their territorial integrity or political independence."[52] On Walzer's view this can be extended to cover cases where the state which poses the threat does not intend to attack the threatened state. He explicitly admits that in this case "it is unlikely that the Egyptians intended to begin the war themselves."[53] Egypt might well have been content to close the Straits of Tiran and remain deployed along the Israeli border. But this would have placed a great strain on Israel. In this situation, argues Walzer, Israel would have to attack. Throughout Walzer's account the accent is on Israel's right to exist. The argument is not formulated in terms of the rights of individuals or threats to these rights. In the situation which existed prior to the war no individual rights had been infringed. It may plausibly be argued that the pre-emptive strike had the effect of infringing many of the rights to life, liberty and property of the Egyptian citizens. The only charge which can be laid against the Egyptians who were killed is that their government might have entrenched an army along the Israeli border and this might have been a severe strain on the military resources of Israel. Once again there is an unresolved strain here between states' rights and individual rights.[54]

Fourth, in general, Walzer's justification for the legalist paradigm is that it is derived from the individual consent (tacit or explicit) of the individual rights holders. But this basic position of his is not compatible with the way in which he deals with interventions, i.e. with the moral question about when it is just for one state to interfere in violent disputes within other states. Such issues arise with regard to secession, civil war, wars of national liberation and so on. He accepts a position proffered by John Stuart Mill according to which states are to be treated as self determining communities "whether or not their internal political arrangements are free, whether or not the citizens choose their government and openly debate the policies carried out in their name."[55] On this view a "state is self determining even if its citizens struggle and fail to establish free institutions, but it has been deprived of self determination if such institutions are established by an intrusive neighbour."[56] The overall picture which emerges from this account is that states ought to be respected, not because they represent a contract freely arrived at by individual rights holders, but because they are an area within which such a contract might emerge. Thus we see that on this view states have a right which is prior to the contract; the right is not derived from the contract. Reasoning along these lines, Walzer says that within states people have no right to be protected against domestic failure to construct free institutions. They have no right to be protected "even against a bloody repression." Similarly, intervention is not warranted wherever there is revolution for "revolutionary activity is an exercise in self determination."[57] Here we see Walzer (following J. S. Mill) sketching a picture within which communities/states (he admits there is a problem here, for community boundaries do not always coincide with state boundaries) have a right to self-determination and the right here is not dependent on a prior contract by individuals. He is not happy with this stark position so he introduces several exceptions to the strong non-interventionist rule.[58] I do not intend to examine these now. I merely wish to point out that there is in his theory a strong sense in which states' rights are not derived from individual contract/ consent but are prior to it. Thus his theory does not reconcile states' rights and individual rights in the standard contractarian way.

I have been looking for a background theory for the list of settled norms in international relations. More specifically I have been looking for a background theory which justifies and reconciles the seemingly antipathetic norms relating to the preservation of the system of states and sovereignty on the one hand, with those norms relating to the protection of individual rights on the other. Contract theory sought to do this by providing us with a picture of a free person who then restricted his freedom through contract/consent. On this view the contract/consent brings about a transfer of powers from the individual to the sovereign state. The sovereignty of the state is presented as a limitation which the people have imposed upon themselves. What has emerged from the foregoing discussion is that the contractarian rights-based theories do not manage to justify and reconcile the norms relating to state sovereignty with those relating to human rights. Is there an alternative way in which this might be done? I think that there is.

5 Reconciling rights and sovereignty: the constitutive theory of individuality

Introduction

I am attempting to construct a background theory which justifies the list of goods currently accepted as settled in international relations. I considered order-based justifications and utilitarian justifications and found them both wanting. I then turned to rights-based theories which used the notion of contract and found that such theories held promise with regard to the justification of several of the items on the list of settled norms. Most obviously it seemed plausible enough to suppose that a rights-based theory would justify the settled norm referring to democratic institutions within states, the settled norm which required that states be both internally and externally concerned with the protection of human rights, and the settled norm asserting that international law is a good thing. However, I argued that at first glance it seemed rather improbable to suppose that the settled norm referring to the preservation of the system of states and the norm establishing that state sovereignty is a good could be justified by a rights-based background theory. There seemed to be a basic tension between those norms concerned with the preservation of the system of states and sovereignty on the one hand, and those norms related to individual human rights on the other. It seemed that human rights norms were best seen as setting limits to the ambit of the sovereignty-related norms, rather than as justifying those norms. In the course of the last chapter I showed how contract theories of rights which held out the promise of reconciling sovereignty and individual rights systematically fail to deal satisfactorily with the tension between the rights-related norms and the sovereignty-related norms.

At this point in the argument, we are still faced with the fundamental problem of constructing a background theory which will enable us to justify and reconcile these two sets of seemingly antagonistic norms on the list of settled norms, viz. the norms which assert that state sovereignty and the preservation of the system of states is a good, and those norms premised upon the notion that individual human rights are a basic good.

Constitutive theory as an alternative to the contractarian approach

In this chapter I shall outline a theory which, I contend, does solve the problem of reconciling these two seemingly antagonistic poles on the list of settled norms. I shall call this theory the constitutive theory of individuality. The construction of this theory also involves an attempt to reconcile state sovereignty with individual rights but it involves a different mode of theorizing to that pursued in the contract tradition. Constitutive theory, unlike contract theory, does not seek to show that the sovereign state is a *device* which protects certain pre-existing rights. Unlike contract theory it holds that rights are not things possessed by individuals prior to entering into social and political relationships. Rather it contends that a person is constituted as a rights holder of a certain sort within the context of a specific social relationship. Contrary to all rights-based theories it argues that rights are not things which a person can be conceived of as having outside of or prior to any and all social and political institutions. A Robinson Crusoe has no rights. Whenever we envisage a person as a rights holder we have in mind a situation in which a person claims a certain kind of recognition from another person or set of people. In a world inhabited by a single being there would be no point in claiming a right to x, y or z.[1] The typical kind of case in which we invoke a right is in a situation in which our entitlement to act in a certain way is challenged by another (or others). We then invoke our right as giving us sufficient entitlement to act. Jane, for example, may claim that John ought not to have been allowed to publish a certain article. John defends his having written and published the article by referring to his right to free speech. In referring to his right we must suppose John to be speaking to some audience who might acknowledge or deny his entitlement to publish the article. Rights talk always presupposes the existence of a speaker and an audience who between them recognize one another as being able to make certain kinds of claims on one another. Another way of putting this point is to say that rights talk always presupposes a practice of rights: a practice, that is, within which people make claims of right upon one another.[2]

Contract theory envisaged institutions as devices for defending pre-existing rights. On that theory the rights were primary and the institutions were designed to protect them. At first glance it might now appear as if I am making the contrary argument, viz. that institutions are primary and that people only come to have rights once they enter into institutions. This is not my position. I want to argue that neither is prior, but that rights and institutions presuppose and imply each other. As an indication of what I mean, consider the following: it is only with the state that people may meaningfully be said to have citizenship rights. To be a person with the rights of a citizen is to be a person who lives within a state-like institution of some or other kind. This might suggest that the state is primary. Yet this is not the case. The state as an institution can only be comprehended within the context of a wider social and political practice. An elucidation of this wider practice would have to refer to citizens, government, police, judges and so on. A state is an institution created and maintained by the people living in a particular territory, i.e. the state depends on there being citizens and citizens exist only within a state.

This difference between constitutive and contract theory has important implications for the way in which the problem of reconciling state sovereignty and individual rights is conceived of in each case. For contract theory the problem is: why would an autonomous rights holder agree to subject himself to a sovereign state? The answer given is the self-interested one that only by entering (or establishing) a state can a person secure certain of his pre-existing rights. The contract model allows one to argue that the constraining aspects of the institution, in this case the state, are actually self-imposed constraints. For constitutive theory the *problem* is quite otherwise. There is no need to show why rights holders perfect in respect of their rights would agree to enter into constraining relationships with other rights holders.[3] For constitutive theory, to be a rights holder at all already presupposes a constraining relationship with other people. To claim a right is to articulate a certain kind of reason justifying an action and constraining the actions of others.[4] A relationship in which rights are recognized is a relationship in which individuals recognize one another as beings who may legitimately constrain one another's actions in certain ways. The problem for constitutive theory is not to show why rights and rights holders should enter into a constraining relationship (for to be a rights holder at all already presupposes such a relationship) but to show how being a rights holder of a certain sort involves the other components of the practice within which the right is situated. The argument will typically not be directed at an outsider who is not a member of the institution in question. It will not be aimed at an outsider in an attempt to convince him that he should enter the institution (this is what contract theory sought to do). Rather it will be aimed at someone who accepts (and acts in accordance with) some components of the practice in question (for example, at someone who accepts and acts in accordance with the norms relating to individual human rights), but who denies another component of the practice (for example, someone who does not accept or act in accordance with the norm in terms of which state sovereignty is a good). The aim of constitutive theory will be to demonstrate to such an interlocutor the connection between his being a rights holder of a certain sort and his being a member of a particular kind of institution. Constitutive theory aims to bring to light the *internal* connections between being an individual rights holder of a particular kind and being a member of a certain kind of social or political institution, where both the rights and the institution are conceived of as being components of a wider practice.

Where contract theory sought to overcome the objections an outsider might offer against his entering into a certain kind of arrangement (viz. a sovereign state), constitutive theory may perhaps be seen as seeking to overcome a different kind of hurdle. A successful argument in constitutive theory seeks to overcome the *alienation* a person might feel with regard to certain aspects of a practice within which she is living. A person is alienated when she experiences certain aspects of a practice (essential to her full flourishing within that practice) as hostile or detrimental to her well-being. Alienation is overcome where it is made intelligible to the person in question that, for example, there is a necessary connection between her being a rights holder of type X (which she values highly) and her living within an institutional arrangement of type Y (which she may experience as imposing a burden on her).[5] John Charvet portrays the task as the one of "making explicit, or recognizing and developing to its full consciousness, what is implicitly true of an individual's relations to others in any scheme of social cooperation."[6]

The problem then is to show how constitutive theory can justify and reconcile the norm asserting that the sovereign state is a good with the norms relating to individual human rights. As we have seen in the previous paragraph the task is not (as it would be for contract theories) to show why an individual who is outside of a social or political arrangement (i.e. in a state of nature or in inter-planetary transit) ought to become a citizen of a sovereign state amongst other sovereign states. The task is rather to make explicit the moral dimension that is already implicit in the simultaneous acceptance of the state and sovereignty norms (norms S1 and S2 on our list in the previous chapter) on the one hand, and the rights-related norms on the other hand.[7] Constitutive theory does not reason from the "mid-air" position occupied by the contractualists: an imagined position outside of any existing society. Rather it takes seriously the truth that when we reason about normative issues we do so from within a standpoint defined by specific institutions such as the state and the inter-state system.

Constitutive theory of individuality

Let us start by returning to a notion which is common both to contract theory and constitutive theory. This is the notion of the value of the individual. Contract theories usually stress the rights of freedom and equality which they take to be grounded in the notion of the autonomous individual striving for authenticity, i.e. as striving to be the author of his own individual, social and political being.[8] The autonomous individual is presented as having value prior to any community. Constitutive theory starts by asserting that a person only has value *qua* individual in a relationship of mutual valuation with another person or other people, i.e. within a community. Constitutive theory then seeks to make explicit the complex system of mutual recognition within which individuality comes to be a value.

The relationship of mutual valuation is not a contractual type of relationship in which one individual approaches another and says, "I'll value you, if you'll value me." In the contractual perspective the parties do indeed only value one another as individuals who can make contracts. But constitutive theory understands mutual valuation in a different way. Individuality only becomes a value where it is the case that two or more people do, through their reciprocal recognition of one another, give concrete practical expression to valuing one another, rather than through merely saying that they value one another. Thus the task for normative theory becomes the one of showing how we as individuals are constituted as such through our participation in a particular set of social, economic and political institutions which in turn are grounded in our adherence to certain norms.[9] What we are called upon to do is to stand back from the multiple institutions in which we live in order to show how each contributes to the kind of individuality we value; to show how the kind of individuality which we value in ourselves could not be, were we not members of certain kinds of institutions. This does not mean that institutions should be conceived as means to the realization of certain ends we may happen to have. Rather the point is that we could not be the individuals we are, were we not members of a specific set of social arrangements which are based upon specified sets of norms.

It is apparent from the previous paragraph that the constitutive approach is holist. It insists that we cannot understand individuality without situating it within a whole within which people constitute each other by recognizing one another in specified ways. No independently existing metaphysical whole need be posited. The social practice or institution as a whole is, of course, a human and historical creation, but people are individuals by virtue of being members of certain kinds of social practices.

The foregoing is unacceptably vague. Let us attempt to make the matter a bit clearer by showing an application of the method in practice. Charvet, following Hegel, shows how individuality is constituted within a hierarchy of institutions, viz. the family, civil society and the state.[10] Both Hegel and Charvet take the state (or, as Charvet calls it, "the self-governing political community") as being the constitutive context of paramount importance. It is only in the state that individuality can be fully realized. Both support this contention by examining how our individuality is partially constituted by subordinate wholes, like the family and civil society, and by showing how the shortcomings of the subordinate institutions are overcome by subsequent and higher institutions. This dialectical process then culminates in the state. I do not intend to give a detailed discussion of the whole hierarchy of institutions because my main concern is with the upper end of the hierarchy, i.e. the state and the system of states. However, in order to demonstrate this constitutive mode of reasoning in operation let us briefly examine some aspects of the hierarchy.

The outline of constitutive theory given below draws heavily on Hegel's political philosophy, but it is what may be termed a secular interpretation of his theory. Constitutive theory does not require of us that we understand or accept Hegel's metaphysical system.

Individuality and the family

Let us examine the historically changing institution of the family. It is within the family that we as individuals first come to be valued. Here we are valued as *members* of the family. An early notion of selfhood is achieved in the recognition accorded to us by the other members of the family. Hegel puts the matter thus:

> The family, as the immediate substantiality of mind, is specifically characterized by love, which is mind's own feeling of its own unity. Hence in a family, one's frame of mind is to have self-consciousness of one's individuality within this unity as the absolute essence of oneself, with the result that one is in it not as an independent person but as a member.[11]

What binds the members of the family together is love, which Hegel elucidates as follows:

> Love means in general terms the consciousness of my unity with another so that I am not in selfish isolation but win my self-consciousness only as the renunciation of my independence and through knowing myself as the unity of myself with another and of the other with me.[12]

We here see that it is within the family that a person gets that special kind of recognition which is to be recognized as a loved self. It is important not to take Hegel as simply making the empirical point that, as a matter of fact, most people do start life as members of families. Rather his point is that in the love between members of a family there is an implicit valuing by each member of the family of the other members; they are ends for us and valuers of our own lives. To put the matter another way: in thinking about the family we recognize that the love of the other members for us is partially constitutive of ourselves and that our loving them is also constitutive of ourselves. We could not be the selves we are and value, were it not for the love we receive from, and the love we give to, the other members of the family. We are partially constituted by the common will that exists in the family.

It is important to notice that there is a critical dimension to Hegel's discussion of the family. Throughout history, as anthropologists have shown, there have been diverse kinds of family structures. Not all of these realize or constitute the beginnings of individuality. Hegel argues, for example, that the early Roman family institution in which the father had the right to disinherit his children, and even to kill them, was an unethical institution.[13] He also says, "A child in slavery is the most unethical of all situations whatsoever."[14] In the ethical family parents recognize their children as nascent autonomous selves who can advance to a more mature form of individuality beyond the family by becoming actors in civil society and citizens of a just state. The Roman family was unethical because it failed to treat children as nascent free people. Although the family is the first on the hierarchy of institutions, it is, nevertheless, a crucial institution at both a micro and a macro level. At the micro level a person who is not recognized within a family as a nascent autonomous individual will not be able to develop into a free individual within the higher institutions. Similarly at the macro level, were the institution of the ethical family to crumble or change it would then no longer be possible for the higher institutions of civil society and the state to persist. These latter institutions are grounded in (have their foundations in) the family.[15] Thus it is that the state must seek to preserve family life. Ethical families partially constitute the individuals who are the citizens of fully formed states.

Viewed in the larger context, however, the family also has inherent defects with respect to the constitution of individuality. Charvet writes:

> But the family, being a small, intimate group, cannot realize the value of the particular personality of its members adequately, for in its intimate bounds there is not the room for the development of the individual's interest that the freedom of civil society provides.[16]

In a general way this may be so, but it does not yet articulate the specific shortcomings of the family. What are these? Two main ones deserve mention. The first is that the family is bound together by love and thus does not provide a fully rational context. About this Hegel says:

> Love, however, is a feeling, i.e. ethical life in the form of something natural. In the state feeling disappears; there we are conscious of unity as law; there the content must be rational and known to us.[17]

Hegel's point here is that a unity based on law, which is consciously recognized as such, forms a more secure bond than a unity based on love. In the family the unit is held together by reciprocal love, but as a feeling this is not something which can be demanded by a member of a family as of right. To summarize this point, the family is deficient in that in it a person's individuality is dependent on something essentially changeable, viz. feeling.

The second shortcoming of the family is that in it the principle of personality is still not fully expressed. Within the family a person is but a member of the family unit. In order to develop, a person has, so to speak, to leave the family in order to seek "the development and realization of his particular needs, interests and purposes."[18] These drawbacks of the family can only be overcome within civil society. In civil society the individual seeks to realize his or her own ends more fully. But what is civil society?

Individuality and civil society

Civil society is, amongst other things, an economic system based on private property, within which people work, acquire things, exchange things and generally seek to satisfy their own needs. Amongst the various components of civil society Hegel distinguishes a system of needs, a system for the administration of justice, the police and the corporation. I am not concerned with the details of civil society, but shall look at a few of the ways in which individuality is constituted in civil society in ways which improve upon what is achieved by the family.

On growing up, an individual in some sense "leaves" the family. His/her emergence from the family is characterized by the acquisition of contractual rights and rights to property. A minor member of a family is typically not allowed to make major contracts without parental consent and the minor's dealings with regard to property are severely restricted. The acquisition of these rights is generally considered to be one of the reasons why "becoming adult" is a sought-after status. But how does our entry into the civil society in which things are made, owned and exchanged constitute us as individuals in ways that would be denied us were we to be condemned to stay as minor members of a family for ever? Or, to ask a slightly different question: "What is the significance of private property for individuality?" There are several levels at which property can be understood. First, a person's appropriating something may be seen as a way in which he (or she) fulfils his (or her) wants. "I make something my own as a result of my need, impulse and caprice."[19] On this level it would seem that the *raison d'etre* of property is the satisfaction of whatever needs a person happens to have. In fact, the satisfaction of wants does not strike us as a particularly important moment in the constitution of individuality (or, as Hegel would put it, in the advancement of freedom). At this level there is not much to distinguish people from animals.

But on a second level, property may be seen as a right of personality as such. Hegel says that prior to owning property a person is but a thing amongst things and does not become a personality (we would say "individual") until such time as he is recognized as such by other people who in turn gain their recognition as personalities from his recognition. Property is an important factor in the progress towards mutual recognition of one another as persons. John comes to recognize Joan as an individual, as someone who can own something in her own right and who can cease to own it by selling it, giving it away or whatever. Thus we can see how participating in the transactions of civil society enables a person to become individual in a way that was not possible within the family.

In civil society the individual gains recognition as a free person able to own property and enter into transactions with other people who are free in the same way. The importance of these rights is recognized in a system of law which is impartially administered and enforced. It is important to notice that the rights of personality which are advanced in civil society depend on the property relations being *private* property relations. Hegel writes in this connection:

> The idea of a pious or friendly and even compulsory brotherhood of men holding their goods in common and rejecting the principle of private property may readily present itself to the disposition which mistakes the true nature of the freedom of mind and right and fails to apprehend it in its determinate moments.[20]

Why is this a mistake? In the Addition to this paragraph Hegel gives his reasons.

> In property my will is the will of a person: but a person is a unit and so property becomes the personality of this unitary will. Since property is the means whereby I give my will an embodiment, prop-

erty must also have the character of being "this" or "mine." This is the important doctrine of the necessity of private property.

In this connection Charvet makes a slightly different point. In order to be fully individual a person needs to be able to distance himself from the collective. Private property is an institution which makes this possible. This aspect of private property is what makes it more satisfactory than family property. On these grounds Charvet rejects collectivist socialism. It would not allow the individual to distance himself from the other members of the community in the way that private property does.[21] There is a lot more to Hegel's conception of civil society than I have indicated here. The details need not detain us. I have briefly introduced the notion of civil society in order to show two things. First, to demonstrate a constitutive theory in operation. It showed how individuality as a particular kind of self is partially constituted by the institutions within which we live. Second, to show how the shortcomings of a particular institution may be remedied by a further institution which does not replace the earlier defective institution, but operates together with it. Hence there develops a hierarchy of institutions. It is thus clear that in order to understand how individuality is constituted within the context of a given practice we need to examine the whole hierarchy of institutions.

Individuality and the state

Civil society, although it advances individuality (free personality) in ways that the family did not, is nevertheless itself subject to certain limitations. A simple way of putting the matter is as follows: within the family what individuals gained was consciousness of themselves as valued members of a whole. Within civil society the individuals gained a consciousness of themselves as independent persons distinct from the whole. In it they experienced the law and other people's competitive cooperation as necessary for the furtherance of their own aims. Although the whole apparatus of civil society depends on the mutual recognition by the participants of one another as rights holders, the others on whom a person's recognition depends are not experienced as co-determinators of a person's individuality, but rather as threats to it. Similarly the law is not experienced as the ground of a person's individuality, but as a curb on it. To put the matter in a nutshell, in civil society, although individuals are grounded in the law and recognition of others, they nevertheless experience them as alien. They feel alienated. It is this tension between the individual and the whole which is resolved in the state. Within the state people participate in the whole as members: as citizens. As citizens they are accorded a form of mutual recognition by their fellow citizens; something which they lacked within the competitive and atomized civil society. As citizens, people know themselves to be constitutive parts of the whole and they are conscious that the whole of which they are part is constituted by them together with their fellow citizens. The state is the creation of its citizens and yet it is only in the state that any given individual can be fully actualized as a citizen. Hegel writes:

> If the state is confused with civil society, and if its specific end is laid down as the security and protection of property and personal freedom then the interest of the individuals as such becomes the ultimate end of their association, and it follows that membership of the state is something optional. But the state's relation to the individual is quite different from this. Since the state is mind objectified, it is only as one of its members that the individual himself has objectivity, genuine individuality and ethical life.[22]

Here we can see the distinctive break between constitutive theory and contract theory emerging. Hegel criticizes the contract theorists' interpretation of the state on the grounds that it presents membership of the state as something *optional* for individuals. What precisely is Hegel getting at here? The contract position supposes that it is possible to conceive of a fully actualized and free moral person who is not a member of any state, and who may then be pictured as having an option about whether to join the state or not. Hegel's counter is that to become a whole, free and fully ethical self a person has to be a citizen of a good state. It is only in that capacity that individuality can be fully realized. Thus citizenship of a good state is not an option for a free person, but is rather a precondition for the existence of a free person. This may seem unduly speculative, but in more mundane historical terms Hegel has, *prima facie,* a good case. Acquiring full citizenship rights has been a major concern for all those who have been denied them over the past hundred and fifty years. Even in those cases where gaining the rights of citizenship has involved taking a fall in welfare, citizenship has been considered a prize worth having. It is, indeed, a commonplace of the modern world that citizenship is of fundamental importance. Those who are denied it are prepared to fight for it. Who, then, would dispute that being deprived of full citizenship rights would be a major threat to a person's sense of self? It is this basic connection between individuality and the state which is at the heart of Hegel's argument.

In the state individuals are conscious that their individuality is grounded in the whole. But this whole, i.e. the state, is not something experienced as alien and external to them, for they know the state and its laws to be that on which their individuality is grounded. This point comes out nicely in Hegel's discussion of patriotism. Patriotism is not mere subjective assurance or feeling, but is "assured conviction with truth as its basis."[23] It (patriotism) is:

> the consciousness that my interest, both substantive and particular, is contained and preserved in another's [i.e.the state's] interest and end, i.e. in the other's relation to me as an individual. In this way, this very other is immediately not an other in my eyes, and in being conscious of this fact, I am free.[24]

It is essential to understand that for Hegel the prior institutions of the family and civil society are not made redundant by the state. The state incorporates and improves upon them yet is also dependent upon them. Here it is relevant to cite *in toto* a whole section from the *Philosophy of Right:*

> As was remarked earlier on, the sanctity of marriage and the institutions in which civil society is an appearance of ethical life constitute the stability of the whole, i.e. stability is secured when universal affairs are the affairs of each member in his particular capacity. What is of the utmost importance is that the law of reason should be shot through and through by the law of particular freedom, and that my particular end should become identified with the universal end, or otherwise the state is left in the air. The state is actual only when its members have a feeling of their own self-hood and it is stable only when public and private ends are identical. It has often been said that the end of the state is the happiness of the citizens. This is perfectly true. If all is not well with them, if their subjective aims are not satisfied, if they do not find that the state as such is the means to their satisfaction, then the footing of the state itself is insecure.[25]

In sum, the crucial feature of the state is that in it citizens come to self-conscious appreciation of the way in which they constitute the whole and are constituted by it.

Patently such individual freedom is not constituted by just any kind of state. In some kinds of state there is no provision made for private willing, private judgement and private conscience: "under the despots of Asia the individual had no inner life and no justification in himself, in the modern world man insists on respect being paid to his inner life."[26] In the fully developed state the citizens perceive a coincidence between what the state requires of them and what they require in order to be free.[27]

It might seem as if the relevant question to ask at this point is: "In what kind of state can individuality flourish?" The answer would enable us to set about building the right kind of constitution. However, asking this question would show us to have missed a fundamental point about constitutive theory. Posing this question presupposes that constitution building may be used as a means to realize a certain kind of end, viz. a world peopled by free individuals. It also suggests that the would-be constitution builders (in this case us) are, so to speak, standing outside of any constitutional form deciding which constitution to implement. But, of course, we the constitution builders are not outside any and all constitutions. We, ourselves, are constituted by a particular constitutional arrangement, viz. the state. Whatever we propose for the future cannot be the creation of a new constitution, *de novo*, but a modification of the old. Any changes in the constitution will have to be premised on a proper understanding of how we the constitution builders already are constituted by the old arrangements. The relevant question to ask must then rather be: "What is the proper understanding of the institutions by which we are presently constituted as individuals?" The answer to this question will have a critical dimension in that the answer will rule out certain kinds of proposal for a new constitution while it will allow others.

Another important point to make here concerns the role of education in constitutional change. A constitution cannot simply be imposed on a people. It is a set of rules in terms of which they constitute each other. The people have to see the constitution as the proper way of doing things. They have to be educated into accepting it. They have to be convinced that it is necessary to their being who they are.[28]

Individuality and the society of sovereign states

I have reached the following point in my argument. I have shown rather sketchily how a free individual is partially constituted by being a member of a family, how the shortcomings of this institution are remedied within the arrangements of civil society and how individuality comes to a more complete form within the state. The state, on this view, should not be seen as a device which protects individual rights, but as a comprehensive arrangement between people who by mutually recognizing one another in certain specified ways come to constitute one another as free individuals. The question which needs to be answered now is: "Given that the state is necessary for the flourishing of individuality, in what way is the system of sovereign states and its associated norms a prerequisite for the flourishing of individuality?" The question may be differently formulated as follows: "What is the proper understanding of the link between free individuality and the system of sovereign states?" Yet another formulation would be: "In what way, if any, can our individuality be said to be constituted by the system of sovereign states?"

These questions can best be answered by reflecting on the respective contributions to, and limitations of, individuality at each level of our hierarchy. In the family members are aware of themselves as parts of a whole, but this limits their development as individuals. This limitation is overcome in civil society within which they come to be recognized as bearers of rights which they may use or not at their discretion. But once again their freedom is limited in that they experience other people and the laws to which they are subject as external constraints on their individual liberty. This feeling of constraint on the individual is resolved within the state in that here the individuals feel themselves to be members of a whole (as was the case in the family). To be recognized as a citizen of a good state and to recognize others as such is to be self-conscious about the way in which you (the "self" in question) and others mutually constitute one another within a system of reciprocal recognition.

But the whole within which the individual is re-united with others as a member (i.e. the state) is a whole amongst other wholes, i.e. a state amongst other states. At the level of international affairs the state is an individual *vis-à-vis* other states and its individuality is reciprocally bound up with the individuality of its citizens:

> Individuality is awareness of one's existence as a unit in sharp distinction from others. It manifests itself here in the state as a relation to other states, each of which is autonomous *vis-à-vis* others . . .[29]

The point here is that within the autonomous state all individuals are constituted as free citizens, but for their citizenship to be fully actualized their state needs to be recognized by other states as autonomous.

Were it not thus recognized their own individuality would not be properly constituted:

> A state is as little an actual individual without relations to other states as an individual is actually a person without rapport with other persons ... [it] should receive its full and final legitimation through its recognition by other states although this recognition requires to be safeguarded by the proviso that where a state is recognized by others, it should likewise recognize them, i.e. respect their autonomy; and so it comes about that they cannot be indifferent to each other's domestic affairs.[30]

The necessity of being recognized as autonomous is well demonstrated by the phenomenon of colonialism. People in colonies are not free, because the political entity in which they live is not recognized as autonomous. Few people would agree to their state becoming a colony even if accepting colonial status brought with it substantial economic gain. The reason for this is that in a colony the people are in a subject position and are not free individuals in a way that citizens of an autonomous state are. In short, it is crucial for the individual that his state be autonomous and be recognized and treated by other autonomous states as such. Or to put the matter slightly differently, it is crucial, in order for a person to be an individual, that he be a member of an autonomous state recognized as such by other autonomous states.

In order to be recognized as an autonomous state, the state must meet certain specific requirements. Not just any arrangement may count as an autonomous state. A family, a horde, a clan, a multitude, a tribe, a robber band, a liberation movement, a tyranny, an oligarchy, a totalitarian order ... none of these is an autonomous state. In order to be recognized as an autonomous state, the state must have what Hegel refers to as "objective law and an explicitly established constitution."[31] He continues the paragraph just quoted:

> It would be contrary even to commonplace ideas to call patriarchal conditions a "constitution" or a people under patriarchal government a "state" or its independence "sovereignty."

I agree. In order to be recognized as a state, a polity must be one in which the people recognize each other as citizens in terms of the law which they in turn recognize as being both constituted by them and as constitutive of them as citizens. In a patriarchal state the people see themselves as subject, not as citizens. In an authoritarian state the people see themselves as the oppressed ones, and so on. An autonomous state is one in which the citizens experience the well-being of the state as fundamental to their own well-being, just as a member of a family experiences the well-being of the family as essential to his (or her) own well-being. Thus a threat to the autonomous state threatens a citizen directly. Such a threat does not threaten those interests which he (or she) might then seek to have satisfied in some other way. To threaten the constitution of the state or to withhold recognition of its autonomy is to threaten directly the way in which the individual is constituted as an individual.

At this point the following objection may be made. The background justification for states and the system of sovereign states which has been presented here grants moral standing to those states within which citizenship rights are well respected in the ways outlined above; but in the world as it exists today, not many states measure up to this standard. If we were to apply this standard to our political world, few states indeed would qualify for recognition because the bulk of existing states fall far short of this standard in that they are either authoritarian, corrupt, anarchic, totalitarian or deficient in any number of other ways. The nub of this objection is that the background theory which I have presented here is too stringent; it does not account for the recognition we give to those many states which Robert Jackson has called "quasi-states."[32]

My reply to this objection is that it misunderstands the image which guides my use of the notion of *recognition* when I talk of one state recognizing another state as sovereign. Those making this objection seem to me to understand recognition in "gate-keeping" terms. The dominant image is of a doorman at a club who either recognizes your credentials and lets you in, or, denies their validity and turns you away. Here there is a barrier to be crossed and conditions to be met before the crossing is permitted. On this view my present endeavour is to be read as an attempt to specify the conditions which a state must meet before it will be admitted to the portals of the community of states. *A fortiori*, then, when thinking about Jackson's quasi-states, what the community of states has to decide is whether this kind of state ought to be allowed membership of the community of states or not. The process is pictured as akin to that which was faced by gentlemen's clubs deciding whether to admit Jews, Blacks or women as members. Recognition in this sense is an all or nothing affair; the relevant category of person is either in or out.

The notion of recognition incorporated in constitutive theory, as I have outlined it, is different in important ways – it does not rely on a notion of gate keeping. Instead it must be understood with reference to a person or group of people learning how to participate in a given practice. Let me start my elucidation of this point with reference (once again) to a two-person game such as chess. If I wish to play chess with you, we need between us to achieve a complicated relationship of mutual recognition within which we each come to recognize the other as one on whom we can rely to make the appropriate moves in terms of the rules of the game. If you are an experienced player we can quickly establish the requisite recognition in all its complexity. But suppose that you are a novice with only a faint grasp of what this game involves, then the task I face is altogether different. If I want you to become a competent player then there is a period during which I have to recognize you as competent even though I know that you are not. My treating you thus is part of what is involved in teaching you the game. I follow the forms to teach you the forms. So, for example, I have to let you mull over your move and let you make it even where I can see that it is the wrong one to make. While you are thinking I have to observe a rule of non-interference. Once you have made your move I might then point out that that piece does not move in that way (if you are a real novice) or that moving that piece to that square does not make a lot of strategic sense (if you are a somewhat more advanced player). But in order for you to advance towards the kind of full recognition which we both seek (the kind that holds between fully competent players) I need to practice forms of non-interference followed by interference. Throughout this process I recognize you as one who wants to become a member of the chess-playing practice. My recognition is not a "once off" gate-keeping act in which I allow you in or turn you away from some bounded area (in this case the domain of those who play chess), but involves a commitment on my part to educate you into this practice. For your part you recognize me as one who can do this and you indicate your willingness to learn in any number of ways.

There are some interesting things in this relationship between me (the initiate) and you (the novice) which I would like to highlight. At certain moments during this process I have to accord you the standing and respect of a fully-fledged chess player even though you are not that yet. When I do this it is not the case that I am committed to a non-interference rule which permits me to ignore or neglect you.[33] For although I must leave you in peace to make your own mistakes I am not indifferent to your actions. I am concerned to find ways of guiding your conduct and helping your development so that you do not make the same mistakes in future. My concern is prompted by the fact that what I ultimately want is for you to become a fully competent player. That you want this too, is indicated by the fact that you actively seek to play with me.

What I hope to have highlighted in the discussion above is that it is important to distinguish between different senses of the concept of "recognition". It might refer to an act of classification (which may be simple or very complex) such as "Is this person (or is this state) a member of this association (such as a club or commonwealth)?" Or, it might refer to a way of treating a person or group of people in order to establish a certain kind of practice between you and them. I contend that the recognition which the developed states of the world give the quasi-states is of this latter kind. States, in recognizing the sovereignty of Jackson's quasi-states, recognize a non-interference rule for the sake of establishing a certain kind of practice between themselves and these states, viz. that practice which exists between fully-fledged autonomous states. These states are recognized as autonomous so that they might become autonomous. The quasi-states themselves seek this kind of recognition.[34] The incorporation of newcomers into most social practices (games, micro institutions like the family, and macro institutions like states) requires this kind of manouevre by initiates and novices.

Summary

The argument has now reached the following point. I have been outlining the ways in which, according to Hegel, sovereign states and the system of sovereign states are necessary to the flourishing of individuality. (This discussion forms part of the wider argument in which I have been seeking a way of reconciling the settled norms relating to the preservation of the system of states and to sovereignty on the one hand, with the norms which refer to individual rights on the other.) From what has gone before it ought now to be clear that a failure by sovereign states to recognize one another as such implicitly threatens the individuality of the citizens of the respective states. That this is so can be seen by considering the alternatives to this mutual recognition of one another's sovereignty. In the most extreme case the denial of another state's sovereignty can take the form of seeking to conquer and incorporate the territory of that state. In such a case, apart from the destruction and loss of life brought about by the conquest, the conquest also negates it in another crucial dimension. The conquering state fails to recognize the common will in terms of which the citizens of the target state constitute one another through the constitution of their state. Even in a hypothetical case in which conquest resulted in the conquered state being better off in every respect except self-determination, the individuality of the citizens of the subject state would be severely impaired.

It is important to notice that what is being recognized where states recognize one another's sovereignty is not the rights of the individuals in the states to form an association (where these rights are envisaged as existing apart from and independently of the state in question). What is recognized (or not) is a common will in terms of which the people involved reciprocally constitute one another as, amongst other things, rights holders by recognizing each other in certain specified ways. Where one state seeks to conquer another it does not merely supplant the government but inevitably seeks to place the people in the target state under domination. It seeks to change them from citizens to subjects. The flourishing of individuality requires free citizens, not a subject people.

In the previous paragraph I mentioned one kind of refusal to recognize the sovereignty of a state, viz. a refusal which takes the form of the conquest and subjection of that state and its people. Consider a different kind of refusal to recognize sovereignty. Consider a situation in which the community of sovereign states refused to recognize a would-be state. Here I have in mind a situation such as that faced by Rhodesia after its Unilateral Declaration of Independence (UDI). It is important to the argument to see that the refusal by the states of the world to recognize Rhodesia as a sovereign state was not merely a matter of practical significance. Of course, non-recognition did have serious practical implications for Rhodesia: the sanctions policy seriously impeded trade; the refusal to recognize passports hindered the opportunities for travel of the Rhodesian people; severed links in the sporting and cultural fields impeded normal activity within these spheres.

However over and above these practical consequences, non-recognition was also of more fundamental significance to the Rhodesian whites who had enjoyed the full benefits of citizenship internally and who had had that status recognized internationally. This group were now denied the *status* which had previously been accorded them. Prior to UDI they had been citizens of a state which had played an honourable role in the recent history of the states in the Western world. Their state had a noble record in the two World Wars, and in the Korean War. It had played an important part in the life of the British Commonwealth of Nations. After UDI the white Rhodesians found themselves to be *outcasts*. Those who had supported UDI suddenly found themselves classed by the international community as criminals in so far as they supported a government which was almost universally condemned as illegal. This loss of status hurt those Rhodesians who supported the rebel government and their hurt was revealed in their repeated assertions that Rhodesia was a member of the "free world." The rhetoric of Ian Smith left no doubt that being recognized as a member of the free world was a major concern for him and his fellow Rhodesians. What was important here was not merely the *results* which recognition would bring (such as the increased trading, sporting and cultural links mentioned above), but the recognition itself. A *de facto* increase in trade and in sporting and cultural contact by clandestine means would not have been a sufficient remedy for the more subtle and basic harm caused by non-recognition – just as *de facto* improvements in the material conditions of the life of a slave would not solve the problem of slavery. What is wrong with slavery cannot be remedied merely by improving the lot of the slaves. It can only be remedied by freeing the slaves, i.e. by according them the status of free persons. Similarly, what the white Rhodesians needed was a certain kind of status within the community of states. This was denied them because their "state" failed to qualify for recognition.

The foregoing discussion has implications for the kinds of ways in which the world polity may justifiably be organized. Any attempt to achieve a world state through imperial expansion would, from the point of view of autonomous states, be unjustifiable. Does this rule out the justifiability of a world state altogether? Not necessarily.[35] A world "state" would be justified if it came about through the voluntary action of all sovereign states. The agreed polity would have to be one in which the autonomy of the parties to the agreement was respected; it would have to be an arrangement arrived at through a confederal or federal procedure. It must be noticed, though, that the world "state" would have to come about through the confederating (or federating) act of states and not by a dissolution of existing states followed by a contracting in of all the individuals of this world into the new global state. In short, any new order must grow from the autonomous action of *states*. It would be a new order growing out of the old rather than a new order replacing a dissolved old order.

The constitutive theory of individuality as a background theory justifying the settled norms of the modern state domain of discourse

In chapter 4 I set out to construct a background theory which justified the list of goods currently accepted as settled in international relations. I examined and found good reason to reject theories stressing order, utilitarian theories and rights-based theories. I subsequently outlined a better background theory derived from Hegel which I called "constitutive theory" in which rights are not conceived of as adhering in individuals divorced from any community whatsoever. Instead, rights are envisaged as what people come to recognize one another as having within the context of a community with specified social and political institutions. Following Hegel, I showed how individuals with the rights which we value are constituted within a system of mutual recognition which includes within it the institutions of the family, civil society, the state and the system of sovereign states. Each of these creates a moral standing which remedies some of the deficiencies experienced at the lower level. The background theory which we have been looking for then is constitutive theory – a theory which demonstrates how individuality is constituted within the context of these institutional arrangements. This theory then makes it possible to reconcile those settled norms relating to the preservation of a system of sovereign states with those norms connected to the notion of individual rights.

I have not worked out this theory in any great detail. A fuller exposition would have to determine the precise ways in which individuality is constituted with the state and the system of states. A fuller theory would have to indicate the criteria in terms of which states recognize one another as fully sovereign. As I have mentioned, not any polity may justifiably be granted full recognition as an autonomous state within which individuality may flourish. In the exposition we saw how a state in which the individual rights associated with civil society were not recognized would not count as a state within which individuality was actualized and would thus not qualify for full recognition. There is a wealth of detail which needs to be filled in here.

The aim of this chapter has been to find a background theory which would justify the settled norms of the modern state domain of discourse. Constitutive theory succeeds in doing this, but it is a theory with its own characteristic style of theorizing. This mode of theorizing involves bringing to light those dimensions of the moral order within which we, together with others in the order, constitute one another as fully-fledged individuals. In the next two chapters I shall give two examples indicating how people who accept this background theory might set about reasoning towards solutions for particular hard cases in the normative theory of international relations.

6 The justification of unconventional violence in international relations: a hard case for normative theory

The purpose of constructing a background theory was to enable us to generate answers to some of the hard cases mentioned at the beginning of chapter 3. In this chapter the aim is to demonstrate a practical application of this method. Let us look at the normative problems posed by various unconventional uses of violence in the modern world.

Unconventional violence as a normative problem in international relations

In the modern world few conventional wars are fought, yet there is a great deal of violence of one form or another in world politics. We are all acquainted with the typical cases. Foreign activists place bombs in stations in major cities. An embassy is raided by guerrillas. The staff is held hostage and demands are made which are of an international nature. Suicide bombers drive trucks laden with explosives into key installations in Israel and the Middle East in order to influence the foreign policy of the USA. The Irish Republican Army (IRA) launch mortars at the runways of Heathrow. States, too, practise various kinds of unconventional violence – for example, sabotage against the installations of neighbouring states, active support of liberation movements engaged in violence of one sort or another in foreign states, and so on.

These diverse forms of violence pose a problem for normative theory in international relations because there are so few settled norms relating to it. This is in sharp contrast to the case of conventional warfare.[1] There is a well-settled body of norms relating to the legitimate causes of and the proper conduct of conventional war. For example, although it is accepted that war is generally not a good, nevertheless it is settled that going to war in response to aggression is justified in specified cases. There is thus a measure of agreement about when conventional forms of violence are justified. However, with regard to modern unconventional forms of violence there seem to be very few established norms. Consider, for example, the moral confusion surrounding the violent activities of groups which are often referred to as "terrorist." Most people intuitively judge such activities to be morally evil. However, we cannot simply point to the almost universal condemnation of terrorism and leave the matter there. For we have to take into account that terrorists do not simply disclaim any and all constraints of morality. Indeed, most terrorist actors overtly proclaim a moral position of their own. This deeper concern is revealed in disputes about how such people ought to be described. The people we normally refer to as "terrorists" usually dispute the label. The label has built into it a negative moral evaluation. People labelled "terrorists" usually call themselves something else: "urban guerrillas" or "freedom fighters," for example. Members of the following so-called "terrorist" organizations (to name but a few) reject the label "terrorist": the Palestine Liberation Organization, the Irish Republic Army, the Red Army Faction, the Red Brigades, the National Resistance Movement in Mozambique (RENAMO) and the Basque Separatist Movement in Spain. That disputes arise about the proper classification of members of such groups alerts us to the fact that significant moral importance is attached to the correct label.[2] Why? The answer is plain. The members think that their description of themselves justifies their group and its actions, whereas the alternative description does the converse; it shows the group and its actions to be unjust. If it is important to such groups how they are described (and it generally is so), then we may dismiss a basket of popular myths about the so-called "terrorist" groups. Examples of such myths are that such groups are totally indiscriminate killers, that they are arbitrary perpetrators of violence, that they have no standards, that they are irrational, that they are barbarous, beyond the pale of morality, inhuman and so on. If it is important for such groups to be described in one way rather than another then they have indicated their participation in the business of moral argument. Against the charge "terrorist" the counter claim is made – "freedom fighter." What emerges here is that the "terrorist" groups want to maintain that their actions are justified.

The key question thus becomes: "When, if ever, are 'terrorist-type' actions justified?" The question is pressing because the kinds of actions in question are dire, viz. killing people, maiming them, instilling terror into them, destroying property, destroying social and political systems. Generally "terrorist" groups would agree that such measures are not normally justified. They argue that theirs is not the normal case, but is a special case and is justified because it is special. No doubt examples can be found of groups who do *not* wish to argue that killing, maiming and so on are usually unjustified. It is difficult to see how such groups would not very soon find themselves in an incoherent position akin to that of the amoralist which was discussed earlier in chapter 2.[3] But most "terrorist" groups about which people are concerned do not argue in this way. Their argument is that the dire acts which I listed are not normally justified, but are so in their exceptional case.

There are many different forms of unconventional violence which raise difficult normative questions. Such questions concern violence against property (for example, sabotage committed by individuals or groups opposed to the state against state-owned installations, destruction of private property for political purposes, violence by the state against the property of individual citizens for political purposes); and violence against persons (for example the maiming or killing of state officials, policemen and women, military personnel, etc., by individuals or groups opposed to the state; the maiming or killing, by such individuals or groups, of civilians in an indiscriminate manner; and the maiming or killing by the state of civilians other than in accordance with the due process of law or in the course of a declared war). All of these forms of unconventional violence get an international dimension when the people committing the violence cross international borders or seek international aid and/or approval.

It is most important at this point to notice that justifications of acts of unconventional violence are not only made by people opposing a state, or the system of states, but may be (and are) made by *states* which do the same kinds of thing against people both inside and outside their territory. Israeli actions against the PLO sometimes fall into this category.

It is not difficult to see why these kinds of unconventional violence raise important normative questions in international relations. Those who commit such acts, be they individuals, groups or states, often act across international borders, they regularly seek international aid and recognition, and the targets of such acts seek political, financial and military aid to combat such violence. Thus most actors in international politics are called upon at one time or another to make difficult normative decisions about unconventional forms of violence. The central question which they have to answer is: "When is the killing, maiming, terrorizing of people, the destruction of their property, and of their social and political systems justified?" This question is too wide and contains within it the question: "When is war justified?" I put it this way to overcome a gut reaction many people have, which is that even to ask whether such acts are justified is silly; to many they seem patently and obviously unjust. But most people recognize that questions such as "When is war justified?" and "What may justifiably be done during the conduct of a war?" are questions worthy of serious consideration. My contention is that the questions about the justification of unconventional forms of violence are in the same class as questions about the justification of war.

Terrorism as a hard case for normative theory

In order to demonstrate the ways in which unconventional violence poses difficult problems for normative theory in international relations, let us consider the normative problems which arise concerning the violent activities of terrorists/freedom fighters. Let us start by contrasting the activities of such people with the activities of mentally deranged persons.

Consider the case of a mentally deranged person who hijacks an aircraft. Such a hijacker carries out this deed (for example, threatens to blow up everybody aboard unless some irrational demand is met) from some or other compulsion. Such a case would be of interest to a psychiatrist. It would not pose any serious moral issues regarding the possible justifiability of the killing and maiming of people and the destruction of property. In the case of a mad hijacker we do not say that the action was justified or unjustified. It was simply the action of a deranged person. Such cases pose no problem for normative theory.[4] The actor has clearly broken the law and acted contrary to our moral norms, but he or she cannot be held accountable for these actions. Psychiatrists will probably be able to indicate in a general way why the act was committed. There is also not much dispute about what ought to be done with such a person once caught. He or she should

not be punished but ought to receive psychiatric treatment of one kind
or another.

Similarly hijackers who are sane but criminal pose no special problems for normative theory. The hijacker who threatens terror in order
to get hostages and so to raise money for private gain presents us
with an easy case of broken laws. If caught, the procedure is clear
and the punishment is prescribed.[5] Were a spate of such crimes to
occur, the problem of how best to enforce the law might arise.[6] This
is a practical problem and not a problem for normative theory.

The major cases in which the normative problems surrounding
unconventional violence arise are not at all like this. They are more
difficult in that the actor in question argues that although his action
would not normally be considered justifiable (indeed his action flouts
the conventional legal norms), his action is nevertheless justified in
this case. Typically such actors reject the legitimacy of the law (or of
the legal system as a whole). The important point here is that in order
to evaluate this more radical challenge we are called upon to produce
a background theory in terms of which the state (and its laws) and/
or the system of states (and the international legal system) can be
evaluated. It is no use in such cases referring the hijacker to the law
and arguing that his action is wrong because he broke the law. The
type of hijacker we are considering here admits that he has broken
the law, but wishes to argue that there is nothing wrong in breaking
the law in his case. Usually he will argue that the law in question is
itself unjust. Thus anyone wishing to enter into argument with the
hijacker has to proceed to a deeper level of argument about the justice
of the particular law (or, more likely, of the whole system of law) by
which his action is judged wrong. In order to make this point
somewhat clearer, imagine a woman who hijacked a plane to take
hostages in order to secure funds for her political cause and to obtain
the release of her comrades who were languishing in jail. Before she
was caught she killed one of the hostages. She is brought to trial.
At some stage in the procedure she is allowed an interview with a
journalist.

Journalist: You admit that you broke the law, terrified the passengers
and killed the steward?

Jill: Yes.

Journalist: Yet you claim that such violent action was justified?

Jill: Yes, because life under the junta is awful. The people are
            starving. They have no real civil rights. They are forced to
            fight in adventurer-type wars which are avoidable. There is
            no free press, so they do not know what is going on. All oppo-
            sition to the state is crushed. My comrades and I are trying
            to change things in the only way that we can. We need funds
            and we need support. What I did was done in order to raise
            funds and publicize our case in the hope of gaining inter-
            national backing.

Journalist: Do you agree that in general it would be wrong to go
            around breaking the law in this way?

Jill: Yes, but this is a special case.

Readers may continue the dialogue themselves. Whatever follows
next has to be some or other normative theory justifying the authority
of the state or setting limits to it. It might justify great state power as
did Hobbes' theory, or it might set more severe limits to it as did
Locke's theory and, more recently, Nozick's and Ackerman's.[7] But it
must be a discourse within the modern state centric domain of discourse. This assertion is challenged by Barrie Paskins and Michael
Dockrill, who argue that our failure to think coherently about terrorism must be attributable to our being blinded by the theory of the
state, blinded by the state centric model of reasoning. Contrary to their
position, I am arguing that there is indeed a prevailing modern state
domain of discourse, and this implies that there is more or less universal agreement that it is right that there be in the world a system of
states. The terrorist/freedom fighter who ignores this consensus risks
being dubbed "mad" or "merely criminal." The serious terrorist/free-
dom fighter must distinguish himself from the mad hijacker.[8] His only
way of doing so is by justifying his case. This is borne out by experience; for example, serious terrorists/freedom fighters generally seek
a high-profile public image in order to put their case across. But, in
order to present a justifiable case at all, they must appeal to arguments
which will be understood and recognized by the audience to whose
attention they have drawn themselves; i.e. they must participate in
the state centric domain of discourse. Groups which argue for the
demolition of the state and the system of states *in toto* and who may
thus be seen as not participating in the state centric domain of discourse at all (such as the erstwhile Red Army Faction in Germany,

the Angry Brigade in Britain and the Weathermen in the USA) were generally considered to be on the lunatic fringe. Such groups are seen as dangerous in the way that an armed madman is seen as dangerous. But they are not seen as posing any moral challenge or interesting problems for normative theory. They are not interesting because they fail in their justification to enter in any profound way the central political debate which is in the state centric domain of discourse.

Much more interesting and challenging are those groups of terrorists/freedom fighters which do enter this debate, groups who set out to make a plausible case in this central domain of discourse. Such groups cannot merely be dismissed as "lunatic." Here I have in mind such groups as the Irish Republican Army, the Palestine Liberation Organization, and so on. I suggest that we are acutely uncomfortable in thinking about these cases because on the one hand we want to reject the kind of deeds they are committing as evil, while on the other hand we do recognize that their political claims are not completely outrageous.

The difficult cases which are posed for normative theory by terrorists/freedom fighters are triply hard. First, they are hard in that we cannot simply deal with the case by subsuming it under an accepted rule (as we did in the case of the criminal hijacker), but are in fact called upon to produce a background justification for the system of rules as a whole. Second, they are hard in that, even in terms of the background theory, they are likely to be borderline cases. The background theory is not likely to provide a straightforward answer. Finally, they are hard in that once we have admitted that, for example, the PLO's activities may be justifiable, then we are called upon to wage the argument in public. In those cases where a terrorist/freedom fighter challenges us (where the "we" is the state, or the community of scholars, or the ordinary citizen), we are not simply called upon to sort the issue out in our own minds, so that we may then take the appropriate action. Rather we are required to take up the argument in public. The terrorist/freedom fighters issue a public and fundamental challenge to accepted interpretations concerning the law and institutions of the state and the inter-state system, and the *arguments* must be publicly rebutted. Once the issue "freedom fighter or terrorist?" is raised in connection with individuals (or groups), then executing them imprisoning them, or having them disappear, or placing them under house arrest, or censoring their written and spoken words will not settle the issue. They have to be shown to have been wrong. Their arguments have to be shown to have been faulty.

Pressing normative issues with regard to other forms of unconventional violence in international relations arise in much the same way. In cases (involving state or non-state actors) of sabotage against state or private property for political purposes, in cases of extra-legal political executions, in cases of arbitrary terror, in cases of clandestine political, financial or military aid to people involved in the aforementioned kinds of activities, the acts would normally be considered to be wrong, but it is claimed by those committing them that in the special circumstances involved their acts are justified. Each of these cases raises core issues within the modern state domain of discourse.

Those committing unconventional acts of violence, as I have mentioned, do not usually confine their activities to the internal affairs of a single state. They often seek material and political aid from other states, and from international organizations. In pursuit of their aims in state A they may commit (or threaten) violent deeds in state B. In acting against state A they may seek bases in state B, and so on. It is thus plain that from the international point of view there is a need to answer questions such as "When are the activities of such groups justified?" and "What ought other states to do when confronted with such actions?"

I have argued that the answer to these questions will have to be within the state centric domain of discourse. More specifically, it will have to be in the form of a background justification for the list of settled norms in world politics. In the previous chapters I have given reasons for rejecting a natural law/community-of-humankind approach to these problems, together with order-based theories, utilitarian theories and liberal human-rights theories. I indicated why I thought that a constitutive theory of individuality seemed best suited as a background theory. Let us now put it to the test and see if it will enable us to find satisfactory solutions to the hard cases posed by unconventional forms of violence.

Constitutive theory applied to unconventional violence

In the discussion of constitutive theory we saw that argument towards the solution of a hard case proceeded by seeking to determine whether the act or institution was a necessary part of the constitution of the community within which certain values are held. Applying this method to the hard cases posed by unconventional violence, the question to ask must be: "Can the practice in question (sabotage, extra-legal political executions, terrorism or whatever) ever be partially constitutive of individuality as we value it?" If the answer is positive then "unconventional violence of type x (under circumstances *a,b* or *c*) is a good" would have to be added to the list of settled goods mentioned at the beginning of chapter 4. This list, it will be remembered, included such things as the system of sovereign states is a good, democratic institutions within states are good, international law is a good, and so on.

At first glance it seems unlikely that it will be possible to reconcile any of the forms of unconventional violence with the goods mentioned on the initial list. They seem so diametrically opposed to many of those goods (such as democracy, human rights, law, property, non-combatant immunity, etc.). The practice of terrorism, for example, seeks to be in fundamental conflict with most of these norms. But "terrorists" usually see themselves as "freedom fighters." "Liberation movements are a good" seems far more likely to find a place on the list of goods than "terrorism is a good." Thus the general question formulated above may be reformulated as: "Is the practice of unconventional violence in the fight for freedom partially constitutive of individuality as we value it?" Phrased in this way the question does not seem to call so clearly for a negative answer.

A possible dialogue on justifiable sabotage

In what follows I shall attempt to show how constitutive theory may be applied to the hard cases posed by unconventional violence. In doing so I shall often present the argument in the form of a dialogue. I need to provide a brief justification for this procedure. Arguments presented in this way have, of course, no exceptional logical force. The arguments contained in the dialogue would be as strong were they presented in a more conventional mode. This way of presenting the arguments, though, does have certain advantages. First, it provides a neat way in which argument and counter-argument can be presented. Second, it provides a way of dramatizing what might otherwise be a longer and more laborious argument. Third, it is particularly useful for keeping us aware of a central feature of constitutive theory, viz. the insight that we reciprocally constitute one another in certain specified ways. Finally, I must point out that although it is often the case that the dialogue form allows the crisp statement of an argument, this is not always so. Even in dialogue form, some arguments are lengthy.

Imagine an ongoing dialogue between a terrorist/freedom fighter, called Joe, and Critic, who would label Joe a "terrorist." In order to justify his acts Joe must show Critic that individuality, as Critic values it, can be partially constituted by the practice of "freedom fighting" as he, Joe, portrays it. For the sake of argument, let us assume that Joe embarks on a series of violent acts, that he does not get caught and that after some of these acts he meets Critic, at which point the dialogues ensue. Both Joe and Critic may be taken to have read the present argument and to agree with the substance of it. They both agree that the list of settled goods is correct and they agree that these are best understood as indicating a social arrangement in which individuality can be constituted as such within a hierarchy of social institutions. Joe and Critic will thus not consider the possibility of order-based justifications for the practice of terrorism, neither will they reconsider utilitarian justifications nor liberal rights theories, nor will they reopen the debate about natural law theories predicated on the existence of a community of humankind.

The first dialogue takes place after Joe has blown up an electricity pylon.

Critic: This is outrageous. You know that it is wrong to cause wanton damage to essential services thereby disrupting the economy. How can you possibly justify this act?

Joe: Yes, it is normally wrong (in terms of the settled norms relating to the maintenance of peace and the protection of property rights), but this is a special case.

Critic: Explain yourself.

Joe: Do you agree that to be a free individual it is important that you be recognized as a citizen of a democratic sovereign state, that it is important that you be recognized as having certain key rights, both civil and economic?

Critic: Of course I do, you know very well that we are agreed upon the list of settled norms which includes norms relating to these matters. But what has this got to do with the pylon you bombed?

Joe: Imagine that you awoke one morning to find that the state had suddenly withdrawn certain key rights from you; for example, your rights to democratic participation in the central law-making authority. You find that you are no longer recognized as a citizen who is entitled to stand for public office and participate in the electoral process. You do not accept the justification for this act proffered by the state as a valid one. Assuming that you are determined to do something about this, what must your ultimate objective be?

Critic: To get people to recognize my rights once again.

Joe: What people? Are you referring only to the members of the government which passed the laws depriving you of your rights?

Critic: No, not only them. The government's act of passing the laws depriving me of rights must be seen as taking place in a community which recognizes the government's acts as authoritative and binding. Internationally the act is seen by the community of states as the act of a sovereign state. The state's arbitrary and coercive acts against me depend for their legitimacy on this wider recognition within the society of states. So in seeking to have the wrong done to me recognized, I have to address the wider community which recognizes that government as entitled to pass laws. If I cannot convince the government which committed the act, but succeed in convincing the wider community, the government itself will come to lose that recognition which entitled it to act in the first place.

Joe: Given that you consider yourself to have been wronged, what means would you be justified in using to rectify the situation? Would you, for example, be justified in seeking *power* so that you could force people to recognize your claim to recognition of the requisite sort?

Critic: Of course not. The kind of recognition I presently have (and which I have been deprived of in your example) is freely given and not forced. It is this kind of recognition which I seek to regain. Were I to coerce people into calling me "brother," "fellow citizen," or "comrade" or whatever, their calling me such would not signify that they recognized me as such.

Joe: What then could you justifiably do to get people to recognize your proper status once again?

Critic: My problem is to get back to the situation of mutual recognition which I was in before. In the prior situation I was recognized as a citizen, voter, property owner, rights holder and

170

so on. I, in turn, recognized my fellow countrymen as having these rights. We constituted one another via this system of reciprocal recognition. It follows that if what I am wanting is a situation of reciprocal recognition, then I cannot get that if I fail to accord to the people I am addressing the requisite recognition. What I want is the recognition of free men and I can only get that if I recognize as free men those whose recognition I seek. This indicates a limit to the means which I can justifiably use to rectify the situation you have hypothetically placed me in.

Joe: Explain.

Critic: I am constrained in the following way. Whatever I do to regain the recognition I seek, I must not do anything which would deprive the recognition of those from whom I seek it of all value. Let me put the most extreme case. To be a free man is to be recognized as such by other free men, thus it would be self-defeating to enslave those from whom recognition is sought.

Joe: What are the implications of all this for the situation in which I have placed you?

Critic: The main one is this: in order to regain my rightful status in the community I need to *convince* those who have deprived me of it that they are wrong in denying it to me. In seeking to convince them I must make clear that what I am seeking is a situation of reciprocal recognition and that I am upholding my side of the desired reciprocal arrangement, i.e. I am recognizing them in the proper way. Notice that this is not only important internally, but is of international significance too. My major source of support against an unjust state is likely to come from the international community of states. It is crucial that they see that I use just means to counter injustice.

Joe: So what may you properly do then?

Critic: Given that my task is not to force people but to convince them, my efforts must be aimed at *arguing* with the people concerned. Thus I would seek to address them in as many ways as possible: in personal conversations, in public debate, at meetings, over the radio, on television, in the daily press, through learned journals, via pamphlets and so on.

Joe: Suppose that all those avenues are progressively blocked to you through government action. Your written and spoken words are censored or banned. You are prevented from addressing people, you are confined to your house. What may you properly do then?

Critic: If I had tried the previously mentioned methods and had failed to have my case heard, then I would have to adopt more unorthodox *methods of communication*.

Joe: Such as?

Critic: Getting my case aired internationally. There is an international consensus that sovereign states, democratic procedures within states, the rule of law, the furtherance of human rights, etc. are goods. It would be reasonable to suppose that if my case were a good one it would find widespread support internationally, both within states and in international organizations, both officially and unofficially. In this way I could communicate with those who wrongfully refused to recognize my case.

Joe: But suppose that your international hearing was ineffective. That your case was not taken seriously and that within your state you were still not allowed to have your say and that others in your position were put into jail.

Critic: I would have to show the audience that I viewed my situation as desperate. I could then properly resort to passive resistance and civil disobedience. In these actions I would break the law (and suffer the consequences) as an act of communication with my government, fellow citizens and the international community.

Joe: Suppose that, once again, this kind of act was treated with the utmost severity by your government, so that you knew that a single act of civil disobedience would be your last communication in the debate. What would you be entitled to do then?

Critic: I might try to think of a drastic act of communication which would leave me free to communicate on another day, such as . . .

Joe: Blowing up a pylon?

Critic: Possibly, but I would have to be sure that the act could not be misinterpreted. It would have to be made clear to my audience that my act was not merely criminal, that it was not an act of straightforward coercion, that although I was breaking the law by destroying state property I was not an anarchist, that I had tried all sorts of more conventional ways of getting my message across, that what I was trying to convey with my act of violence had widespread support both internally and internationally, that I had been careful not to harm any people, that I would not endorse this kind of action in normal circumstances and so on.

Joe: I agree with you and my case satisfies all the conditions which you laid down. I deserve local and international support for what I have done. Let me explain the history ...

In this dialogue we see how Joe got Critic to reveal that he (Critic) was prepared to justify, in certain circumstances, that very act of Joe's which Critic had sought to morally condemn, viz. the blowing up of a pylon. In broad outline, Critic's response may thus serve to show how this act could be reconciled with the settled body of goods and with the background theory justifying those goods. At no point does he repudiate the settled core or background theory. Moreover, these arguments are aimed at Joe *and* the reader. The implicit contention of the dialogue is that between the reader and the author (me) there exists a community within which we constitute one another in certain ways. We constitute one another in all the usual ways by recognizing one another as citizens, voters, rights holders and all those other ways indicated in our list of settled beliefs. We do not, however, usually recognize one another as having a right to blow up state property. What the dialogue sought to bring out (make apparent) is that we do recognize one another as having this right in exceptional circumstances, and that this right can be made to cohere with our usual norms of reciprocal recognition.

Second, the dialogue brought out the centrality of reciprocal recognition. This works at two levels. For the argument to work the reader needs to be convinced that in making out a case for this limited act of sabotage any protagonist of such means is not failing to recognize the reader in all the normal ways which constitute him as a free individual (as a citizen in a sovereign state amongst sovereign states, in a state which is democratically organized and in which basic rights are respected, etc.). In short, a person seeking to defend such violent action has to demonstrate his allegiance to the list of settled norms. At a second level, a protagonist of such violence must at all times show those against whom his violence is aimed that he recognizes them in the same way. For what he seeks is the just recognition which is wrongly denied him. If he wrongly denies this recognition to those who deny it to him, then neither party has a case and all talk of justification becomes otiose. Slaves who seek to enslave their masters are not engaged in justified action.

Third, the dialogue shows us that whether or not an action is justified depends on a prior history of graduated acts. In this case it clearly would not have been justified for Joe to resort to sabotage as a first step. In other words, this norm justifying sabotage in specified circumstances is a conditional one. It only applies after the failure of a series of less drastic measures.

Fourth, notice that there is a whole series of ways in which the case for justified sabotage could be weakened. If it could be shown that the saboteur had not been denied access to the media, then no case could be made for advancing to such drastic means of communication as blowing up state property. Similarly, if it could be shown that his arguments, although clearly heard by all those at whom they were aimed, had not elicited much support, then his case would be considerably weakened. For then it is reasonable to assume that what he was arguing for was not consistent with the body of settled goods and its background justification. Thus if the saboteur's message did not find favour within the internal or international community in spite of unimpeded communication, then the odds are that his case is a weak one. If in such a situation he still wanted to maintain that his case was a strong one, he would be entitled to continue arguing for his position, but he would not be warranted in resorting to sabotage as a stronger form of communication. The justification for resorting to acts of sabotage is not that other forms of communication did not *succeed* in convincing the target audience, but that the avenues of communication were blocked. Force is not justified as a stronger form of argument, it is justified when it is the only form of argument available.

Sabotage strategies: two case studies

Let us apply the conclusions of the previous section to two actual examples of sabotage strategies. In both cases although the sabotage campaigns took place within states they nevertheless had implications for international relations. States and individuals not directly the target of the campaigns had to decide whether to aid the terrorist/

freedom fighters, or, whether to engage actively in attempts to bring such campaigns to an end.

The comparison enables us to see how constitutive theory enables us to distinguish clearly between a justified campaign of sabotage and an unjustified campaign.

Consider the Red Army Faction, which received international notoriety in West Germany during the seventies. This was a clandestine group of revolutionaries who engaged in the following kinds of acts in support of their programme: robbery, arson, bombing, kidnapping and murder. Their aims were, amongst other things, to "hit the system in the face; mobilize the masses; and maintain international solidarity."[9] To what extent were their actions justified in terms of the approach I have outlined? The Red Army Faction (RAF) did attempt to justify their actions, but did so in a somewhat eclectic way. Three main *leitmotifs* to their arguments were identified: first, a strong identification with the armed struggle for the liberation movements in the Third World; second, an argument according to which their own state (at that time West Germany) was identified as democratic only in form, while in fact being fascist, in the way the Nazi state had been; third, the rejection of the consumer society. The *leitmotifs* were not brought into any overall coherence and no clear plan for an alternative social arrangement was offered by the group. The RAF was against "the system," but it was not clear what kind of alternative system it stood for.

The RAF's acts could not be justified in the way that it was possible to justify limited sabotage in the dialogue. It is not possible to construct an argument in terms of constitutive theory which clearly shows that the members of the RAF were being denied a form of recognition which ought rightfully to have been granted them. In terms of the accepted norms they were accorded all the rights which were due to them; their personal, civil and property rights were all well respected. Furthermore, the RAF were not able to make the point that they had been unable to state their case in their national community and the international community. They could not point to a past record of attempts to communicate their case in a peaceful manner and could not refer to a past in which their attempts at such communication had been systematically blocked. The acts of the RAF could not be interpreted as clearly signifying their respect for those institutions in terms of which individuals are constituted as free in the modern world. Nor could their acts be interpreted as acts of communication to an audience whose rights were being respected in the act of communication. Quite understandably, opinion polls during the period in question consistently revealed minimal support for the "terrorists" among ordinary citizens.[10] Nor was there any international consensus that the RAF were fighting for a good cause. We may thus conclude that the RAF policies were unjustified.

Let us contrast the activities of the RAF with those of the African National Congress (ANC) which embarked on a programme of sabotage (and other violent acts) in South Africa during the period 1960–1990. The aims of the ANC as formulated in its 1943 Constitution were:

a. To protect and advance the interests of the African people in all matters affecting them.
b. To attain the freedom of the African people from all discriminatory laws whatsoever.
c. To strive and work for the unity and cooperation of the African people in every possible way.

The constitution of the ANC included a Bill of Rights with such provisions as the right to vote, freedom of residence, prohibition of police raids on homes, free and compulsory education, equality in social security schemes, collective bargaining rights and equal opportunity rights. The ANC considered that the African people in South Africa were denied their legitimate rights. Initially the organization sought to state its case through conventional channels. For example, at a meeting in December 1951 in Bloemfontein it was decided to write to the government, requesting it to repeal six specific laws which the ANC regarded as discriminatory. In an exchange of letters with the Prime Minister the ANC mentioned a long series of efforts "by every constitutional means" to bring to the notice of the government the legitimate demands of the African people. It served notice on the government that it was contemplating a course of passive resistance against "unjust laws which keep in perpetual subjection and misery vast sections of the population."[11] They made it clear that their action would not be aimed at specific groups, but was a protest against specific laws. The campaign went ahead. African volunteers broke petty laws and then allowed themselves to be arrested, tried and punished, without showing any resistance to these subsequent procedures. The resisters were severely punished by the state, leaders of the organization were detained and banned, the advocating of passive resistance techniques was declared illegal by a new Act of Parliament. Subsequently new legislation and the activities of the police made it ever more difficult for the ANC to operate as a legitimate political group. Finally, it was declared an illegal organization, thus terminating all further options to pursue its aims in open and constitutional ways.[12] At this stage a clandestine branch of the ANC was formed with the express aim of using sabotage as a means of communicating its aims. These aims were still the aims originally propagated. Umkhonto we-Sizwe ("Spear of the Nation"), as this organization was called, set out to sabotage government installations without endangering human life. It carried out many such acts over a period of thirty years. Clearly in terms of the dialogue the ANC had a much better case for engaging in such sabotage than did the RAF. The ANC's case is strengthened by the fact that at about the same time as it embarked on this campaign it sought and gained widespread international support. This support was forthcoming because of international recognition of the strength of the ANC's case which I claim rested (even if tacitly) on the kind of ethical position I have outlined. At all times it was made quite clear to those who were being addressed that the organization did respect their rights and did not want to deprive any group of their existing rights.[13]

A dialogue on unconventional violence against people

If the kind of justified sabotage discussed in the previous section fails to convince the internal and international audience to whom it is addressed, individuals and groups who claim that they are being denied the recognition which is justly theirs might turn towards more drastic strategies, strategies which involve maiming and killing selected military and official personnel. The IRA is one well-known organization which has adopted such a strategy. The question we must face then is: "When are such strategies justified?"

In a second dialogue Critic confronts Joe after the latter has shot a policeman.

Critic: Joe, you have now taken matters too far. Last time I agreed with you that, in certain special circumstances, an act of sabotage might possibly be a justifiable act of communication. But murder is murder and is always unjustified.

Joe: No, this is just another step in the process which you yourself outlined. For a long time we have restricted our actions to this kind of sabotage and have avoided all violence against persons, especially civilians. But this has been to no avail. Saboteurs who have been caught have been treated with the greatest severity. What is worse, the people of the country have had their rights eroded even further. The government has cracked down on the people's freedom of speech and freedom of movement. Thus the time has come when our cause requires of us that we go further than sabotage alone. We regret the use of violence against individuals. Such violence would normally be wholly unjustifiable, but in our circumstances this is the only possible way open to us.

Critic: Is your task the same one we envisaged in the previous dialogue, i.e. is it to convince those who are denying you the recognition due to you of their mistake and to convince the international community of the justness of your cause?

Joe: Yes, it is.

Critic: If you grant this, then you must agree that your murder of the policeman could only be justified were it possible for you to portray it as an act which did not in any way indicate a desire on your part to reject the basic norms in terms of which you and your audience constitute one another.

Joe: Yes.

Critic: How then by killing a policeman did you convey to your audience that you are still at base committed to the norms of the settled list? For on the face of the matter killing a policeman signifies a rejection of several of the most fundamental norms. For example, it indicates a rejection of the authority of the sovereign state within which you live, a rejection of law, and a rejection of the norm according value to human rights.

Joe: Yes, but it symbolizes my rejection of *this* state and *these* laws, not all states and all laws.

Critic: But the message your deed conveyed was that you espoused lawlessness. Contrast this message with the one conveyed by acts of passive resistance or civil disobedience. What happens in a typical case of passive resistance is that a person breaks a law and accepts the punishment meted out. In doing this he communicates to his audience that although a breach of the law has been committed, he remains loyal to a more fundamental rule – to which both he (the passive resister) and his audience (which includes the police) subscribe. Thus someone who burns a pass book to register his rejection of laws which compel him to carry such documents communicates his rejection of a specific law. But by accepting the consequences he also communicates his acceptance of the rest of the legal system. Compare this type of action to your killing the policeman. There is no way in which by killing the policeman you could be said to be breaking a law at one level in order to refer to a shared value at a deeper level. The dead policeman shares no deeper values with you. The rest of the audience would be justified in interpreting your act from the policeman's point of view.

Joe: I did not kill just anyone; I killed a policeman as a symbol of the corrupt target state and I did not kill just any policeman, but singled out one from the special squad which has been created to suppress the activities of my group. Furthermore, we had given ample warning to the state that such attacks might take place. It was not in any way a random killing.

Critic: Your argument, then, is that your commitment to the basic common norms is revealed in having given public warning that such killings would take place (and why they would take place) and in your choice of target. Is that right?

Joe: That's correct.

Critic: Do you agree that even in this state within which you live the police uphold some norms listed in our settled list: that some of the laws which they uphold would be essential in any kind of political organization which happened to spring up here in future within which individuality was secured?

Joe: Yes.

Critic: Thus you cannot be opposed to every law upheld by this government.

Joe: I suppose so, yes.

Critic: Do you agree that the killing of a policeman in this state does not make it clear that you accept some of the laws and reject others?

Joe: Yes.

Critic: It is exceptionally easy for your opponents to represent what you have done as unjustified anarchism or mere criminality, is it not? (Contrast this case with the pylon bombing case we discussed earlier. It is very difficult for opponents of your pylon bombing act to represent it as mere criminality or vandalism).

Joe: Yes.

Critic: Thus the killing of the policeman appears unjustifiable on two counts. It is a crude gesture capable of too many interpretations, and far more importantly it undermines one of the basic values which unite you and your audience, viz. respect for one another's right to safety of their persons. Do you agree that if I can indicate a different deed which would have had the same or greater effect as killing a policeman and which would not have been open to misinterpretation in the way that killing a policeman is, then your case for killing a policeman would be undermined?

Joe: Of course.

Critic: Would the taking of a policeman hostage accompanied by a detailed notice of why it was undertaken have had an equally dramatic significance?

Joe: Yes.

Critic: Would it not possibly be more effective than the killing because it would hold public attention for a longer period of time?

Joe: Possibly.

Critic: Would it be possible to interpret such a hostage taking exercise as a straightforward criminal act?

Joe: No.

Critic: Would it show more or less respect for the rights of the victim than killing him?

Joe: More.

Critic: Thus you cannot argue that killing was the only option left to you in this unjust state in which you live. For there is at least one other option. Nor can you argue that killing is the only effective option left, for there is at least one better one available.

There are some further points which may be made to strengthen Critic's case that Joe's act was unjustified. The move justifying sabotage in the earlier dialogue was opened when the other avenues of communication were effectively blocked to Joe. The move from sabotage to killing cannot be similarly justified. If it is possible for Joe to undertake the murder of a policeman, then it is possible for him to undertake further sabotage of the pylon-bombing type. It is not possible for a state to block effectively *all* attempts at sabotage. Furthermore, if sabotage over a period of time did not convince a large number of people of the case being put by Joe, then we have a *prima facie* reason to believe that his case must be a weak one and that by increasing his activities to include killing he is not trying an alternative method of convincing his audience, but is trying to coerce them. He no longer seeks recognition for legitimate claims, but seeks to enforce subservience. The former process requires that he seek to convince his adversary on the basis of certain shared premises. Throughout the argument he needs to make apparent his continued acceptance of these. The latter process does not necessarily involve argument at all, it also does not seek a relationship of mutual respect of one another's rights. If Joe's campaign of sabotage has not, after a period of time, gained much support then we would be justified in interpreting any further bombings of his as the frustrated ravings of an eccentric. Quite different is the situation in which more and more people come to declare their support for the policies pursued by Joe and his movement. Such an event would clearly increase the strength of Joe's claim, especially if it could be shown that the consensus behind his movement was not forced, but arrived at in some or other more or less open way. The greater the consensus about the justice of Joe's position, the greater the opportunities would be for effective non-violent methods of opposition such as strikes, go-slows, refusal to cooperate with the implementation of the unjust laws, passive resistance, civil disobedience and finally very widespread and repeated minor acts of sabotage.

In the second dialogue we once again see the constraints placed on normative argument by the condition that in order for a norm to be justified it has to be shown how it may be obeyed while at the same time the actor shows due recognition for the other rights specified in the settled list of norms. Joe's act was indistinguishable from that of a criminal in so far as it did not reveal a clear appreciation of this need for coherence between norms.

It might be argued that in the discussion of violence against persons in the previous dialogue no attention was paid to justifications which can be made for *violence*, i.e. no attention was given to those situations in which a group may reject the legitimacy of a whole regime and seek to overthrow it by all means possible, including violence. In such cases those committing the revolutionary violence may be seen (so the argument goes) as seeking not so much to convince the internal state officials who are denying them their rights, but to gain international recognition and aid for their cause. The dialogue ignored, so this argument runs, cases such as that which pertained in Warsaw in 1944 when the Poles of Armia Krajowa rose up against the Nazis. They expressed their rejection of the Nazi regime *in toto* and used violent means, including the killing of Nazi soldiers and officials. Was their action justified? Did it indicate the Poles' fundamental respect for the core values contained in constitutive theory? What does this example reveal about normative theorizing in revolutionary situations?

The context in which the uprisings occurred was not a stable civil one in which the Poles formed a minority protesting about certain forms of recognition which were denied them. Poland was an occupied state in a highly unstable wartime environment. The occupying Nazis were facing the inevitable advance of the Russian army. The Nazis' treatment of their enemies had always been morally atrocious. It could scarcely be said that there existed a domain of discourse between the Nazis and this Polish underground army at all. The question facing us is: "Given the situation that existed, what forms of violent opposition to the Nazis were justified?" What actions were open to the Poles which would show their commitment to the basic settled norms? Passive resistance and civil disobedience would not work because they require a stable context within which, over time, the effect of these actions may become known and gather support. In a war such acts by a minority would hardly be noticed. Similarly acts of sabotage, hostage-taking and other acts which depend for their effectiveness on national and international publicity would not be effective in a time of war when news of great battles totally eclipses any such puny events. In the event it was clear that *no* act by the Poles would be successful. Anything they did would have failed to convince the Nazis of the justice of their cause. With regard to the international community, we may argue that the Poles did not have to make a case because the justness of the Polish cause was well established. They did not face the task of convincing the international order that their methods of opposition to the Nazis were just. A major portion of the international community was already engaged in a conventional war against the unjust Nazi regime. The international community of states was thus likely to regard whatever form of opposition the Poles adopted as a justified form, provided that it adhered to the just war constraints with regard to the selection of targets and to certain restrictions dictated by international law with regard to the kinds of weapons which could legitimately be used.

The choices which faced the Poles in Warsaw at the time were fundamentally stark: they could either resist the Nazis in whatever way possible, or they could give up all attempts to maintain themselves as moral beings constituted as such within a practice of reciprocal recognition. This latter option would involve sinking into total apathy and retreating from all discourse and action. They were presented with no subtle moral problems at all. They were denied all forms of freedom constituting recognition by the Nazis and denied all the normal means of asserting claims to such recognitions. In such circumstances the choice of violence was not one possible choice amongst a wide range of possibilities. It was almost the only option left.

Contrast the limited choice of means available to those in the Warsaw ghetto with the choices available to the Polish opposition group, Solidarity, thirty-five years later. Solidarity faced an authoritarian communist regime which it sought to overthrow. In deciding how to oppose the authoritarian communist rule it had a whole range of means of opposition from which it could choose. Here constitutive theory would not allow a simple choice for violence against such tyranny. If the leaders of Solidarity had opted for violence, constitutive theory would have required of them that they show that their violent action did not erode state sovereignty, law, democracy, human rights, and so on through the list of settled norms. Because Poland was at the time a relatively stable modern industrial state, there were a variety of different non-violent forms of opposition available to Solidarity. In the event Solidarity did, indeed, choose the non-violent methods which it used against the communist regime with telling effect. What was noticeable about Solidarity was the extent to which its political and moral strength derived from its choice of non-violent means of protest. Part of the wide international support which Solidarity enjoyed was attributable to the scrupulous care which that organization showed in the choice of its methods of opposition. The adherence by Solidarity to the fundamental tenets of the modern state domain of discourse (as formalized in constitutive theory) was beyond doubt. Its case would not have been so strong if it had used more violent means of opposition.

The methods of legitimate opposition used by Solidarity in Poland were used even more spectacularly in the 1980s by the citizens of the Baltic states within the Soviet Union and within the satellite states dominated by the Soviet Union. Here the citizens made use of mass marches, strikes and many other forms of mass action to oppose communist rule.

These actions showed exactly the kind of ethical subtlety called for by constitutive theory. In opposing the tyranny of their existing governments these people were careful to embody in their oppositional action respect for the kinds of values which they hoped to see realized in new polities. The almost unanimous support which these movements enjoyed internationally stemmed not merely from the fact that they opposed tyranny, but from the means which they used to do so.

A dialogue about the use of indiscriminate terror

Let us consider a more serious kind of terrorism. Here I have in mind those acts in which someone like Joe commits random deeds of violence such as indiscriminate bombing and shooting attacks on people. A typical case would be the planting of a bomb in a crowded pub. Can a case be made out justifying this type of violence? This brings us to the third dialogue.

Joe: I planted a bomb in the Pig and Whistle today. Killed several people and got a lot of media time. It gave us more publicity than we have ever had. Even the quality newspapers have several good discussions about what can be said for and against our cause. The debate is now alive in a way that it was not before. We need some similar bombings in some of the great cities of the world to ensure an international debate. I'm off to New York tomorrow.

Critic: Joe, how can you bring a norm justifying this despicable act into coherence with the norms on our settled list and the background theory justifying those norms? Central to that theory was the link established between being an individual and living within a system of law. The norms relating to the state, to the system of states, to citizenship in a democracy, to human rights and many of the other items on the list all presuppose the centrality of law. Crucial to all law is the purpose of regulating human conduct so that people in their day-to-day relations with one another will know where they stand. Your act of terrorism goes contrary to that central purpose of law which in turn is a central feature of so many of the settled goods on our agreed upon list. Any member of the audience you are addressing with your terrorist act could be a target for your next attack. By your own confession you do not discriminate between your victims. Thus it is quite impossible for you to claim with regard to any member of your audience that in committing the act you were respecting values which you have in common with them.

Joe: In all our talks we have been discussing what methods may justifiably be used. Now I want to stress that we have tried the other methods which we have discussed. We tried the ordinary methods of political mobilization using the media and so on. The conventional channels were closed to us. We then tried passive resistance, civil disobedience, sabotage and kidnapping. All to no avail. We are turning to indiscriminate violence as a last resort. We are still committed to the core values we have so often discussed, but this is the only means left by which we can realize those values. By this means we can push up the costs to the government (and its supporters) of maintaining their repressive policies. To use the jargon of political science, what we want to do is nudge along the "asset to liability shift."[14] When the costs of maintaining an asset become too high it becomes a liability and the owner will dispose of it.

Critic: Your argument is that the other methods have failed and you are trying this as a last resort.

Joe: Yes.

Critic: We need to know precisely in what ways it is the last resort. Are you in a position similar to that of the Poles in Warsaw in 1944 where all other modes of opposition (passive resistance, civil disobedience, sabotage) would not have communicated anything significant over the surrounding din of war? They simply would not have been noticed.

Joe: No, the situation we face is not like that, we are not involved in war. The state is relatively stable; it is simply unjust.

Critic: So the other means that you have tried were noticed, but they did not bring about the desired result.

Joe: Yes. We are now trying what we hope will be a more effective method.

Critic: Throughout our conversations we have agreed that your aim is to convince your audience of the justness of your claims. This is what is to count as being effective.

Joe: I have never denied this.

Critic: For the sake of argument then, imagine that I am a member of the audience you are addressing (I may be a citizen of your state, a member of the ruling group in your state, or a foreign policy-maker in the wider international community). I noticed your earlier drastic communications (sabotage, etc.), carefully considered your case and decided that your position was unjustified. In short, you failed to convince me. By escalating your activities to include random terror killings are you likely to strengthen your case in my eyes?

Joe: Clearly not, for you are already opposed to our case.

Critic: Consider the converse case, viz. the situation in which I was impressed by your earlier attempts. I noticed your passive resistance, civil disobedience and sabotage, considered your case and decided it was a good one. Your efforts have succeeded in convincing me. (By the way, the actions of Solidarity in Poland impressed me in just this way.) I am determined to support you. Do you need to adopt the methods of random violence against people to strengthen my conviction of the justice of your cause?

Joe: No, of course not, for you are already convinced of the worth of our cause.

Critic: So you admit that such violence will not instil a sense of the justice of your cause in those who were not convinced by your earlier methods, and such violence is not needed to convince those who were impressed by your other methods. How do you justify random violence then?

Joe: It is aimed at getting the ruling group to relinquish their unjust policies. We seek to raise the costs to them of maintaining those policies.

Critic: Your aim, then, is not to convince them of the justice of your case (you have already admitted that violence will not do that if the other methods did not succeed), but to *force* them to change their practices. Violence here is no longer a drastic means of communication to be used in specific circumstances but has become a means of coercion.

What emerges from the foregoing dialogue, taken together with the earlier discussion of the Polish rising in Warsaw during the Second World War, is that more drastic violent measures are only justified when the less drastic measures are not available as options which will be heard at all. For example, passive resistance is only a justifiable option when other more orthodox avenues of communication have been closed to the aggrieved group; similarly, sabotage is only justi-fied after the method of passive resistance has been crushed, and so on. Finally, methods of violence against specified classes of people (as in Warsaw) are justified when the situation is such that all the less drastic methods are not feasible avenues of communication at all. Here violence of this kind was the only avenue of expression still open. It is crucial to note that tougher measures of unconventional violence are not warranted in those cases where the "softer" measures were heard by the audience, but simply failed to convince them. The correct metaphor for the conclusions we have reached here is that forms of violence are lines of communication which may only be justifiably used when all the other lines are down. The erroneous metaphor is the one which pictures the forms of violence as a graded set of wea-pons such that where the small weapon fails to bring down the quarry the hunter may switch to a larger weapon.

There is one final small point to make about the previous dialogue. Where Joe describes random terror as a method of last resort he is clearly thinking in terms of the weapons analogy just mentioned. His is a means/end argument. He is advocating the use of a force as a means to the desired end. There is a major problem with this approach from the point of view of constitutive theory. The end which Joe wishes to achieve (viz. the just state in which people recognize one another in certain good ways) cannot be reached in the way he describes. The just state consists in people reciprocally recognizing one another in the ways we have already discussed. This state of affairs can only come about when people do recognize one another in the requisite ways. Where people fail to do so, the only way of remedying the situation is to bring them to see the error of their ways through a process of argument. A person cannot be forced to believe that X is his equal. He may be forced to say it, but not to believe it; hence the importance of argument and education *en route* to the just state. At the end of an indiscriminate terrorist campaign there would not be a people properly educated to be citizens of a free state. The means used would have made the end impossible.

Uses of unconventional violence by the state

In the foregoing set of dialogues we have considered the case of the individual terrorist against the state. Let us now consider whether a case can be made out defending a norm which justifies the state in using similar methods against individuals within the state or against the people of neighbouring states.

Consider a hypothetical situation in which the agents of a state like South Africa when it was under white minority rule (or of a state like Israel) enter into the territory of a neighbouring state (here after referred to as Neighbouring State) and commit deeds of sabotage against state installations there. There is in international relations clearly no settled norm authorizing sabotage by one state in the territory of another. This would be counter to the well-established norms of non-interference and non-aggression. A state which undertook such actions would have to show that its acts constituted a special case. Before considering whether it is possible to construct a coherent argument in support of such acts let us consider the general justification for the non-interference and non-aggression norms. It is the justification articulated in the previous chapter according to which these norms are justified in so far as they provide a framework within which individuality can flourish. States, by recognizing one another's sovereignty, make it possible for the citizens in those states to recognize one another as citizens in a sovereign state. This is an important component of individuality. Not doing this would involve regarding the neighbouring territory as a conquered territory, a subject state or a colony (to mention but a few of the possibilities). People in a subjected state do not feel themselves recognized as free individuals *vis-à-vis* those in the dominant state. In order to justify unconventional violence in a neighbouring state, South Africa would have to argue that the relationship of reciprocal recognition between states had already broken down in specified ways and that it was this breakdown which warranted South Africa's resorting to sabotage in Neighbouring State. South Africa might make the following allegations against Neighbouring State:

1. That Neighbouring State sought wrongfully to undermine South Africa's legitimacy in the eyes of the community of states.
2. It openly advocated the overthrow of the government in South Africa and gave material assistance to those who sought to achieve this.
3. It refused to discuss matters of common concern with the government of South Africa.

In the normal course of events it is clear what legitimate avenues are open to a country like South Africa (as represented in this hypothetical example) in seeking redress of such grievances. The usual approach would be to address the target state through normal diplomatic channels. Besides the normal bilateral channels recourse could be made to the forums of international organizations. In all of these endeavours South Africa's (or Israel's) task would be to convince Neighbouring State and the international community that its (Neighbouring State's) actions are not justified. It would seek to show that Neighbouring State's behaviour is not in accordance with the settled norms and the background theory of constitutive individuality.

But suppose that the normal channels of communication were blocked to South Africa. Suppose that Neighbouring State refused to have diplomatic relations with South Africa, that the key international organizations did not allow South Africa to participate in their day-to-day proceedings, that special emissaries sent to put the case for South Africa were not granted travel documents and access to the key people they wished to address. What might South Africa (Israel) do in such circumstances? Here once again is a situation with which we are now familiar, in which a participant in a constitutive practice is denied the normal channels of communication and has to use unorthodox methods of putting his case. What might a state thus placed legitimately do?

There are unorthodox methods which fall short of sabotage which are available to a state like South Africa (Israel) in this example; methods which show a full commitment to the settled norms of the constitutive practice. For example, South Africa could attempt to influence public opinion within the neighbouring state by buying space and time in its media in order to publicize its grievances. It could invite leaders from Neighbouring State's political, religious, economic, cultural and other spheres to visit South Africa in order to have the opportunity of putting South Africa's case to them. Similarly, it could send prominent citizens to foreign states as informal ambassadors seeking to convince the international community of the justice of South Africa's cause.

Imagine that these avenues of communication were also effectively blocked. Foreign powers might introduce measures to discourage their own nationals from visiting South Africa. This could be done by ostracizing sports players who went to South Africa. Conversely, measures could be introduced to curtail South African sportsmen and women travelling to play in other states. Similar measures could be applied to other kinds of informal diplomats. For example, organizations in South Africa could be excluded from international umbrella bodies. International contact between academics in South Africa and academics in other states could be limited in various ways. Multinational companies with interests in South Africa might be obliged to limit their activities there or even to withdraw altogether. In all these diverse ways South Africa's opportunities for putting its case might be curbed. In cases like this, with so many lines of communication damaged, what might a state like South Africa justifiably do to make its voice heard? Would it be justified in resorting to unconventional forms of violence, like sabotage, against the vital installations of Neighbouring State?

The answer must be negative. Consider how implausible the example I have sketched is. South Africa is presented as adhering to the fundamental norms of the modern state domain of discourse. Neighbouring State is presented as wrongfully failing to accord South Africa proper recognition and as actively promoting the overthrow of the South African state. Then the community of states as a whole is portrayed as imposing progressively more stringent curbs on South Africa's right to participate in the discourse of the community of states. At the end of the story South Africa, a lone just state in a world of injustice, seeks to use extraordinary means to communicate with the world of the deaf. The story is supremely implausible because the steps taken against South Africa by Neighbouring State and the community of states at large would only be possible if they acted in concert. Such concerted action in a world of many sovereign states would only be possible after the fullest possible discussion of the issues surrounding the claims and the counter-claims of South Africa and Neighbouring State. If, *mirabile dictu*, it were possible to achieve such an international consensus against South Africa, this, it seems reasonable to assume, would be a *prima facie* indication that South Africa's case was not a strong one.

In this example, as in all the other examples which I have introduced, whether the act of violence is justified or not depends on what is communicated by the act of violence in question. It would be justifiable if it could be interpreted as being in accordance with the settled norms and the background theory. I have argued that it cannot coherently be suggested that the violent act is a desperate attempt at communication following the closure of all other avenues of communication. The consensus required to block the other avenues necessitated extensive debates about the merits of the cases of South Africa and Neighbouring State. How then ought we to interpret such an act? The most plausible interpretation is that it must be seen as an act aimed at intimidating Neighbouring State in order to get her to act in accordance with South Africa's purposes. If my analysis of this kind of case is correct (i.e. if it is true that this kind of unconventional violence cannot be made to cohere with the settled norms of the state centric practice), then it seems reasonable to expect that South Africa would always seek to deny in the public forum any involvement with such deeds. Complicity in such deeds would be kept secret. Conversely Neighbouring State would seek to publicize sabotage attempts by South Africa as widely as possible. Let us now, in conclusion, look at a more difficult case.

South African special forces entered Maseru, the capital of Lesotho, in the dead of night and attacked several places of residence within which lived members of the African National Congress army (Umkhonto weSizwe) who had mounted sabotage attacks on installations within South Africa. The ANC soldiers were exiles from South Africa who were fighting for the rights denied them by the South African government. The aims of the ANC had achieved widespread international recognition and were approved of by the majority of the domestic population within South Africa. After years of attempting to convince the government of South Africa of the justice of their case through conventional means and after the government of South Africa had effectively closed down most of the channels of communication open to the group, the ANC resorted to passive resistance, civil disobedience and, finally, reluctantly turned to sabotage. That the ANC pursued a policy of sabotage was well known. Lesotho, knowing this (and acting in concert with other Front Line states) continued to allow the members of the group to live in and operate from its territory. Prior to the night raid South Africa had repeatedly requested the government of Lesotho to curtail the activities of the saboteur group, but this had not been done. On several occasions it had warned Lesotho that if the activities of the saboteurs were not curtailed, South Africa might resort to force to settle the matter. Again this was to no avail. Finally, before the raid the government of Lesotho was notified by South Africa that a raid was going to take place, that no harm was intended towards Lesotho itself, its government or its people. In the actual raid the action was confined to the residences which had previously been identified as being the places where the saboteurs lived. Several non-ANC people who happened to be sleeping in the same residences were killed in the raid.

Ethics in international relations

In the following dialogue, Critic confronts Ben, who is to be imagined as a member of the government of South Africa, but party to the previous dialogues with Joe:

Critic: How can you justify your government's action of sending troops into a neighbouring state in order to slaughter some of its residents in their sleep? Surely it is in flagrant contravention of the non-interference norm?

Ben: Those whom we aimed to kill were not ordinary residents of Lesotho; they were saboteurs bent on fomenting revolution in South Africa. As the government of South Africa we are obligated to protect law and order, and the security of our citizens generally. These people were seeking to undermine it. We had tried several more orthodox means of curbing their activities in order to give due recognition to the sovereignty of Lesotho, all to no avail. Lesotho refused to curb the activities of these saboteurs; it repeatedly allowed them to stage sabotage raids into our state. In this way they forced us to take more extreme measures which were nevertheless justified in the circumstances.

Critic: Let us consider the position of the ANC saboteurs you refer to. Is their position the same as the one which confronted you some years ago when we had our first dialogue, i.e. do they claim that you as a government are failing to recognize certain important rights of theirs, that they had tried all the orthodox channels of addressing you about this matter, and that you have systematically blocked these, that they tried less orthodox, but still peaceful, channels such as an underground press, and the seeking of international recognition, and that they have at all times taken pains to reassure you that they do not wish to threaten your basic rights? Have they achieved quite significant success in their attempts to gain international recognition and have they gained significant underground support within South Africa?

Bem: Yes, they have done all these things, but we still maintain that the case which they are arguing is wrong.

Critic: What is your main aim throughout this process?

Ben: At its broadest I would say that we aim to establish the legitimacy (both internally and internationally) of our government and of the policies which we pursue. The counter side of this is that we would seek to refute those critics who deny the legitimacy of our government and its policies. Their arguments and actions undermine our international standing and our internal security.

Critic: In short, what you aim at is a situation of reciprocal recognition in terms of which your standing and your acts are recognized as legitimate and where you grant similar recognition to the standing and acts of other states in the community of states.

Ben: That's right. To act justly is to act in ways that are recognized as such within the modern state domain of discourse.

Critic: Then you must admit that you cannot achieve your aim by brute force. If you are accused of not being a just state worthy of recognition, you can shoot the accuser, but that will not remove the accusation.

Ben: That's correct. We have been through all this before. What I need to do is convince my critics that their criticism is unfounded. Only if we do so will our actions be recognized as legitimate, and recognized in the desired way.

Critic: But there are two different criticisms to be dealt with in this case, are there not? First, there is the criticism raised by many in the international community of the way in which you entered Lesotho to deal with the saboteurs with force of arms. Second, there is the criticism raised by the ANC cadres themselves which refers to the way in which your government denies them their rights. These two are closely interlinked. Now I can see that you have some defences which you can offer against the charges of the first kind of criticism. You can with some justification say that you took great pains to make it clear to all concerned that your raid was not a challenge to the state of Lesotho itself. You warned the government of Lesotho beforehand that the raid was to take place, that it would be limited and that you intended no harm to Lesotho itself. These arguments may go some way towards convincing the community of states that your state is committed to recognizing certain ground rules of the community, for example the non-interference rule. But it will not silence the second kind of criticism, which refers to the denial of rights to certain groups within your state. Shooting the critic leaves the criticism either untouched, or more likely, it reinforces it.

Ben: Let me ask you a question. What kind of argument from us would weaken the case of the ANC saboteur?

Critic: Well, consider his claim that he is forced to sabotage because the normal channels of communication between him and the community at large within South Africa are denied him. If you could demonstrate that this charge was unfounded, his case would be weakened. If you could show that he and his fellows had full freedom of speech, access to the media, the right to attend and convene meetings, that he was not threatened with kidnappings or house arrest and the like, then his reasons for turning to bombs would be shown to be spurious and your case seeking to counter the sabotage would be considerably strengthened.

Ben: It so happens that we can erode the saboteurs' position in much the way that you have outlined. Within our state we have an exceptionally free press. There is a range of newspapers catering to most tastes. There is nothing to prevent entrepreneurs setting up new newspapers. Open discussion is tolerated among the people. There are universities within which the whole range of political and social questions may be discussed. The only curbs placed on freedom of speech are those which prevent people propagating ideas which would undermine just those rights and liberties which need to be preserved to make freedom of speech possible.

Critic: It is this last contention of yours which is crucial. The saboteurs argue that they have made it plain throughout their campaign that they are committed to all the core values on your list. They are not aiming to bring about a breakdown in the rule of law, they do not aim to infringe your basic rights, they do not intend jeopardizing your *bona fides* in this regard. For example, in their passive resistance campaign they demonstrated their respect for persons by avoiding harm to humans, and to private property. They have avoided arbitrary terror, assassination campaigns and the like. In all this they do not look like people bent on undermining the basic preconditions for a free state. In all this they acknowledged that what they are seeking is a relationship of mutual recognition within

the state and they have shown their commitment to recognizing you in the requisite way. Your action against them has not
shown a similar commitment. Instead of seeking to induce
them to recognize you, in the way you require, through
reasoning, you have attempted to put a stop to their argument, by censorship, bannings, arrests and now finally you
have sought to put a stop to their arguments by killing them.
Will this not weaken your position in the eyes of those you
wish to convince? It seems to me that there is no interpretation
of your action which you could have offered the saboteurs
killed in the raid which would have shown them that at base
you were committed to common core values and a common
justification for the core. The most plausible interpretation of
your act is that you were trying to frighten the saboteurs into
silence; not that you were trying to convince them of the justice of your case. Compare this case with the quite different
one in which troops from opposing states who are at war with
one another meet in battle. Here in manifold different ways
the troops recognize one another as participants in a practice
which embodies fundamental values and ground rules which
they both endorse. War is a practice within the international
community which under certain specified conditions is considered just. There are broad conventions governing how wars
might legitimately be fought. Within war there is a strong
element of mutual recognition between the antagonists. I mention but one small facet of this: mutual recognition is revealed
in according a killed enemy soldier a decent military burial.
Your action in this case has shown that you do not recognize
the people involved as rights holders at all. You cannot seriously be seeking recognition from people you portray in such
a light, no matter what you protest yourself to be doing. It
might be said that you are a true terrorist, in that you seek to
frighten people rather than convince them.

Conclusion

Several interesting things emerge from the foregoing discussion of
various cases of unconventional violence. First, we have seen in each
case how important it is, from the constitutive theory point of view,

for the person seeking to justify his violent act that he show his audience how his act coheres with the other values in terms of which he and his audience constitute one another as individuals.

Second, a particular link between argument and force has emerged in the discussion. Violent acts which are acts of force *simpliciter* are not justifiable. In general, only those acts of force which may be interpreted as acts of communication are justified. Violent acts of communication are only justified in those cases in which all other avenues of communication have been blocked. An implication of this is that acts of unconventional violence are only justified where freedom of speech has been curtailed. It follows that a central imperative of constitutive theory is that the channels of communication between people be kept open at all times. The only exception to this is provided by those cases where the use of force is the only remaining means available for asserting one's freedom (the case of the Warsaw ghetto).

Third, the common adage that violence is justified as a means to a good end blurs more than it reveals. This style of talk suggests that any means to a good end is warranted. However, we have seen in our discussion that violence is justified only when it is used as a *means of communication* or when it is the *last remaining means at hand for protecting a person's or polity's freedom*. It is not justified as a means of coercion.

Fourth, it has emerged that acts of *random* killing and maiming are never justified because such killings fail to show due respect for the aspect of reciprocity required by justifications in constitutive theory. Even in the case of the Poles in the Warsaw ghetto, the killing which took place was rightfully not indiscriminate, but was aimed at the functionaries of the Nazis. This is not to suggest that all killing of people is always unjustified. In some forms of combat (examples range from formal feuds to wars) there is a form of mutual recognition involved between the parties and it is only in such cases that killing is ever justified. In the relationship between the terrorist killer (or maimer) and his victim there is no such reciprocal constituting of one another as values. Soldiers meeting on the battlefield see one another as representing opposing states in battle. By seeing one another as representatives of their respective states they confer a certain dignity upon one another. The relationship between a terrorist and his random human target involves no such recognition. It is akin to the relationship between a hoodlum and his victim.

7 Who gets what state where? The Bosnian conflict

The marketplace massacre in Sarajevo: the ethical issues

As a final practical application I now wish to use constitutive theory in order to answer some of the difficult moral problems the international community encounters in the territories of former Yugoslavia. A central problem there (and elsewhere in Eastern Europe) revolves around the question: "Who is entitled to what state, where?" I intend approaching this topic obliquely by focussing on recent developments in Bosnia and more specifically on a single event which demanded an international response, viz. the mortar bomb attack on civilians in a marketplace in Sarajevo in February 1994. Such a study will be useful more generally in that there is every reason to suppose that similar cases are likely to arise in the future both there and elsewhere in the world.[1]

The mortar attack on the marketplace was seen as a *moral* outrage by the international press who, no doubt, anticipated that readers would view it in a similar light. A glance at any of the "quality" newspapers in London in the immediate aftermath of the attack reveals a number of expressions of moral outrage at the killing of sixty-eight civilians. Notice the unmistakably moral character of the terms used. The reports and comments were not spelled out in terms of a cold calculation of national interest – a concept fundamental to the analyses of realist international relations. Here are some of the words and phrases used in *The Times* and the *Independent* that week: the deed was labelled an "atrocity" (note that this is not merely a descriptive term; those acts we label "atrocities" are ones deemed particularly obnoxious from a moral point of view), there was mention of the need for "revenge for the slaughter", outrage was expressed at the "killing of civilian targets," reference was made to this "cruelty, not to be condoned." Rees-Mogg in his column in the *The Times* wrote of "murderous tribes," President Clinton was reported to have urged people to give the United Nations time to "identify the guilty,"[2] commentator Robert Fisk wrote in the *Independent* of a "war crime."[3] In writing about what should be done, mention was made of the need to punish, the necessity of intervention, the possibility of pre-emptive military action, and there were calls for retribution. Throughout, the suggestion was that some military action should be taken as a response to this unjustified killing of civilians.

In spite of this widespread moral condemnation of the Sarajevo bombing it is far from clear how, from a moral point of view, we ought to think about what happened there. Should we think about it as murder or in terms of "just war" theory? Another possibility would be to conceive of it in terms of the morality used by those fighting wars of national liberation. Whatever line of thinking we adopt will, in the end, determine what we think we ought to do, and, finally, what we do do in response to the killing. What we end up doing includes, of course, the possibility of our doing nothing. The "we" I refer to here includes you, me, presidents, foreign ministers, decision-makers in the United Nations, etc. We (you and I) are in exactly the same boat here as presidents, prime ministers, foreign ministers and all the others who may become involved directly or indirectly in what happens there. They have more power to wield by virtue of their positions, than we do. But we may be called on to support or oppose the policies of our governments with regard to that region. We may be called on to provide material or political assistance to the groups involved there and so on. Whatever our involvement we all have to make some moral judgements about what happened in Sarajevo and to make some decision about what a justified response would be. If our presidents and prime ministers reach conclusions which we think are fundamentally wrong then we can bring pressure to bear on them through public opinion and the democratic process. How then, from a moral point of view, should we think about the bomb in the market place at Sarajevo?

Let me start by pointing out that it does not help much to say, as a thoroughgoing realist would, that moral questions do not come into the picture; that each state ought to make a quick calculation about its core interests and act accordingly. According to this account no moral questions arise for statesleaders or citizens. This will not do, for the debate has already been couched and understood in moral terms in the public domain, as indicated above. Anyone entering the debate will have to do so in the idiom of moral discourse. In terms of this discourse the realist response, "We have no interest in Bosnia, let them slaughter one another," will not do.

However, simply asserting the commonplace that there are moral issues at stake here, does not take us very far. Ought we to evaluate this act as an act of murder? Or as a wrong understood in terms of just war theory, (i.e. a failure to adhere to the *ius in bello*)? Or ought it to be understood in terms of the moral theory which underpins liberation struggles? Or is it best seen as a crime against humanity? None of these presents itself as being an obviously correct answer. We find ourselves then in the puzzling position of being in broad agreement that we morally condemn those who killed the civilians, but we are not quite clear about the moral basis from which we make this moral judgement.

We are not likely to suggest, and none of the commentators in the British newspapers suggested at the time, that the appropriate way of understanding this deed was in terms of our ordinary concept of murder. We do not think that the problem is one of finding out who did the deed, bringing that person (or group of people) to trial to be charged with the crime of murder and then handing down an appropriate sentence.[4]

Similarly neither we nor the commentators are likely to spend time wrestling with just war theory as being applicable to this case.[5] The first part of that theory, the *ius ad bellum*, is inappropriate for it concerns the justice of any given war itself. That theory would have us decide, in the light of the appropriate criteria, which party to a given war was the belligerent and which the victim. This would then enable us to support the party which had been wronged. This part of the theory seems inappropriate to this case for in Bosnia there is no conventional war in progress. Whatever is happening in Bosnia, it is not a war of one state against another.

The second part of the just war theory, the *ius in bello*, initially seems more promising in that it focusses on the justice of the means used in war. Yet even this component of the theory hardly seems appropriate because, to repeat an earlier point, there is no conventional war in progress. It is not that the parties to the dispute are generally engaged in fighting a war according to the just war canon, and that all we need to guard against are periodic infringements of the rules of war. The battles of this "war" have from the outset not been between rival standing armies pitting themselves against one another. Throughout, what we have witnessed are militias directing their violence at civilians. The massacre of civilians and the rape of innocents have been the basic methods of fighting in the conflict. This is not a just war within which some of the actors are behaving as war criminals. Nor is it, in just war terms, an unjust war, within which are to be found a few war criminals. Just war theory does not seem to be of use here at all. It does not help us make any discriminations other than to allow the global judgement that everything that is happening in the region is wrong.

I conclude this part of the argument then by suggesting that just war theory must be understood as providing standards for judging conventional wars and that, because this conflict is not at all like a conventional war, the just war tradition has no purchase here.

It seems initially more promising to consider this case from the point of view of those more recent phenomena which we have come to know as wars of national liberation. Is this not a case of unconventional violence which ought to be understood along the lines described in the previous chapter? A practice of moral judgement has arisen around wars of liberation which is significantly different from just war theory. What made wars of national liberation unconventional was that in them one found, on the one side, a traditional state with a conventional army, facing, on the other, a national liberation movement using unconventional military formations. Usually the national liberation army fought not only across the borders of the state under attack, but from within the state itself. Because of internal repression and lack of economic and military resources the liberation armies did not identify themselves as soldiers through the wearing of uniforms and they did not form permanent standing armies. Instead they fought wars in a clandestine way; attacking and hiding. Terror tactics were often used. The aim was to demoralize and weaken the oppressor while empowering the oppressed. The just war tradition of reasoning was not particularly useful in understanding these wars. Once again the core problem, as in Bosnia today, was that the war was not between two conventional powers. Quite the contrary, these wars were often between the powerful (in conventional terms) and the powerless within a single state. They were wars waged between standing armies and unconventional forces of one kind of another.

From a moral point of view the unconventional armies demanded that they be judged by criteria somewhat different from those used in just war theory. They (for example, the African National Congress in South Africa, the Irish Republican Army in the United Kingdom and the Palestinian Liberation Movement in Israel – to mention but three) claimed in their defence, the justice of their cause. In arguing for the legitimacy of their cause and the justice of the means which they used in pursuit of their cause, they appealed to criteria contained in the Charter of the United Nations – especially those criteria relating to human rights, the right of self-determination of peoples and the United Nations resolutions against racism and colonialism. As often as not they would appeal to democratic theory (especially the majoritarian principle) by pointing to a majority which supported their cause. They would seek to justify their present actions by reference to historical injustices such as conquest and colonial rule. The cases made out in terms of these criteria often won for these "armies" considerable international support.

The main point though is that in all these wars of national liberation the "struggle" was (and is) waged on the basis of moral considerations. The international community which was called upon to participate in these wars (directly or indirectly) had, perforce, to evaluate the moral claims of the liberation movements before deciding whether to support or oppose such wars.

The African National Congress's (ANC) war against apartheid in South Africa provides a good example of the practice of moral judgement which I have been describing. In order to make my point I would ask you, the reader, to judge the ANC's case against your own (possibly unsystematized) moral judgments. You would probably judge white minority rule in South Africa post-1948 as unjust. You would easily find moral courage and merit in the mass non-violent protests mounted by blacks in the early 1950s. Similarly you would probably judge the strike actions directed at the minority rulers as justified. Turning now to the international sphere you would no doubt judge the worldwide condemnation and the diplomatic actions which followed from that (all of them aimed at bringing an end to apartheid) to have been morally correct. Turning now to economic sanctions, judging these is more difficult because with regard to these it could be alleged that they harmed the oppressed as much as the oppressor. Violence against the property of the rulers which did not harm people, could be justified as extreme measures. When all these failed to bring the unjust order to an end, it became possible to make a case (plausible at least) that violence against targeted personnel who worked in the service of the government was justified. Once again (as we saw in the last chapter) what was far more problematic were exercises of indiscriminate violence which hurt civilians.

What I would draw your attention to is the way in which the ANC (like other liberation movements) made its case by appealing to widely held standards in the international community. There is amongst the international community in general widespread agreement on the criteria which I referred to in the previous paragraph. These norms include, as we have seen, those to the effect that: people have a set of fundamental rights, and *a fortiori* that a minority forcefully depriving a majority of their fundamental rights is wrong, that one of these rights is the right to participate as an equal in the democratic process through which the government of one's country is elected, that self-determination is a good, that the rule of law is a value to be cherished, that peace is better than war, and so on. These I have discussed in much greater detail in chapter 4 above. They are the settled norms of our international community. They are the norms in terms of which we constitute ourselves.

The judgement made by the international community (that is, you and humankind everywhere outside of South Africa) about South Africa under apartheid was straightforward. Little intellectual sophistication was needed to make the moral judgement about who occupied the moral high ground. There were, as is well known, disputes about what ought to be done against the apartheid government; for example, about whether to impose mandatory economic sanctions against South Africa. But on the basic issue concerning the injustice of apartheid rule there was little dispute. It was, you may say, an easy case. It was easy because the well-established criteria cohered in a way which made a quick judgement possible. Some cases are not so easy. Bosnia is an example of a hard case.

Bosnia: a hard case for international ethics

The Bosnian case is a hard one for us to judge from the moral point of view.[6] A discussion of what makes it thus will edge me towards the central topic of this chapter which concerns the criteria governing the granting of statehood to peoples.

In 1989 it all seemed so simple. There was a sequence of events in Eastern Europe which was easily understood in terms of well-known principles. We in the international community approved the breakdown of communist tyranny and the successful liberation struggle of the peoples in those areas. The actions of the people there seemed to be guided by the well-established principles against tyranny, in favour of democracy, human rights, self-determination and the free market. The newly formed states were welcomed into the international community by the United Nations.

The ease with which we were able to make judgements ended when cases arose where the peoples/nations demanding self-determination did not neatly coincide with the given borders of states. Suddenly we were faced with irredentism, drives to secede, and civil wars.

Two well-known principles to which we might normally turn for guidance did not provide much help in this case. First, the freedom of association principle (which would clearly allow Christians to associate together in a way that excludes Muslims, and, conversely would allow Muslims to associate together and exclude Christians, and so on for other religious and national groups) seemed suddenly very problematic. The people and parties in Bosnia knew with whom they wanted to associate, but they could not agree on which association was entitled to live where. The people freed from communist tyranny seemed unable to agree on who should live in what state.

Second, the principle of self-determination, as a settled norm of international relations, showed itself to be similarly problematic. What "self's" claim to which territory was to be regarded as legitimate? Our democratic belief that the will of the people should settle major political problems seemed of little use in clarifying these cases. To which people's will in what area should we have turned for a settlement of the problem? In a dispute between one group demanding autonomy in one area and another demanding autonomy in a different, but overlapping area, how should this be settled? Here the hard question was not about the moral relations between states in the international community, but about the prior question: Which people, are entitled to live, in what area, under what state?

These questions would have been difficult enough to answer without war having broken out between the parties to these disputes. Once this happened we were faced with the problem of deciding whose cause was the just one in such conflicts.

Finally, compounding an already complicated picture, if all the parties to these disputes used methods of war which breached all our established rules about how wars should be waged (massacre, rape and torture), how ought we to conceive of our own moral obligations to those involved in such wars? None of these questions could be construed as merely academic. They had been put to us by all the parties involved in the Bosnian conflict (and those involved in other conflicts in the region too). They were couched as appeals to the international community for political, material and military support – these appeals were based on the cry of "foul" against the methods used by the opponents of each group. The claims were not the well-known ones so often produced by liberation movements – namely, claims which refer to their long-term oppression by colonial, authoritarian or totalitarian rulers. Rather they were about immediate cruelties and acts of barbarism. Similar claims were made by all the parties to the dispute.

What are we, in the international community to do in such cases? How are we, from a moral point of view, to conceive of such events? We, of course, condemned the massacre, but in trying to decide what ought to be done about it we found several settled norms of international relations pulling in different directions.

First, the principle referring to the sovereignty of states and their rights to non-interference in their internal affairs suggested one course of action. It suggested that we should refrain from intervening in the civil war in Bosnia-Herzogovina unless asked to do so by the government. In this case the government did call for international aid in putting down the militias of the Serbs and Croats. On this principle we should have given them the aid which they requested. But this would have required of us that we ignore a second settled principle which is the principle of self-determination. This principle rules that we ought to provide aid to the ethnic groups (peoples) in Bosnia who seek to secure their self-determination by attaching themselves and their territories to Croatia and Serbia respectively. According to this principle, if we had given military aid to the Bosnians (enabling them to repress the drive to self-determination of the Croats and Serbs in the area) we would have been supporting a tyranny over the minorities. Obeying this principle would itself have been problematic. For following this principle (requiring of us that we support the rights of self-determination of minorities) would require of us that we ignore a third principle.

This third principle demands of us that we respect human rights. It requires of us that we protect and enforce human rights against offenders wherever these offenders may be found. This principle would take no cognisance of the competing political claims of the state and the rival peoples in Bosnia mentioned above. The problems with regard to applying this principle, to cases like Bosnia, are particularly acute because all the belligerents were guilty of gross human rights abuses. Are we, in such cases, required to punish all those that abuse human rights?

These principles tug in different directions. The knotty problem at the heart of this "tug of principles" centres around the problem of statehood. The key question is, "What ought we to do about people who were previously subject to tyranny, *but who now cannot agree on what people should live under what state in what territory?*" If we are to answer this question we need to resolve the tension among the three principles I have identified.

Let me attempt to make the nature of the problem clearer by bringing the discussion back to the events in Bosnia which I described. Croatians in Bosnia claimed their right to self-determination and indicated their willingness to fight to excise bits of territory from Bosnia with a view to joining these to Croatia. Serbs in Bosnia desired to excise specific territories in order to attach them to Serbia. Bosnian Muslims argued that either of these actions would involve minorities wrongfully dismembering Bosnia. They refused to accept a package negotiated with the other two. They sought to gain international military support for their war by building up international outrage against the means used by the other parties. Finally we need to remember that all the groups involved in this dispute sought international support. Thus, international actors had to assess the merits of the different moral claims made by each of the groups involved in the dispute.

What emerges from the above is that it is not possible to judge and respond to the marketplace massacre in Sarajevo without making some decisions about which claim, by what group to which territory is justified. It is not possible in practice to keep these substantive questions about the merits of the ethnic territorial claims quite separate from questions about the justice of the means used by Croats, Muslims and Serbs. In Bosnia it was not possible for the international community (us) to take firm action against the Serbs and Croats without *de facto* supporting the military efforts of the Muslims to hold onto the whole territory of Bosnia (and thus end up taking sides against the

Croatian and Serbian pleas for self-determination). Similarly if we sided with the Bosnian Croats (or Serbs) we would *de facto* be supporting their territorial claims. It is crucial that we notice that what each group sought was not merely redress for war crimes committed by the other parties to the dispute. Each sought support for its substantive long-term goals in the region.

Any military action at all in the region (and in any of the other regions of central Europe) required of us that we have some answer to the question: Whose claim to statehood over what territory is a just one?

Nations, territories and states: the ethical links

What entity should we recognize as a state? With regard to the old established states this is normally no more than an academic problem. For we normally recognize as legitimate states those entities which we have always recognized as states. Here we might suppose that there is good reason for this practice, but we are not usually called upon to articulate the reason. However, when would-be states start claiming statehood we are forced to think more deeply about the matter; about what the moral basis for statehood is.

It is here that constitutive theory is of use. The core insight of constitutive theory is that people constitute one another as free people within a hierarchy of institutions. The core institutions which we have discussed in previous chapters are the family, civil society, the state and the community of sovereign states. In each of these we find that people, by recognizing one another in specified ways, create for themselves a valued form of moral standing. In constitutive theory we saw how moral claims are often claims for a certain kind of recognition from others. Constitutive theory showed how certain forms of moral standing can only be established through reciprocal recognition. For me to be a citizen I need to be recognized as such by others who I, in turn, recognize as citizens. It would be no use to me in this regard to be recognized as a citizen by those whom I recognize as subjects or slaves. Similarly a state needs to be recognized as such by those which it recognizes as sovereign states. The same point could be made about civil society and the family. In sum then, at the heart of constitutive theory is the notion of a complex reciprocity of recognitions.

Let us apply this notion of complex reciprocity to the Bosnian case in hand. We are faced with people who, we may assume, are well constituted within family structures. Beyond this they may be partially constituted within a more or less well-formed civil society. As was elucidated earlier, civil society is largely composed of those relationships which hold between rights holders within the sphere of the economic market. At the time of writing, the institutions of civil society (the market and non-governmental institutions) in the territories of former Yugoslavia were functioning to some degree. People bought and sold. Contracts were made. People associated with one another through a range of associations. In short, people recognized one another as rights holders. In this way they constituted an area of freedom between them. But given the immediate history of the region it is clear that the market relations were, at the time, less than stable. But in spite of their partial constitution as free people within their families and within civil society, the people in Bosnia had not established their freedom within a stable state within which they all recognized one another as citizens. This form of mutual constitution had yet to be established.

The question which faces us then in this type of case is what ought we, as people more or less well constituted within free states, to do about those who lack a well-constituted state?

First, in terms of constitutive theory it is clear that we may not seek to exert power to force people to start constituting one another as citizens of a state, for a relationship of mutual constitution cannot be forced upon people. Just as a marriage made under duress (the so-called shotgun wedding) does not establish a marriage properly so called, in like manner a state-like structure forced upon a people will not establish a fully fledged state. A good demonstration of the truth of this point is to be found in the state-like arrangements which were forced upon people by the South African government in its attempt during the period of apartheid to create ethnic states (the so-called Bantustans). This attempt to force states into being failed completely to provide freedom constituting relationships between the people in those territories.

Second, we as outsiders cannot dictate to those who have not yet constituted themselves into a state whether they ought to create one, two or more states. How many states (understood as relationships of complex recognition between people in an area) the people in a given area will form is a contingent matter. There is no known tablet on which is engraved how many states there should be. What states the people create will depend on any number of contingent considerations such as what common understandings of their histories the people share, what languages they speak, what the history of regional economic cooperation is, what the ancient enmities between people in that area are, what the geographical spread of people within the region is like, what the present arrangements of infrastructural factors are, and so on. It follows from this that there is nothing sacrosanct about the boundaries of previously existing states or state-like arrangements.

Third, just as we as outsiders may not attempt to force a state into being at the point of a gun, we may, for the same reason, reject any attempt by a single group in the region unilaterally to force the others in the region into a state-like arrangement. If, in the case we have been discussing, the Serbs, for example, sought to impose their rule on the Croats and Muslims we would not regard this as a legitimate exercise of state formation. (For the same reasons, we would reject a similar imposition by the Croats or Muslims). Any such attempt would be a case of the subjugation of a people or peoples. Such a process would create subjects, not citizens.

Fourth, constitutive theory suggests that we as outsiders should do all we can to encourage certain kinds of procedures for the establishment of a state (or states) in the region. Our preferred procedure would be one in which the people negotiate with one another about what state (or states) should be created. For only such a procedure embodies within it an acknowledgement of the fact that freedom can only be created where each person reciprocally constitutes others (and in turn is constituted by them). The kind of recognition required in the state has to be freely given. The very notion of citizenship suggests free reciprocity and the absence of force. Internally the only procedure which can bring this about is negotiation towards the establishment of a constitution acceptable to those who are to live under it.

Fifth, constitutive theory suggests a range of procedures we might use to secure the process of negotiation mentioned in the previous paragraph. The means by which we as outsiders may seek to encourage such processes of constitution building through negotiation are legion. We might provide conference facilities (in our capital cities) where these negotiations might take place. We might reward progress in such negotiations with high profile occasions of commendation (signing ceremonies in Washington, London, Paris, etc). Material impediments could be put in the way of attempts to subjugate groups internally – such impediments might include the imposition of sanctions against arms sales. Resources might be provided for the conduct of referenda in which the people are consulted about constitutional proposals. Monitors may be provided for referenda and elections. We might provide people of stature to act as third parties, counsellors, facilitators, and intermediaries in the negotiation process and so on. This list of suggestions could easily be extended. The general idea, though, is clear. *From a moral point of view the task of outsiders in a dispute like the Bosnian one is to provide a dynamic framework (through the means suggested above) within which the people may constitute themselves as citizens in a state or states.* In short, the moral requirement is not for some brave, brief military solution, but calls for patient persistence over a long period which might well be boring, slow and painstaking.

Sixth, where the parties involved in trying to set up a state (or states) not only fail to achieve this, but start warring in a way that destroys those other institutions which are constitutive of freedom (the family and civil society) then those in the outside community may do whatever they can to prevent this destruction of these freedom-creating institutions. But what can be done in this direction is limited by the constraint I mentioned earlier – the external community (in this case, us) cannot force people into establishing the systems of reciprocal recognitions required in a system of family life and civil society. Here again, constitutive theory limits what outsiders can do. They must confine themselves to the creation of the circumstances within which people may come to recognize one another in the requisite ways. This may be done through education, facilitation or by providing suitable inducements and disincentives.

Seventh, what does constitutive theory advise us about the claims of ethnic groups to be self-determining in their own states? Constitutive theory implies the following with regard to claims made for ethnic self-determination. Constitutive theory asserts that people can only establish themselves as free when they are self-determining, i.e. when they reciprocally constitute one another as citizens within a state. It does not specify that only an ethnically defined state will do. But, by the same token it does not rule out the legitimacy of ethnic states. If it is the case that the people about whom we are concerned (the people of Bosnia) through an appropriate procedure of negotiation (as described above) find that for a significant section of the population ethnicity is an important factor, they may find that the only structure of recognition they can agree on is the establishment of three largely ethnically defined states. This would be quite congruent with constitutive theory *provided that no group of people is forced into an arrangement within which they effectively become subjects rather than citizens.* No group, whether it be defined in ethnic terms or in terms of some other criterion (religion, for example) has a right to self-determination where this involves subjugating others.

It is important to spell out precisely what follows from the last paragraph. For constitutive theory the self-determining entity is the state; within it citizens recognize one another as beings who through their reciprocal recognition jointly constitute a self-determining sovereign entity, viz. the state. In trying to establish this entity, ethnicity may be one of the contingent factors which comes to play an important role in the process. But the ethnic unit has no right to override all the claims of other people with a view to denying them full participation in a state. Negotiations may establish that these others may best be accommodated within a separate state, or it may be found that some form of federal structure may solve the problem of the minority. An ethnic group, just like any other group, has no right to deny to the members of other groups the freedom which comes through being a fully fledged citizen within a state.

The corollary of the point made in the previous paragraph is that people who refuse group labels (such people may refer to themselves as living in a plural society, a liberal society, a "melting pot" type society, an open society, and so on) have no right to force an ethnic group into a state which the latter refuses. Domination by ethnic groups and forced assimilation are both unacceptable in terms of the canons of constitutive theory.

Concluding remarks

What constitutive theory recommends as the appropriate ethically grounded forms of action in cases such as Bosnia, in fact, quite closely matches the policies which have been pursued by the major external actors involved there (the UN, Britain, the European Union, Russia and France). In other words, the explicit theory which I have outlined matches quite closely the principles implicit in their practice. Saying this though is not an admission that this theory has no critical edge. Constitutive theory, as I have articulated it, is sharply critical of many of the moral stances which have been taken by newspapers and public opinion in the West. These have often been couched in the language of the just war tradition. Here the call has been for firm action against an enemy state guilty of aggression against the peace-loving Croats or Muslims. At other times the language of human rights has been used. Here the call has been for the punishment of those who have abused human rights. In each case the call is for firm, military action against the wrongdoer. The failure of the international community to take such firm military action is then construed as showing military weakness or weakness of will. There are often derogatory references in the newspapers to the futile wringing of hands which takes place in the corridors of power. What I hope to have shown in this chapter is that this kind of call is based on inappropriate theories of international ethics. They involve applying just war theory to circumstances to which it does not apply. Alternatively they involve applying human rights criteria to a situation in which a civil society (in which such rights are embedded) does not exist. Both of these calls do, indeed, refer to norms which are settled in world politics, but we ought not to accept recommendations based on them because such appeals fail to bring the norm in question into coherence with the other settled norms of world politics. It is my claim that constitutive theory succeeds in doing this. Having done so it then provides prescriptions for action in cases like Bosnia. Such prescriptions highlight the need for creating *framework conditions within which the institutions of reciprocal recognition may grow*. The institutions within which free people are constituted cannot be forced into existence; such equal relationships need to be nurtured. What is required are certain forms of encouragement, certain forms of facilitative practice, material aid, and educational measures. What has to be remembered at every point though is that what has to be created is a set of reciprocal *relationships* between the target group of people themselves and between them and us. At the end of the day such relationships can only be created by the actors themselves. It cannot be imposed upon them. People cannot be forced to become valued members of families, rights holders in civil society, citizens, and finally, *via* their states, good members of the community of states.

Conclusion

I have tried to do two things in this book. First, I have sought to examine the reasons why ethics is accorded such a marginal place within the discipline of international relations and to show that these reasons are not good ones. Second, I have put forward a substantive normative theory which I have dubbed *constitutive theory*. In seeking to achieve this latter objective I followed a model of argument first set out by Ronald Dworkin in the context of legal reasoning. This model of argument starts from the settled norms within a given domain of discourse and seeks, on the basis of these, to construct a background theory which will enable us to find solutions to hard cases. I started with a list of what most actors in international relations accept as settled norms and then sought to construct a background theory which would enable us to achieve a coherence between the different items on the list of settled goods. In the course of this attempt it was found that the following did not suffice as background theories: order-based theories, utilitarian theories and rights-based contract theories. The best background theory which emerged was a secularized Hegelian approach which I have called the constitutive theory of individuality.

In the last two chapters I applied constitutive theory to two sets of ethical problems which arise in international relations. The first had to do with normative questions which arise with regard to the use of unconventional violence in world politics. In particular I examined the use of those methods which are often referred to as "terrorist" methods. The use of these methods provides hard cases for normative theory both because there are no settled norms specifying whether (and under what circumstances) such acts are justified, and because a norm justifying such acts of violence seems to be contrary to so many of the settled norms of international affairs. For example, on the face of it these acts of violence are opposed to the norms relating to democracy, human rights, international law, peace and state sovereignty, to mention but a few. In the course of my argument I show how it is possible to justify a limited class of such violent actions. The argument proceeds from the shared premises contained in the list of settled norms and the background theory and demonstrates how individuality is constituted through reciprocal recognition of the list of settled norms to conclusions about various difficult norms relating to unconventional violence. In seeking to justify the contentious norms relating to unconventional violence I showed how these norms could be brought into coherence with the other norms which are crucial to the constitution of free individuality. The major substantive conclusion about acts of unconventional violence was that they are only justified when it is possible to interpret them as acts of communication from those who have been unjustly treated aimed at those who have systematically denied the people in question the opportunity of having their case heard. But such extreme acts of communication are only justifiable when they are of such a nature that they demonstrate an ongoing commitment to the corpus of settled norms by which they judge that an injustice has been done them. I have thus outlined a method which enables us to come to grips with a set of normative issues which, at first glance, seemed so difficult to accommodate within our normal modes of moral discourse.

In the final chapter I applied constitutive theory to the ethical questions which arise with regard to the notion of self-determination. Recent events in Bosnia-Herzogovina afforded me a practical case study which brought forth just such questions. Here I was able to show how constitutive theory requires of us that we recognize from the outset that our ethical task is to establish certain kinds of relationships of reciprocal recognition among all the parties involved in the dispute about self-determination. This immediately brought to light that what is required are procedures of negotiation and education rather than procedures aimed at forcing others to do certain things. The argument showed that with regard to producing ethical outcomes there are severe limits to what can be brought about through the use of power, force or coercion. Ethical action in international relations is better understood as "doing therapy" than as doing battle.

I contend that it would be possible and fruitful to apply constitutive theory to all the other hard cases for international ethics mentioned in chapter 3. For the present, the constraints of space and time prevent me from continuing this important and interesting task.

Notes

Introduction

1 Similar violent disputes have arisen in the territories of the former Soviet Union.

2 Mervyn Frost, *Towards a Normative Theory of International Relations* (Cambridge: Cambridge University Press, 1986), p. 1

3 See Chris Brown's "International ethics: fad, fantasy or field," in *Paradigms* (Special Issue on International Ethics 8, 1, 1994, for a discussion of the new flowering of interest in international ethics).

4 The following is a selection of books published since 1986 on international ethics: L. Brilmayer, *Justifying International Acts*, (New York: Cornell University Press,1989); Chris Brown, *International Relations Theory: New Normative Approaches:* (New York: Columbia University Press, 1992); Chris Brown, ed. *Political Restructuring in Europe: Ethical Perspectives* (London and New York: Routledge, 1994); Allen Buchanan, *Secession: The Morality of Political Divorce* (Boulder: Westview Press, 1991); James Child, *Nuclear War: The Moral Dimension* (New Brunswick: Transaction Books, 1986); Anthony Ellis, *Ethics and International Relations* (Manchester: Manchester University Press, 1986); John Finnis, J. Boyle, and G. Grisez, *Nuclear Deterrence, Morality and Realism* (Oxford: Clarendon Press, 1987); Paul Keal, ed., *Ethics and Foreign Policy* (London: Allen and Unwin, 1992); F. Kratochwil, *Rules, Norms and Decisions* (Cambridge: Cambridge University Press, 1989); A. Linklater, *Men and Citizens in the Theory of International Relations*, 2nd edn., (London: Macmillan, 1990); Terry Nardin and David Mapel, *Traditions of International Ethics* (Cambridge: Cambridge University Press, 1992); Joseph Nye, ed. *Nuclear Ethics* (New York: The Free Press, 1986); Nicholas Onuf, *World of Our Making: Rules and Rule in Social Theory and International Relations* (Columbia, SC: University of South Carolina Press, 1989); T. Pogge, *Realizing Rawls* (Ithaca: Cornell University Press, 1989); John Vincent, *Human Rights and International Relations* (Cambridge: Cambridge University Press, 1986).

The key journals are: *Millennium: Journal of International Studies; Review of International Studies; Ethics; International Organization; Ethics and International Affairs; Philosophy and Public Affairs; Journal of Applied Philosophy;* and *Social Philosophy and Policy.*

5 See, for example, William O'Brien and John Langan (eds.), *The Nuclear Dilemma and the Just War Tradition,* (Lexington, MA.: Lexington Books, 1986); James Child, *Nuclear War: The Moral Dimension;* Joseph Nye, ed., *Nuclear Ethics.*

6 President Reagan's references to the "evil empire" are illustrative here.

7 On such issues see Chris Brown, *Political Restructuring in Europe.*

1 The place of normative theory in international relations

1 For a short succinct account of this history, see Martin Hollis and Steve Smith, *Explaining and Understanding International Relations* (Oxford: Clarendon Press, 1990), ch. 2. See also *Millennium: Journal of International Studies* (Special Issue: The Study of International Relations), 16, 2 (Summer 1987); K. J. Holsti "International Relations at the End of the Millennium," *Review of International Studies,* 19, 4 (October 1994) pp. 401–8.

2 For a classification and discussion of some of the competing traditions see Timothy Dunne, "Mythology or Methodology? Traditions in International Relations", *Review of International Studies,* 19, 2 pp. 305–18.

3 See Martin Wight *International Relations Theory: Three Traditions,* volume eds.: Gabriel Wight and Brian Porter (Leicester University Press/Royal Institute of International Affairs, 1991).

4 Terry Nardin and David Mapel, *Traditions of International Ethics,* (Cambridge; Cambridge University Press, 1992).

5 The distinction between the classical and scientific approaches was most clearly stated by Hedley Bull, "International Theory, the Case for a Classical Approach" in K. Knorr and J. N. Rosenau, eds., *Contending Approaches to International Politics* (Princeton University Press, 1970).

6 Recent exponents of the scientific approach are: J. W. Burton, *Deviance Terrorism and War* (Oxford: Martin Robertson, 1979); Robert O. Keohane, ed. *Neo-Realism and Its Critics* (New York: Columbia University Press, 1986); Stephen D. Krasner, *Structural Conflict: The Third World Against Global Liberalism* (University of California Press, 1985); and Michael Nicholson, *Rationality and the Analysis of International Conflict* (Cambridge: Cambridge University Press, 1992).

7 See Robert L. Rothstein, *The Evolution of Theory in IR* (Columbia: University of South Carolina Press, 1991).

8 In 1984 a survey showed conclusively that the broad scientific tradition is still dominant; see Hayward R. Alker and Thomas J. Biersteker "The Dialectics of World Order: Notes for a Future Archeologist of International Savoir Faire," *International Studies Quarterly,* 28, 2 (June 1984), pp. 121–42. More recently in 1992 Alan Gilbert talked of "the still prevailing empiricist methodology of political science which stresses 'testing' single hypotheses, suitably specified or 'operationalized,' against '[radically theory-external]

data' " in his article "Must Global Politics Constrain Democracy? Realism, Regimes, and Democratic Theory" in *Political Theory*, 20, 1 (February 1992), p. 17. Other regular examples of the scientific approach are to be found in the *International Studies Quarterly* journal. For a good selection see vol. 35 (1991). A survey of current approaches in international relations can be found in Margot Light and A. J. R. Groom, eds., *International Relations: A Handbook of Current Theory* (Boulder, CO: Lynne Rienner, 1985). On the dominance of the American "scientific" approaches to International Relations see Steve Smith, "The Development of International Relations as a Social Science," *Millennium: Journal of International Studies*, 16, 2 (Summer 1987). pp. 189–206.

9 It is probably fair to say that most British students of International Relations are more classical than scientific in their approach to the subject. See Hedley Bull, *The Anarchical Society* (London: Macmillan, 1977); E. H. Carr, *The Twenty Years Crisis 1919–1939* (London: Macmillan, 1946); D. C. Watt, *A History of The World in the Twentieth Century* (London: Hodder and Stoughton, 1967); Martin Wight, *Systems of States* (Leicester University Press, 1977); Martin Wight, *Power Politics*, volume eds.: Hedley Bull and Carsten Holbraad (Harmondsworth: Penguin Books, 1979).

10 For some Marxist writing pertaining to International Relations see the article and bibliography by Tony Thorndike, "The Revolutionary Approach" in P. G. Taylor, ed., *Approaches and Theory in International Relations* (London: Longman, 1978) p. 54. Also see V. Kubalkova and A. A. Cruickshank, *Marxism–Leninism and the Theory of International Relations* (London: Routledge and Kegan Paul, 1980), and for a theorist making use of Marxist insights, but seeking to move beyond them see Andrew Linklater *Beyond Realism and Marxism: A Critical Theory of International Relations* (London: Macmillan, 1990).

11 In this connection see: Hedley Bull, "International Theory"; and Morton Kaplan "The New Great Debate," in K. Knorr and J. N. Rosenau, eds., *Contending Approaches to International Relations*, p. 39.

12 In this connection see J. D. Singer, "The Level of Analysis Problem in International Relations," in K. Knorr and S. Verba, eds., *The International System: Theoretical Issues* (Princeton University Press, 1961), pp. 72–92; K. N. Waltz, *Man, the State and War* (New York: Columbia University Press, 1959); and K. N. Waltz, *Theory of International Politics* (London: Addison-Wesley, 1979).

13 See, for example, K. J. Holsti, *International Politics: A Framework for Analysis*, (Englewood Cliffs: Prentice Hall, 1967). A more recent work which looks at frameworks of analysis is R. D. McKinley and R. Little, *Global Problems and World Order* (London: Frances Pinter, 1986).

14 "In the present stage of its evolution, international theory is engaged in an extremely costly, laborious, and slow process of accumulating data which do not, so far, clearly fit into any plausible general framework." Joseph Frankel, *Contemporary International Theory* (London: Oxford Univer-

sity Press, 1973). The implication was, presumably, that this is a necessary stage prior to theory building.

15 It is not important for my purposes to go into the disputes between the strict verificationist theories of science and the Popperian falsificationist approach (or the subsequent introduction of the notion of "verisimilitude"). For a brief discussion of these see Paul Diesing *How Does Social Science Work* (Pittsburgh: University of Pittsburgh Press, 1991), sections 1 and 2.

16 See Thomas Kuhn, *The Structure of Scientific Revolutions* (Chicago: University of Chicago Press, 1970, 2nd edn); Steve Smith "Paradigm Dominance in International Relations: The Development of International Relations as a Social Science," *Millennium: Journal of International Studies*, 16, 2 (Summer 1988), pp. 189–206.

17 Modern textbooks start out by introducing students to the competing paradigms in the discipline; see, for example, Paul R. Viotti and Mark V. Kauppi, *International Relations Theory: Realism, Pluralism and Globalism* (New York: Macmillan, 1993).

18 It is not even clear within International Relations whether any of these approaches is a paradigm, properly so called, at all. In other words it is not clear whether they have the features of a normal stable scientific practice. A case may be made that the different approaches are all in a pre-paradigm phase.

19 Writing about "the predominantly positivist cast of the discipline" Richard Price states that "scholarship in the field has been grounded in the quest for theories of causal explanation for behavioural outcomes." See Price, "Interpretation and Disciplinary Orthodoxy in International Relations," *Review of International Studies*, 20, 2 (April 1994), p. 202.

20 The distinction to which I am referrring is clearly articulated in a recent textbook by Paul R. Viotti and Mark V. Kauppi, *International Relations Theory: Realism, Pluralism, Globalism* p. 5. Here they distinguish normative theory from empirical theory: "Unlike empirical theory, however, propositions in normative theory are not subject to empirical test as a means of establishing their truth or falsehood." For an early example of this view, see A. F. K. Organski, *World Politics* (New York: Alfred Knopf, 1968), p. 5 who wrote "A scientific study must be concerned with empirical facts, that is, it must be testable by evidence available to the senses." He continues: "but during the course of his investigation, the scientist lays aside his values and treats his data objectively as if it did not matter to him what he found." Relevant here, too, is Karl W. Deutsch, *The Analysis of International Relations* (Englewood Cliffs: Prentice Hall, 1978, 2nd edn), p. vii, "As the practice of International Relations has become more difficult and decisive, its study has moved to keep pace. The dramatic advances in the field over the last three decades include changes in basic concepts and theories, changes stimulated by a meeting of the newer behavioural sciences of psychology, sociology and anthropology with the longer estab-

lished disciplines of political science, history and economics. These changes in theory have been accompanied by the development of new methods of research, the development of statistical procedures for analysis and the growing availability of *testable empirical data*" [emphasis added]. On the next page he states: "... knowledge is different from values.

Values motivate the search for knowledge and make some of its results more salient to us than others. Knowledge tells us which of our values may conflict and where and when our means begin to injure and destroy our ends instead of serving them. My own values are made plain throughout this book. *You may share or reject them*" [emphasis added]. A forceful statement of this position by James Rosenau in "Thinking Theory Thoroughly" has recently been republished (presumably approvingly) in Viotti and Kauppi, *International Relations Theory: Realism, Pluralism and Globalism*, p. 25. Rosenau says "Progress in the study of international affairs depends on advances in both empirical and value theory. But the two are not the same. They may overlap; they can focus on the same problem; and values always underlie the selection of the problems to which empirical theories are addressed. Yet they differ in one overriding way: empirical theory deals essentially with the 'is' of international phenomena, with things as they are if and when they are subjected to observation, while value theory deals essentially with the 'ought' of international phenomena, with things as they should be if and when they could be subjected to manipulation. This distinction underlies, in turn, entirely different modes of reasoning, a different rhetoric, and different types of evidence."

21 For someone with a Kuhnian understanding of science, "seeing" the facts requires some prior theoretical training, but for the initiate of the practice the facts are objectively given and the links between conclusion and evidence (or hypothesis and verifying data) are inter subjectively verifiable and objective. The observer within the paradigm cannot stipulate a fact to be as he or she wishes it to be. The observable world, even though it may be circumscribed by theory, is independent of the theorist. What the instruments reveal may surprise him/her.

22 For a discussion of the fact/value distinction see Fred M. Frohock, *Normative Political Theory* (Englewood Cliffs: Prentice-Hall, 1974, ch. 1); W. D. Hudson, ed., *The Is/Ought Question* (London: St Martin's Press, 1969); Karl Popper, *The Open Society and Its Enemies*, vol. 1 (London: Routledge and Kegan Paul, 1945), p. 62; Peter Winch, *Ethics and Action* (London: Routledge and Kegan Paul, 1972), p. 50.

23 The two approaches, the traditional and the scientific, differ in their respective claims about what can be done with the facts and about the way the facts can be incorporated into an explanation. The traditionalists claim that it is not possible to subsume the facts under general theories, whereas those adopting the scientific approach view the production of covering laws (or at least general theories) as the final goal of the enterprise. But, at the end of the day, it is, for both of these approaches,

the perceived facts which are supposed to underpin the objectivity of the inquiry. See Hedley Bull "International Theory," and J. David Singer "The Behavioural Science Approach to International Relations: Payoff and Prospects" in J. N. Rosenau, ed., *International Politics and Foreign Policy*, (New York: The Free Press, 1969). The ongoing Correlates of War (COW) project led by Singer is an ongoing example of the positivist bias being discussed here. In the abstract of a recent critical article about COW, David Dessler writes "The modern scientific study of war relies primarily on correlational studies aimed to uncover the recurring patterns of actions, events, and conditions associated with interstate conflict. The goal is an explanatory theory of war grounded in reproducible evidence, free of subjective biases that have plagued traditional analysis. . ." See Dessler, "Beyond Correlations: Toward a Causal Theory of War," *International Studies Quarterly* 35, 3, (September 1991), p. 337. Looking at political science in general Gabriel Almond wrote in 1988 that the bulk of political scientists ". . . have a deep-rooted and unshakable firmness in our commitment to the search for objectivity." See Almond, "Separate Tables: Schools and Sects in Political Science," *PS: Political Science and Politics*, 21, 4 (Fall 1988), p. 840.

24 They made a distinction between factual propositions, which picture reality, and analytic propositions, which do not. The distinction was most forcibly argued by the logical positivists of the Vienna Circle. See John Passmore, "Logical Positivism," in Paul Edwards, ed. *Encyclopaedia of Philosophy*, vol. 5. (New York: Macmillan, 1967) p. 52. But those who understand science in terms of Kuhn's analysis quite clearly do not accept this view, although they still hold to a strong distinction between facts (which for them are, by definition, overdetermined by theory) and values. See note 21 above.

25 See W. D. Hudson, *Modern Moral Philosophy* (New York: Doubleday, 1970).

26 Vernon Pratt, *The Philosophy of the Social Sciences* (London: Methuen, 1978) p. 93.

27 This is not the only reason for the characteristic avoidance of debates about norms. Other reasons are discussed in the next chapter – one of the more important of these being ethical scepticism.

28 See especially the sources referred to in notes 1 and 2 above. See also Stanley Hoffman, "An American Social Science: International Relations," *Daedalus*, 106, 3 (Summer 1977), p. 54. Here he states: "The champions of a science of international affairs have, on the whole, declared their independence from philosophy and their allegiance to objective empiricism." In H. Greisman's "The Paradigm that Failed" in R. C. Monk, ed., *Structures of Knowing* (New York: University Press of America, 1986) p. 286, he states: "Within contemporary definitions of normal science, moral arguments violate the most important taboo of all. Although philosophers and sociologists of science have shown that value-neutrality is at best a chimera and at worst a cynical ideology, its power has not diminished in the slightest." Note that Hayward Alker and Thomas Biersteker found that the bulk of

works in reading-list citations are in the behavioural paradigm (70%) and that the traditional paradigm accounts for 20%. The two together thus make 90%! See their "The Dialectics of World Order: Notes for a Future Archeologist of International Savoir Faire," *International Studies Quarterly*, 28, 2 (1984), pp. 121–42.

29 See the quotations at note 20 above, where Organski writes of the scientist laying aside "his *values*" [emphasis added], and Holsti writes about the "*biases*" [emphasis added] of scholars in international relations.

30 Martin Hollis and Steven Smith, *Explaining and Understanding International Relations*, (Oxford: Clarendon Press, 1990). W. V. O. Quine, "Two Dogma's of Empiricism" in his book *From a Logical Point of View* (New York: Harper Row, 1961). See also W. V. O. Quine and J. S. Ullian, *The Web of Belief* (New York: Random House, 1978).

31 Hollis and Smith, *Explaining and Understanding International Relations*, p. 55.

32 ibid., p. 61.

33 ibid.

34 I. Lakatos, "Falsification and the Methodology of Scientific Research Programmes," in I. Lakatos and A. Musgrave *Criticism and the Growth of Knowledge* (Cambridge: Cambridge University Press, 1970) and Roy Bhaskar *A Realist Theory of Science* (Brighton: Harvester, 1978).

35 ibid. p. 64.

36 ibid. p. 66.

37 See Francis Fukuyama, "The End of History," *The National Interest*, 16, 3; Paul Kennedy, *Preparing for the Twenty-first Century* (London: Harper Collins, 1993)

38 R. D. McKinlay and R. Little, *Global Problems and World Order*, (London: Frances Pinter, 1986.

39 ibid. pp. 24, 54 and 71.

40 Some of the criticisms of positivism made from this point of view overlap somewhat with those made in the previous sections, but in general it is fair to say that *Verstehen* provides a distinct criticism of the positivist approach to social science.

41 Peter Winch *The Idea of a Social Science* (London: Routledge and Kegan Paul, 1958). The *Verstehen* approach was originally worked out by Wilhelm Dilthey. See Dilthey, *Selected Writings*, ed. H. P. Rickman (Cambridge: Cambridge University Press, 1979), Part IV, especially pp. 218ff; and Max Weber, *The Theory of Social and Economic Organization*, trans. A. Henderson and T. Parsons (London: W. Hodge, 1947) ch. 1. The topic is critically discussed by Jurgen Habermas in the set of discussion papers edited by Marello Truzzi, *Verstehen: Subjective Understanding in Human Sciences* (Reading, MA: Addison-Wesley, 1974). For a collection of articles on this approach see Paul Rabinow and William M. Sullivan eds., *Interpretive Social Science: A Reader* (Berkley: University of California Press, 1979). A good recent general introduction is to be found in Paul Diesing, *How Does Social Science Work: Reflections on Practice*, 2nd edn (Pittsburgh: University of Pittsburgh Press, 1992), ch. 5.

42 For a recent discussion of the application of the method of *Verstehen* within international relations, see Martin Hollis and Steve Smith, *Explaining and Understanding International Relations*. They are not, however, concerned with spelling out the implications of this method for normative theory.

43 The notion of the "internal point of view" was introduced by H. L. A. Hart in his book *The Concept of Law* (London: Oxford University Press, 1961).

44 It is not the case that any such act can be *identified* from a non-initiate point of view, but only properly *understood* from the point of view of an initiate. To identify the act requires that the investigator be at least partially initiated into the practice. Of course further initiation into the practice will bring a deeper understanding of the act.

45 A partial appreciation of the importance of the internal point of view has been achieved by some behaviouralist scholars in International Relations who have articulated a need to take note of the different *perceptions* of different actors in world politics, see for example, Robert Jervis, *Perception and Misperception in International Politics* (Princeton: Princeton University Press, 1976). But interpretative social science would see this method as too individualistic and psychologistic and would argue that in order to determine how, for example, policy-makers in Russia perceive the USA, an understanding of the practice within which the actors are participating is required.

46 Brian Fay, *Social Theory and Political Practice*, (London: Allen and Unwin, 1975) ch. 4; John Hughes, *The Philosophy of Social Research* (London: Longman, 1980); Peter Winch, *The Idea of a Social Science*, p. 89.

47 John Hughes, *The Philosophy of Social Research*, p. 83.

48 Those theories in International Relations that focus on perceptions are positivist in a similar way. The facts to be ascertained are the perceptions of the actors in question. See Robert Jervis, *Perception and Misperception in International Politics*.

49 A. R Louch *Explanation and Human Action* (Oxford: Basil Blackwell, 1966), p. 207.

50 Following the example of Brian Fay, *Social Theory and Political Practice* (ch. 5), I use the labels, "critical theory," "critical approach," and "critical social science," to refer to a rather broad class of thinkers – a class broader than those contained within what has come to be called the Frankfurt School. I am aware of the great differences in thought between scholars within the tradition of critical theory. Aspects of these differences are well set out in David Held, *Introduction to Critical Theory* (London: Hutchinson, 1980). In this section I do not intend to provide a general survey of this school of thought, but merely intend to look at some aspects of the approach which are pertinent to my purpose.

51 Charles Taylor, "A New Realism" (lecture given in the Department of Political Studies, Rhodes University, Grahamstown, South Africa, 25 September 1980).

52 For a portrayal of the main features of the critical model see Brian Fay *Social Theory and Political Practice*, p. 92. See also Paul Diesing, *How Does Social Science Work*, part 1, section 5.

53 Justin Rosenberg, "The International Imagination: IR Theory and 'Classic Social Analysis'," *Millennium: Journal of International Studies*, 23, 1 (1994), pp. 85–108.

54 With the break-up of Yugoslavia several new states were given recognition by the international community of states. One of these was Bosnia-Herzogovina. In 1993–4 brutal conflicts raged between those who supported the government of Bosnia and those groups which sought to excise parts of Bosnian territory and attach these to the lands of the neighbouring states. Another feature of this conflict was the attempts made by the different groups to "ethnically cleanse" certain geographical areas of people belonging to other ethnic groups.

55 Making an arbitrary choice would be akin to a social scientist deciding through the flip of a coin whether a game she was observing was chess or checkers.

2 Sceptical and realist arguments against normative theory in international relations: a critical appraisal

1 Charles Beitz, *Political Theory and International Relations* (Princeton: Princeton University Press, 1979), p. 62.

2 Bernard Williams, *Morality: An Introduction to Ethics* (Cambridge: Cambridge University Press, 1972), pp. 17–27.

3 A consistent amoralist person would be considered insane. Can we conceive of an insane state?

4 In the popular mind this is often a position attributed to Machiavelli. Whether or not Machiavelli in fact held this position is not our concern here.

5 John Mackie, *Ethics: Inventing Right and Wrong* (Harmondsworth, Penguin Books, 1981).

6 Ibid. p. 15.

7 Ibid. pp. 36–42.

8 See pp. 45–7 above, and chapter 5 below.

9 Ibid.

10 It is to be doubted whether on a strong relativist position there could be inter-practice disputes at all. In order to have a dispute there has to be *some* common ground. Thus disputes imply the existence of a practice (even if it is only an emerging one). Thus wherever there is a dispute, relativism has already broken down; practices are emerging.

11 Bernard Williams in *Morality* calls this argument "the anthropologists' heresy, possibly the most absurd view to have been advanced even in moral philosophy." (p. 34) I follow Williams' line of argument in refuting the relativist position. For a detailed rejection of the argument that relativism requires a commitment to tolerance see Geoffrey Harrison, "Relativ-

ism and Tolerance," in Peter Laslett and James Fishkin, eds., *Philosophy, Politics and Society,* 5th series, (Oxford: Blackwell, 1979).

12 Bernard Williams, *Morality,* p. 40 and following pages.

13 See pp. 45–7 above.

14 The realist rejection of the idealism that surfaced after the First World War was motivated by just such wariness.

15 As an example of this kind of rejection see E. H. Carr's discussion of idealism in *The Twenty Years Crisis* (London: Macmillan, 1946).

16 See, for example, Ernst Haas, *Beyond the Nation State* (Stanford University Press, 1964); D. Mitrany, *A Functionalist Approach to World Politics* (London, Martin Robertson, 1975); J. P. Sewell, *Functionalism and World Politics* (Princeton: Princeton University Press, 1961); R. Keohane and R. O. Nye, *Power and Interdependence* (Boston: Little, Brown, 1977).

17 For examples of such theories, see V. I. Lenin, "Imperialism the Highest Stage of Capitalism" in *Selected Works of Lenin* (Moscow: Progress Publishers, 1977); A. G. Frank, *Capitalism and Underdevelopment in Latin America* (Harmondsworth: Penguin, 1971); Samir Amin, *Accumulation on a World Scale* (Hassocks: Harvester Press, 1974).

18 For a thorough-going structural analysis of international relations in which this point is put very strongly, see Kenneth Waltz *Theory of International Politics* (London, Addison-Wesley, 1979) pp. 73 ff.

19 Ibid.

20 Kenneth Waltz, *Man the State and War* (New York: Columbia University Press, 1959).

21 In *Theory of International Politics,* Waltz elucidates systemic approaches in international relations. The great merit of his argument is that it articulates the main weaknesses of earlier systemic theories. First, there was a failure to delimit the borders of the international "system" being posited. If these are not clearly defined then it is not possible to explain the interactions between the system and its environment. This makes it impossible to explain either the effect of the system on the environment or of the environment on the system. It also leaves the way open to supposing that everything is included within the system. This makes systems analysis self-defeating, for it is then necessary to assume that the theory of the system's theorist is itself determined by the system and cannot be a good theory or a bad theory, but simply the theory which the system requires. It becomes definitionally impossible to envisage contending theories of international relations. Second, there was a failure to distinguish between theory and reality. Systems theories are often confusing in that it is not clear whether they are simply describing a system of international relations which exists, as it were, "out there" in the world, or whether this "system" is a theory used to explain the facts of the world. Waltz accuses Stanley Hoffman of not making it clear whether "system" is an analytic postulate or a reality to be investigated. This difficulty is, in fact, one which is common to much international relations scholarship. See

Waltz's discussion of this problem in chapter 3 of *Theory of International Politics*. The issue is also well discussed in Charles Reynolds, *Theory and Explanation in International Relations* (London: Martin Robertson, 1973) pp. 36ff. The prevalence of this confusion is also commented on in J. Rosenau *et al.*, "Of Syllabi, Texts, Students, and Scholarship in International Relations," *World Politics*, 29, 2 (January 1977), p. 263. The authors carried out a survey of 26 major international relations textbooks and found that the vast majority of authors wrote as if they were *describing* an existing international system.

If systems theory is no more than description and redescription of the international system, then there can be no conflict between such systems theories but only arguments about which description best fits the international system. Either some or all of the parties to the dispute must be mistaken or under some illusion. On this view, changes of the international system are not to be explained but merely noticed. If systems theory is not descriptive, but consists of theories seeking to explain the way things are in the world and to predict changes in the status quo by using systemic notions as analytical postulates, then the whole enterprise has to be seen in a different light. In particular a very different process for evaluating such theory itself is indicated. This involves the discrete steps of theory building, hypothesis formation and procedures for confirmation or falsification of the hypotheses.

22 Kenneth Waltz, *Theory of International Politics*, p. 73.
23 Ibid., ch. 5.
24 Ralph Pettman, *State and Class* (London: Croom Helm, 1979), p. 148.
25 Ibid. p. 636.
26 Ibid. p. 689 (emphasis added).
27 Ibid. pp. 689–90 (emphasis added).
28 Ibid. pp. 718ff.
29 Ibid. p. 725.
30 Ibid.
31 V. I. Lenin, *Selected Works*, p. 92.
32 See note 15 above.
33 The most famous statement by Marx of his position is contained in the Preface to *A Contribution to the Critique of Political Economy*, reproduced in T. B. Bottomore and M. Rubel, eds., *Karl Marx: Selected Writings in Sociology and Social Philosophy*. (London, D. C. Watts, 1963), p. 51. Marx wrote: "In the social production which men carry on they enter into definite relations that are indispensable and independent of their will; these relations of production correspond to a definite stage of development of their material powers of production. The totality of these relations of production constitutes the economic structure of society – the real foundation, on which legal and political superstructures arise and to which definite forms of social consciousness correspond."
34 See Samir Amin, *Accumulation on a World Scale*, pp. 6 and 32.

35 The most widely accepted definition of the state – that proposed by Max Weber – makes the element of coercion *the* major aspect of states which distinguishes them from other modes of organization. On this view the state is that power which successfully claims the monopoly of coercive force within a given territory. See H. H. Gerth and C. Wright Mills, eds., *From Max Weber* (London: Routledge and Kegan Paul, 1970), p. 78.

36 Of course the form of state may vary from case to case. Some may be democratic while others may be authoritarian and so on.

37 Just as games of one kind or another always involve participants playing according to a given set of rules. There could be no games if people did not recognize the rules constitutive of the games in question.

38 See pages 45–7 above.

39 The most well known of such utopian thinkers was, of course, President Woodrow Wilson in the USA. Two of the major figures who reacted against this kind of thinking were Martin Wight and E. H. Carr.

40 For example see P. A. Reynolds, *An Introduction to International Relations* (London: Longman, 1976), ch. 4; Hans Morgenthau, *Politics Among Nations* (New York: Knopf, 1973), ch. 9; and K. J. Holsti, *International Politics: A Framework for Analysis* (Englewood Cliffs: Prentice-Hall, 1967), ch. 7.

41 For a similar analysis of power, see Hanna Arendt, *On Violence* (Harmondsworth: Penguin Press, 1970).

42 Here we see the practice of social science and the practice of politics merging as we did in another context at the end of ch. 1.

43 The term "post-modern" is used loosely here to indicate a range of authors who do not form a tight-knit school of thought. The authors I have in mind quite often differ amongst themselves. Yet they have enough in common to justify my grouping them under a single heading. Writers in this tradition are to be found in the following edited volume: James Der Derian and Michael Shapiro, eds., *International/Intertextual Relations: Postmodern Readings of World Politics* (Lexington: Lexington Books, 1989). See also Richard Ashley and R. B. J. Walker, 'Speaking the Language of Exile, Dissidence in International Studies," in *International Studies Quarterly* (Special Issue) 33, 3, 1990; and Pauline Rosenau, "Once Again into the Fray: International Relations Confronts the Humanities," *Millennium: Journal of International Studies*, 19, 1 (Spring 1990), pp. 83–110.

44 See Jacques Derrida, *Writing and Difference*, trans. Alan Bass (Chicago, University of Chicago Press, 1978); Michel Foucault, *The Order of Things* (London: Tavistock, 1970); and Jean-Francois Lyotard, *The Postmodern Condition: A Report on Knowledge*, trans. Geoff Bennington and Brian Massumi. (Minneapolis: University of Minnesota Press, 1984).

45 Richard Ashley, "The Geopolitics of Geopolitical Space: Toward a Critical Social Theory of International Politics," *Alternatives* 12, (1987), p. 409 (also quoted in Cochran, "Neutralizing the Positive," p. 4.

46 William Connolly, *Identity/Difference: Democratic Negotiations of Political Paradox* (Ithaca: Cornell University Press, 1991) p. 12.

47 For more on the distinction between rules governing conduct within the sphere of private morality and rules operative in the political sphere see the selection of articles and sources cited in S. Hampshire, ed., *Public and Private Morality*, (Cambridge: Cambridge University Press, 1978).

48 See pp. 45–7 above.

3 Normative issues in international relations: the domain of discourse and the method of argument

1 John Rawls, *Theory of Justice* (London: Oxford University Press, 1972), preface.

2 See James Mayall, "International Society and International Theory," in Michael Donelan, ed., *The Reason of States*, (London: Allen and Unwin, 1978), especially pp. 133ff.

3 Hans Morgenthau, *Politics among Nations* (New York, Knopf, 1973), p. 259. See also K. J. Holsti, *International Politics* (Englewood Cliffs, Prentice-Hall, 1967), pp. 234ff.

4 Morgenthau, *Politics among Nations*, p. 259.

5 Michael Walzer, *Obligations: Essays on Disobedience, War and Citizenship* (Cambridge, MA: Harvard University Press, 1970). More recently in *Thick and Thin: Moral Argument at Home and Abroad* (Notre Dame: University of Notre Dame Press, 1994) Walzer argues that maximalist (thick) moral arguments are only possible within the shared meanings of closely bound communities and that in the international sphere there is, at best, a minimal (thin) morality to guide us.

6 Barrie Paskins and Michael Dockrill, *The Ethics of War* (London, Duckworth, 1979), p. 207.

7 Ralph Pettman, *State and Class* (London: Croom Helm, 1979), p. 72.

8 For a lucid exposition of the communitarian position see Timothy Allen, "Liberals, Communitarians and Political Theory" *South African Journal of Philosophy*, 11, 4 (1992) pp. 77–91.

9 K. J. Holsti, *International Politics*, p. 234.

10 C. Wright Mills, *The Sociological Imagination*, (Oxford: Oxford University Press, 1959), p. 77.

11 See Karl Marx's description of the way in which the "freedom of labour" principle was interpreted in nineteenth-century industrial states in his *Capital* (London: Dent, 1972), ch. 8.

12 See Ralph Pettman, *State and Class*, ch. 3.

13 See Michael Oakeshott, "The Language of the Modern European State," *Political Studies*, 23 (December 1975), p. 409.

14 James Mayall "International Society and International Theory," p. 136.

15 Recent developments in the ongoing debate between liberals and communitarians lend support to the point which I am making here. In the face of criticism from an anti-foundationalist perspective John Rawls has indicated that his theory of justice is not premised on a metaphysical foundation (according to which there are certain transcendent principles appli-

cable to all people and communities across time), but is a political conception rooted in an existing overlapping consensus amongst many different states and peoples. See Rawls, "The Idea of an Overlapping Consensus," *Oxford Journal of Legal Studies*, 7, 1 (1987) p. 1; and Rawls, "The Law of Peoples," in Stephen Shute and Susan Hurley, eds., *On Human Rights* (New York: Basic Books, 1993), pp. 41–82. Michael Walzer, responding to the opposite kind of criticism (namely, that he confined moral theory too narrowly to what was accepted and believed *within* communities) has put forward a position in which he argues that there is a thin moral consensus across the plurality of our communities.

16 Maurice Keens-Soper, "The Practice of a States System," in Donelan, ed., *The Reason of States*.

17 James Mayall, "International Society and International Theory," p. 135.

18 Michael Donelan, "The Political Theorists and International Theory" in Donelan, ed., *The Reason of States*; John Finnis, *Natural Law and Natural Rights* (Oxford: Oxford University Press, 1980).

19 Michael Donelan, "The Political Theorists and International Theory," p. 90.

20 John Finnis, *Natural Law and Natural Rights*, Section IV: 2. On p. 155 he says there is a common good for human beings inasmuch "as life, knowledge, play, aesthetic experience, friendship, religion and freedom in practical reasonableness are good for any and every person."

21 Ibid. p. 71.

22 Ibid. p. 74.

23 Ibid. p. 69.

24 Is it not possible to use a similar argument against the position which I have been arguing? For in support of my argument that there is an international state centric domain of discourse I pointed to the fact that most actors in world politics profess, *inter alia*, a commitment to democracy. Might it not be argued against me that the different actors have widely divergent views of democracy? Against this I would argue that there is a core of concepts common to those who profess a commitment to democracy. There is no such core of common concepts across cultures with regard to the goods isolated by Finnis.

25 Michael Donelan, *Political Theorists*, p. 86.

26 Ibid.

27 Ibid. *passim*.

28 Ibid. p. 76.

29 On sovereignty generally, see Wladyslaw Jozef Stankiewicz, *In Defence of Sovereignty* (London: Oxford University Press, 1969). See also J. Barkin and B. Cronin "Changing Norms and Rules of Sovereignty," *International Organization*, 48, 1 (1994) p. 107.

30 Barrie Paskins and Michael Dockrill, *The Ethics of War*, p. 207.

31 Where a bargain is struck between two or more parties there is no question of the bargain being right or wrong. It is simply what is agreed to. We may say that the bargain favours one party more than the other, but this is quite different from saying that the bargain was wrong.

32 A view in many ways similar to that articulated in this paragraph is put forward in much writing emerging from the so-called "post-modern" tradition. See, for example, R. B. J. Walker *One World, Many Worlds: Struggles for a Just World Peace* (Boulder: Lynne Rienner, 1988), especially ch. 2; and the survey article by Pauline Rosenau "Once Again into the Fray: International Relations Confronts the Humanities" *Millennium: Journal of International Relations*, 19, 1 (Spring 1990) pp. 83–110.

33 The key articles for my purposes are those taken up in his book, *Taking Rights Seriously* (London: Duckworth, 1981).

34 In particular, Dworkin developed his position through a critique of the work of H. L. A. Hart, *The Concept of Law* (London: Oxford University Press, 1961).

35 Ronald Dworkin, *Taking Rights Seriously*, p. 101.

36 Ibid. p. 132.

37 Ibid. p. 103. Also see W. B. Gallie, "Essentially Contested Concepts," *Proceedings of the Aristotelian Society*, 56 (1965), p. 167.

38 Ronald Dworkin, *Taking Rights Seriously*, p. 103.

39 Ibid. p. 104

40 Ibid.

41 Ibid.

42 This applies even where the institution within which the dispute is being decided has a further rule which specifies that the referee's decision will be final – a party involved may well accept the decision as binding, yet still argue that it is wrong. In short, any theory of argument, which asserts that talk of there being a single correct answer is only proper where there is a clear rule supplying that answer, cannot account for most of the arguments people take seriously in chess, the law, and international relations, and many other institutions. See also Dworkin, *Taking Rights Seriously*, ch. 13 and p. 331 for discussion of the "right answer" question.

43 Ch. 1, pp. 13ff.

44 Ronald Dworkin, *Taking Rights Seriously*, pp. 159ff; John Rawls *Theory of Justice*, pp. 48–51.

45 See above pp. 94ff.

46 Ronald Dworkin, *Taking Rights Seriously*, pp. 160ff. Note that Dworkin's portrayal of what judges do in hard cases is not supposed to be a description of what judges in fact do in every case. He admits that the task he set the judge is impossibly huge, thus he calls his imaginary judge "Hercules." Dworkin may be seen as using an ideal type argument.

47 Ernest Gellner, *The Legitimation of Belief* (Cambridge: Cambridge University Press, 1974), ch. 3. Gellner worked out his criticism against the Wittgensteinian and neo-Wittgensteinian positions and has, as far as I know, never specifically focussed on Dworkin's work. But that he would be critical of it is beyond doubt.

48 Ernest Gellner, *Spectacles and Predicaments* (Cambridge: Cambridge University Press, 1980), ch. 3, pp. 98ff.

49 Ernest Gellner, *Words and Things* (London: Gollancz, 1959), p. 44.
50 Ibid. pp. 247–9.
51 H. L. A. Hart "Between Utility and Rights," in Alan Ryan, ed., *The Idea of Freedom*, (London: Oxford University Press, 1979). Hart comments on how radical (unconservative) Dworkin's rights thesis is and compares it to a much more conservative one, viz. that of Robert Nozick, *Anarchy, State and Utopia* (Oxford: Blackwell, 1974).
52 See the general argument of Richard Rorty, *Philosophy and the Mirror of Nature* (Oxford: Blackwell, 1980).
53 Ernest Gellner, *Words and Things*, pp. 217–8.

4 Towards the construction of a normative theory of international relations

1 See Ronald Dworkin, *Taking Rights Seriously* (London: Duckworth, 1981), p. 135, for a discussion of the concept/conception distinction.
2 Although Marxist theory envisages the withering away of the state in a communist society, it was the case that during the Cold War Marxist states both in their domestic and foreign policies used to act in accordance with the norm that the preservation of the international society of states is a good. The states in the Soviet bloc used to formulate their own policies and criticize the actions of others in terms of this norm. Support for this is to be found in Vendulka Kubalkova, "Moral Precepts in Contemporary Soviet Politics," in Ralph Pettman, ed., *Moral Claims in World Affairs*, (London: Croom Helm, 1979), p. 185.
3 See Jan Pettman, "Race, Conflict and Liberation in Africa," in *Moral Claims in World Affairs*, p. 185.
4 See G. Poggi, *The Development of the Modern State* (London: Hutchinson, 1978); Cornelia Navari, "The Origins of the Nation-State," in Leonard Tivey, ed., *The Nation State*, (Oxford: Martin Robertson, 1981); Barbara Tuchman, *A Distant Mirror* (London: MacMillan, 1979); and Hedley Bull, *The Anarchical Society* (London: MacMillan, 1977), p. 9.
5 The content of the corpus of international law must, of course, be seen as resting on the norms which have been mentioned in the list. On international law see G. Schwarzenberger and E. D. Brown, *A Manual of International Law*, 6th edn (London, 1976): Ian Brownlie, *Principles of Public International Law* (Oxford, 1979) and Patrick Moynihan, *On the Law of Nations* (Cambridge, MA: Harvard University Press, 1990).
6 This point was already made forcibly by J. G. Fichte in the last century. See his section on "The Characteristics of the Present Age," in W. Smith, ed., *The Popular Works of Fichte* (2 vols., London: John Chapman, 1849), 2, pp. 221ff.
7 Before considering some possible answers to this question I must attempt to allay certain objections. It may be argued that the primary question for a normative theory of international relations is *whether* the system of sovereign states is a justifiable way of organizing the government of the

world. (Michael Donelan argues in this vein in "The Political Theorists and International Theory" in Michael Donelan, ed., *The Reason of States* (London: Allen and Unwin, 1978).) By contrast my formulation of the primary question might be held to assume that the preservation of a system of sovereign states is justifiable. My formulation would thus seem to avoid the most fundamental problem which is: Are the norms referring to the preservation of the system of states and to the value of sovereignty justifiable at all? My answer to this objection is implicit in all that I have argued up to now, but it is probably as well to recapitulate two important points. First, a natural lawyer may wish to argue that there exists a practice more basic than that of the system of states, viz. the community of humankind. This, he would argue, provides a basis from which the system of states can be evaluated. Earlier I argued that it is not plausible to assert the existence of such a community. (See the discussion of the arguments advanced by Michael Donelan and John Finnis, chapter 3, pp. 84–8) The world is characterized by a diversity of moral communities. There is no single moral community, apart from the communities of people who are citizens of states living in a system of sovereign states. The only community of humankind at present is the community of people within the system of sovereign states. In short, the base from which natural lawyers seek to criticize the system of sovereign states is non-existent. Second, and related to the first point, in this book I have given an account of what is involved in normative argument. In terms of this account (see chapter 3 above) the only way in which settled beliefs, such as the one according to which the preservation of the system of states is a good, can be challenged is by showing that it does not fit the background theory which best justifies most of the other settled beliefs within the practice in question. What is not possible is a simultaneous critique of all the settled items of belief within a domain of discourse. Thus if someone wishes to cast doubt on the settled status of item 1 on the list given above, he has to produce a background justification which justifies most of the other items on the list excluding the one he seeks to challenge (in this case the belief that the preservation of the system of states is a good). There is good reason to believe that this would not be possible. One such reason is that a background theory which requires of us that we reject this item requires that we reject several other bits of the settled core which are related to item 1. Of all the items on the list only five could possibly be thought of as totally independent of item 1. In such a case we are being asked to reject too many settled beliefs and are not left with a basis for argument at all.

8 On balance of power theory generally, see the collection of texts collected by Moorehead Wright, *The Theory and Practice of the Balance of Power* (London: Dent, 1975).

9 See Phillip Windsor, "The Justification of the State," in *The Reason of States.*

10 Quoted in Moorehead Wright, *The Theory and Practice of the Balance of Power*, p. 2.
11 Ibid. p. 39.
12 Ibid. p. 40.
13 Ibid. p. 48.
14 Ibid. p. 72.
15 Hedley Bull, *The Anarchical Society*, p. xii.
16 Ibid.
17 Originally the answer may have been "A Christian one," but for various reasons related to the secularization of modern societies this theological answer became less acceptable and the authors in seeking some more "neutral" answer introduced the notion of order.
18 Hedley Bull, *The Anarchical Society*, p. 5.
19 Ibid. pp. 17–19.
20 Ibid. p. 20.
21 Ibid. p. 20.
22 Ibid. p. 22.
23 Hedley Bull, "Human rights and World Politics," in *Moral Claims in World Affairs*.
24 Kenneth Waltz, *Theory of International Politics*, (London, Addison-Wesley, 1979).
25 Ibid. pp. 112–113.
26 As far as I know there has been no detailed attempt to justify the system of states on utilitarian grounds.
27 John Rawls has worked out the best known critique of utilitarianism on these grounds. In *A Theory of Justice* (London: Oxford University Press, 1972) he sought to construct a theory which fits our considered judgements about fairness and social justice better.
28 See H. L. A. Hart, "Between Utility and Rights" in Alan Ryan, ed., *The Idea of Freedom*, (London: Oxford University Press, 1979).
29 On rule utilitarianism, see J. J. C Smart and Bernard Williams, *Utilitarianism: For and Against* (Cambridge: Cambridge University Press, 1970), p. 9. For a critique of rule utilitarianism see D. H. Hodgeson, *The Consequences of Utilitarianism* (London: Oxford University Press, 1967).
30 For a very brief but useful portrayal of the utilitarian theory of democracy, see J. Roland Pennock, *Democratic Political Theory* (Princeton: Princeton University Press, 1979), p. 126.
31 For a defence of democracy along these lines see Carole Pateman, *Participation and Democratic Theory* (Cambridge: Cambridge University Press, 1970).
32 There may be other possible background theories, but the ones I have considered are currently the main ones in the field.
33 Thomas Hobbes, *Leviathan* (London: Dent, 1962); John Locke, *The Second Treatise of Government* (Indianapolis: Bobbs-Merrill, 1952); Jean Jacques Rousseau, *The Social Contract* (London: Dent, 1973); John Rawls, *Theory*

of Justice; Robert Nozick, *Anarchy, State and Utopia* (Oxford: Blackwell, 1974).

34 This kind of conclusion is supported by C. B. Joynt and H. Corbett, *Theory and Reality in World Politics* (London: Macmillan, 1978).

35 For the argument presented here against this way of thinking about the relationship between rights holders and the state I am indebted to John Charvet, *A Critique of Freedom and Equality* (Cambridge: Cambridge University Press, 1981).

36 There are significant differences between the ways in which the different theorists picture the initial situation but these are of no importance to the present argument.

37 John Locke, *The Second Treatise of Government*, ch. 13.

38 For a detailed account of the problems involved with the notion of tacit consent, see John Plamenatz, *Consent, Freedom and Political Obligation* (London: Oxford University Press, 1968).

39 Walzer's consent theory of obligation is spelled out in his *Obligations: Essays on Disobedience, War and Citizenship* (Cambridge MA: Harvard University Press, 1970) and is implicit in his book *Just and Unjust Wars* (New York: Basic Books, 1977).

40 *Just and Unjust Wars*, p. 29.

41 Ibid. p. 61.

42 Ibid. p. 72.

43 Ibid. p. 135.

44 Ibid. p. 136.

45 Ibid. p. 61.

46 Ibid. pp. 61–2.

47 Ibid. p. 53.

48 Ibid. p. 61.

49 Ibid. p. 107.

50 Ibid. p. 72, emphasis added.

51 Ibid., emphasis added.

52 Ibid. p. 85.

53 Ibid. p. 83.

54 What argument could Walzer advance to show that the individual rights of the Egyptians were not wrongly infringed by the pre-emptive strike of the Israelis? The only one compatible with his general position I suggest is this: the Egyptian citizens and soldiers may be taken to have tacitly consented to an act which their government might have come to intend against Israel and this act in the long run might have infringed Israel's right to political sovereignty. This seems to me a highly implausible argument. The notion that a person may relinquish a right by *tacitly* consenting to an act which *might* have the effect of damaging a third party's right is far-fetched indeed.

55 *Just and Unjust Wars*, p. 87.

56 Ibid.

57 Ibid. pp. 88–9.
58 Ibid. p. 90.

5 Reconciling rights and sovereignty: the constitutive theory of individuality

1 Imposing sets of rights and duties on oneself in such a situation is a sophisticated activity which would involve imagining oneself to be two persons. The two might be envisaged as an actor and a conscience. The actor might claim a right *vis-à-vis* the conscience to do x on Sundays. This way of thinking is derivative from the normal social context in which rights involve mutual recognitions of certain kinds.

2 This point is well argued in R. Flathman, *The Practice of Rights* (Cambridge: Cambridge University Press, 1976), pp. 65ff. See also Bruce Ackerman, *Social Justice and the Liberal State* (New Haven: Yale University Press, 1980), p. 5.

3 For contract theory rights holders are "perfect in respect of their rights" in that, as Thomas Paine puts it, "the state grants men nothing . . ." (*The Rights of Man*, London: Dent, 1979), p. 44.

4 Bruce Ackerman makes a similar point where he portrays rights talk as constrained dialogue. See *Social Justice and the Liberal State*.

5 G. W. F. Hegel, *The Philosophy of Right*, trans. T. M. Knox (London: Oxford University Press, 1973), para. 187. See also the Preface at pp. 7 and 12.

6 John Charvet, *A Critique of Freedom and Equality* (Cambridge: Cambridge University Press, 1981), p. 164.

7 At this point the objection might be offered that this way of going about things is to presuppose what has to be justified; to presuppose that the system of sovereign states is justified, when what is called for is an attempt to find out whether it is justified. The objection here is that all I am doing is looking for a justification of the *status quo* and so will not have any critical dimension. This objection is not well founded. The actors within the system of sovereign states may be acting according to a partial or incorrect understanding of the moral dimension implicit in their social arrangements. These actors will, of course, be guided in action by their partial and incomplete understandings. Where a more satisfactory understanding of the moral dimensions implicit in the existing arrangments is produced, this will serve as a criticism of the previous understandings and will also guide their actions in new ways. Thus the charge that constitutive theory merely endorses the *status quo* is unfounded.

8 See E. M. Adams, "The Ground of Rights," *American Philosophical Quarterly*, 19, 2 (April 1982), p. 191.

9 Talking about laws and institutions, Hegel says in para. 147 of the *Philosophy of Right* that they are not something alien to the subject: "On the contrary, his [the subject's] spirit bears witness to them [the laws and institutions] as to its own essence, the essence in which he has a feeling of his self-hood, and in which he lives as in his own element which is not

distinguished from himself. The subject is thus directly linked to the ethical order by a relation which is more like an identity than even the relation of faith or trust." A pagan thus *feels* himself part of the pagan order in which he finds himself. But reflection may lead him to have an *insight* about his relation to the order, and thinking may lead the subject to have knowledge of the identity between himself and the ethical order. What is important for my purposes in all of this is that the reader notice that Hegel portrays the philosopher's task as being that of revealing the *internal* relationships between the subject and the institutions under which he (the subject) lives. The philosopher's task is to make intelligible how the subject's feeling of self-hood is bound up with the institutions under which he lives.

10 Hegel uses an architectonic metaphor. See *The Philosophy of Right*, p. 6.
11 Ibid. para. 158.
12 Ibid. Addition to para. 158.
13 Ibid. Addition to para. 118.
14 Ibid. Addition to para. 174.
15 Ibid. Addition to para. 265.
16 John Charvet, *A Critique*, p. 174.
17 Hegel, *The Philosophy of Right*, Addition to para. 158.
18 John Charvet, *A Critique*, p. 177.
19 Hegel, *The Philosophy of Right*, para. 45.
20 Ibid. para. 46.
21 John Charvet, *A Critique*, p. 179.
22 Hegel, *The Philosophy of Right*, para. 258.
23 Ibid. para. 268.
24 Ibid.
25 Ibid. Addition to para. 265.
26 Ibid. Addition to para. 261.
27 Ibid. Addition to para. 261, where Hegel refers to this as a conjunction of duty and right.
28 Education here is not to be confused with so called "re-education" as was practised, for example, by the Pol Pot regime in Cambodia.
29 Hegel, *The Philosophy of Right*, para. 323.
30 Ibid. para. 331.
31 Ibid. para. 349.
32 This is a term coined by Robert Jackson in his *Quasi States: Sovereignty, International Relations and the Third World* (Cambridge: Cambridge University Press, 1990) to refer to those Third World states which are recognized by states external to them as being sovereign even though internally they are underdeveloped as states on almost every measure.
33 I do not maintain that learning to play chess is something which you can only do by yourself. In the picture I have sketched I allow you space to make your move, but then I seek ways to nudge you forward in ways that will make a better player of you. I am concerned about your progress at

every moment. Applying this insight to the relationship between fully fledged states and quasi states I am not following J. S. Mill's approach to the non-intervention rule in international relations which he says is justified because freedom is something which people within states have to achieve strictly by themselves.

34 That quasi states actively seek to participate in the system of sovereign states is shown in any number of ways. The new states which were formed on the break-up of the Soviet Union have eagerly sought out membership of the major institutions of international politics and have shown themselves eager to recognize other sovereign states and be recognized by them. Similarly the states formed in Africa after decolonization have actively sought out recognition and membership of the international community of states.

35 Similar conclusions are reached by Andrew Vincent, "The Hegelian State and International Politics," *The Review of International Studies*, 9, 3 (July 1983), pp. 191–207.

6 The justification of unconventional violence in international relations: a hard case for normative theory

1 See the sources cited in Geoffrey Best, *Humanity in Warfare* (New York: Columbia University Press, 1980). Also W. V. O'Brien, *Conduct of Just and Limited War* (New York: Praeger, 1981) and Robert L. Phillips, *War and Justice* (Norman, University of Oklahoma Press, 1984).

2 The BBC World Service does not use the word "terrorist" in its broadcasts, so indicating its sensitivity with regard to this point.

3 See chapter 2, pages 45–7.

4 Michel Foucault has argued most plausibly that the discourse in which we specify what is to count as "mad" is itself a human practice – a set of power relations which benefit some rather than others. An implication of this is that it now becomes possible to ask whether this discourse itself is justifiable or not. Foucault gives us no measure by which we could judge our present practices in this way. What he does show though is that, with hindsight, some of our previous discourses for classifying people as mad fare very badly when judged by our present standards. See Michel Foucault, "Nietzsche, Genealogy, History," in Donald F. Bouchard, ed., *Language, Counter-Memory, Practice: Selected Essays and Interviews*, (New York: Cornell University Press, 1977), pp. 139–65. In this section I am not going to attempt to evaluate our present practice with regard to the classification of people as sane or not. For the sake of argument I accept this as unproblematic at this point.

5 I am ignoring problems of *legal jurisdiction* which might arise.

6 This practical problem has given rise to several attempts on the part of the community of states to deal with it. One such was the setting up by the United Nations of the "Ad Hoc" Committee on International Terrorism.

7 Thomas Hobbes, *Leviathan* (London: Dent, 1962); John Locke, *The Second Treatise of Government* (Indianapolis: Bobbs-Merrill, 1952); Robert Nozick,

Anarchy, State and Utopia (Oxford: Blackwell, 1974); Bruce Ackerman, *Social Justice and the Liberal State* (New Haven: Yale University Press, 1980).

8 Examples of movements which would be concerned to distinguish themselves from mere criminals are: the Irish Republican Army in Ireland, the Red Brigades in Italy, the Sendero Luminoso in Peru, the Sudan People's Liberation Movement in Sudan, and the Rwanda Liberation Front in Rwanda.

9 Geoffrey Pridham, "Terrorism and the State in West Germany during the 1970's," in Juliet Lodge, ed., *Terrorism: A Challenge to the State.* (Oxford: Martin Robertson, 1981), p. 25.

10 Ibid. p. 43.

11 Gwendolen Carter, *The Politics of Inequality* (London, Thames and Hudson, 1958), p. 370.

12 Rodney Davenport, *South Africa: A Modern History* (London: Macmillan, 1977), pp. 285ff.

13 These cases of sabotage are easy to justify. The indiscriminate killing of civilians through the placing of bombs in public places poses far more difficult ethical problems.

14 On "the asset to liability shift" see Maurice Tugwell, "Politics and Propaganda of the Provisional IRA" in Paul Wilkensen, ed., *British Perspectives on Terrorism*, (London: Allen and Unwin, 1981), p. 17.

7 Who gets what state where? The Bosnian conflict

1 By the time this is read this particular event will have receded from public consciousness, but this does not matter because the argument can be easily transposed to cover more recent examples of this kind of act. My purpose is to make clear the kinds of arguments which constitutive theory legitimates (and conversely to specify what arguments are not acceptable in terms of the theory).

2 *The Times*, Monday 7th February 1994.

3 *Independent*, Monday 7th February 1994.

4 For although we may be agreed that the killing of innocents is generally wrong across the board, we do acknowledge the difference between murder under conditions of peace and the killing of innocents in the circumstances of war. The licence to kill is wider in wartime and thus the criteria for wrongful killing are significantly different during a war than in times of peace. What makes the Bosnian case so difficult is that it is not quite clear whether, from a moral point of view, we should regard what is happening there as war or not. The complexity of what is involved here is explained in what follows.

5 On just war theory, see Barrie Paskins and Michael Dockrill, *The Ethics of War* (London: Duckworth, 1979), and Michael Walzer, *Just and Unjust Wars* (New York: Basic Books, 1977).

6 Similarly difficult cases have arisen in areas formerly under the jurisdiction of the Soviet Union.

Bibliography

Ackerman, B. *Social Justice and the Liberal State*. New Haven: Yale University Press, 1980.

Adams, E. M. "The Ground of Rights." *American Philosophical Quarterly* 19, 2 (April 1982).

Alker, Hayward, and Thomas Biersteker. "The Dialectics of World Order: Notes for a Future Archeologist of International Savoir Faire." *International Studies Quarterly* 28, 2 (June 1984): 121–42.

Allen, Timothy. "Liberals, Communitarians and Political Theory." *South African Journal of Philosophy* 11, 4 (1992): 77–91.

Almond, Gabriel. "Separate Tables: Schools and Sects in Political Science." *PS: Political Science and Politics* 21 (Fall 1988): 840.

Amin, S. *Accumulation on a World Scale*. Hassocks: Harvester Press, 1974.

Arendt, H. *On Violence*. Harmondsworth: Penguin Press, 1970.

Ashley, Richard. "The Geopolitics of Geopolitical Space: Toward a Critical Social Theory of International Politics." *Alternatives* 12 (1987): 403–34.

Ashley, R. and R. B. J. Walker. "Speaking the Language of Exile, Dissidence in International Studies." *International Studies Quarterly* 33, 3 (1990).

Barkin, J. and B. Cronin. "Changing Norms and Rules of Sovereignty." *International Organization* 48, 1 (Winter 1994).

Beitz, Charles. *Political Theory and International Relations*. Princeton, NJ: Princeton University Press, 1979.

Best, G. *Humanity in Warfare*. New York: Columbia University Press, 1980.

Bhaskar, R. *A Realist Theory of Science*. Brighton: Harvester, 1978.

Brilmayer, L. *Justifying International Acts*. New York: Cornell University Press, 1989.

Brown, C. *International Relations Theory: New Normative Approaches*. New York: Columbia University Press, 1992.

"International Ethics: Fad, Fantasy or Field?" *Paradigms* 8, 1 (1994).

ed. *Political Restructuring in Europe: Ethical Perspectives*. London and New York: Routledge, 1994.

Brownlie, Ian. *Principles of Public International Law*. Oxford, 1979.

Bibliography

Buchanan, A. *Secession: The Morality of Political Divorce*. Boulder: Westview Press, 1991.

Bull, H. "International Theory, the Case for a Classical Approach." In K. Knorr and J. N. Rosenau, eds., *Contending Approaches to International Politics*. Princeton University Press, 1970.

The Anarchical Society. London: Macmillan, 1977.

"Human Rights and World Politics." In Ralph Pettman, ed., *Moral Claims in World Affairs*. London: Croom Helm, 1979.

"Human Rights and International Relations." *Daedalus* Spring, 1982.

Burton, J. W. *International Relations: A General Theory*. Cambridge: Cambridge University Press, 1965.

Deviance, Terrorism and War. Oxford: Martin Robertson, 1979.

Carr, E. H. *The Twenty Years Crisis 1919–1939: An Introduction to the Study of International Relations*, 2nd edn. London: Macmillan, 1946.

Carter, G. *The Politics of Inequality*. London: Thames and Hudson, 1958.

Charvet, J. *A Critique of Freedom and Equality*. Cambridge: Cambridge University Press, 1981.

Child, James. *Nuclear War: The Moral Dimension*. New Brunswick, N.J.: Transaction Books, 1986.

Cochran, M. "Neutralizing the Positive: Ethics and Post Modern International Relations Theory." *Millennium: Journal of International Studies* (1994).

Connolly, W. *Identity/Difference: Democratic Negotiations of Political Paradox*. Ithaca: Cornell University Press, 1991.

Davenport, R. *South Africa: A Modern History*. London: Macmillan, 1977.

Der Derian, James and Michael Shapiro, eds. *International/Intertextual Relations: Postmodern Readings of World Politics*. Lexington, MA: Lexington Books, 1989.

Derrida, J. *Writing and Difference*. (Trans. A. Bass.) Chicago: University of Chicago Press, 1978.

Dessler, D. "Beyond Correlations: Toward a Causal Theory of War." *International Studies Quarterly* 35, 3 (September 1991).

Deutsch, K. W. *The Nerves of Government*. 2nd edn. New York: Free Press, 1966.

The Analysis of International Relations. 2nd edn. Englewood Cliffs; Prentice-Hall, 1978.

Diesing, Paul. *How Does Social Science Work? Reflections on Practice*. 2nd edn. Pittsburgh, PA: Pittsburgh University Press, 1992.

Dilthey, W. *Selected Writings*. (ed. H. P. Rickman.) Cambridge: Cambridge University Press, 1979.

Dogan, A. *Philosophy of History*. New York: Macmillan, 1965.

Donelan, M. "The Political Theorists and International Theory." In Michael Donelan, ed., *The Reason of States*. London: Allen and Unwin, 1978.

Dunne, Timothy. "Mythology or Methodology? Traditions in International Relations Theory." *Review of International Relations* 19 (July 1993): 305–18.

Dworkin, R. *Taking Rights Seriously*. London: Duckworth, 1981.

Ellis, Anthony, ed. *Ethics and International Relations*. Manchester: Manchester University Press, 1986.

Fay, B. *Social Theory and Political Practice*. London: Allen and Unwin, 1975.

Federking, B. "The Power of Poststructuralism." *Millennium: Journal of International Studies* (1994).

Feyerabend, P. *Against Method*. London: New Left Books, 1975.

Fichte, J. G. *The Popular Works of Fichte*. (Ed. W. Smith), 2 vols., London: John Chapman, 1849.

Finnis, J. *Natural Law and Natural Rights*. Oxford: Oxford University Press, 1980.

Finnis, J., J. Boyle, and G. Grisez. *Nuclear Deterrence, Morality and Realism*. Oxford: Clarendon Press, 1987.

Flathman, R. *The Practice of Rights*. Cambridge: Cambridge University Press, 1976.

Foucault, M. *The Order of Things*. London: Tavistock, 1970.

"Nietzsche, genealogy, history." In Donald F. Bouchard, ed., *Language, Counter-Memory, Practice: Selected Essays and Interviews*, 139–65. New York: Cornell University Press, 1977.

Frank, A. G. *Capitalism and Underdevelopment in Latin America*. Harmondsworth: Penguin Books, 1971.

Frankel, J. *Contemporary International Theory*. London: Oxford University Press, 1973.

Frohock, F. M. *Normative Political Theory*. Englewood Cliffs: Prentice-Hall, 1974.

Frost, M. *Towards a Normative Theory of International Relations*. Cambridge: Cambridge University Press, 1986.

Fukuyama, Francis. "The End of History." *The National Interest*, 16 (Summer 1989).

Gallie, W. B. "Essentially Contested Concepts." *Proceedings of the Aristotelian Society* 56 (1965).

Gardiner, P. *Theories of History*. Glencoe: The Free Press, 1959.

Gellner, E. *Words and Things*. London: Gollancz, 1959.

The Legitimation of Belief. Cambridge: Cambridge University Press, 1974.

Spectacles and Predicaments. Cambridge: Cambridge University Press, 1980.

Gilbert, Alan. "Must Global Politics Constrain Democracy?" *Political Theory* 20, 1, (February 1992): 8–37.

Greisman, H. "The Paradigm That Failed." In R. C. Monk, ed., *Structures of Knowing*, New York: University Press of America, 1986.

Haas, E. B. *Beyond the Nation State*. Stanford: Stanford University Press, 1964.

Habermas, J. *Knowledge and Human Interests*. London: Heineman, 1971.

Hampshire, S. *Public and Private Morality*. Cambridge: Cambridge University Press, 1978.

Harrison, G. "Relativism and Tolerance." In Peter Laslett and James Fishkin, eds., *Philosophy Politics and Society*, Oxford: Blackwell, 1979.

Hart, H. L. A. *The Concept of Law.* London: Oxford University Press, 1961.
"Between Utility and Rights." In Alan Ryan, ed., *The Idea of Freedom,* London: Oxford University Press, 1979.
Hegel, G. W. F. *The Philosophy of Right.* (Trans. T. M. Knox.) Oxford: Oxford University Press, 1973.
Held, David. *Introduction to Critical Theory.* London: Hutchinson and Co. 1980.
Hobbes, T. *Leviathan.* London: Dent, 1962.
Hodgeson, D. H. *The Consequences of Utilitarianism.* Oxford: Oxford University Press, 1967.
Hoffman, S. *Contemporary Theory in International Relations.* Englewood Cliffs: Prentice Hall, 1960.
"An American Social Science: International Relations." *Daedalus* 106, 3 (1977): 41–60.
Hollis, Martin and Steve Smith. *Explaining and Understanding International Relations.* Oxford: Clarendon Press, 1990.
Holsti, K. J. *International Politics: A Framework for Analysis.* Englewood Cliffs: Prentice-Hall, 1967.
"International Relations at the End of the Millennium." *Review of International Studies* 19, 4 (October 1994): 401–8.
Hudson, W. D. *The Is/Ought Question.* London: St Martin's Press, 1969.
Modern Moral Philosophy. New York: Doubleday, 1970.
Hughes, J. *The Philosophy of Social Research.* London: Longman, 1980.
Jackson, Robert. *Quasi States: Sovereignty, International Relations and the Third World.* Cambridge: Cambridge University Press, 1990.
Jervis, R. *Perception and Misperception in International Politics.* Princeton: Princeton University Press, 1976.
Johnson, R. W. *How Long Will South Africa Survive?* London: Macmillan, 1977.
Joynt, C. B. and H. Corbett. *Theory and Reality in World Politics.* London: Macmillan, 1978.
Joynt, C. B. and J. E. Hare. *Ethics and International Affairs.* London: Macmillan, 1982.
"The New Great Debate." In K. Knorr and J. N. Rosenau, eds., *Contending Approaches to International Relations.* Princeton University Press, 1970.
Kaplan, M. *System and Process in International Politics.* New York: John Wiley, 1957.
Keal, P. *Ethics and Foreign Policy.* London: Allen and Unwin, 1992.
Keens-Soper, M. "The Practice of a States System." In Michael Donelan, ed., *The Reason of States,* London: Allen and Unwin, 1978.
Kennedy, Paul *Preparing for the Twenty-first Century.* London: Harper Collins, 1993.
Keohane, R. O., ed. *Neo-Realism and Its Critics.* New York: Columbia University Press, 1986.
Keohane, R. and R. O. Nye. *Power and Interdependence.* Boston: Little, Brown, 1977.
Kindleberger, C. P. "Scientific International Politics." *World Politics* 11, 1 (1958).

Knorr, K. and S. Verba. *The International System*. Princeton: Princeton University Press, 1961.

Krasner, S. D. *Structural Conflict: The Third World Against Global Liberalism*. University of California Press, 1985.

Kratochwil, F. *Rules, Norms and Decisions*. Cambridge: Cambridge University Press, 1989.

Kubalkova, V. "Moral Precepts in Contemporary Soviet Politics." In Ralph Pettman, ed., *Moral Claims in World Affairs*, London: Croom Helm, 1979.

Kubalkova, V. and A. A. Cruickshank. *Marxism–Leninism and the Theory of International Relations*. London: Routledge and Kegan Paul, 1980.

Kuhn, T. S. *The Structure of Scientific Revolutions*. 2nd edn. Chicago: University of Chicago Press, 1970.

Lakatos, I. "Falsification and the Methodology of Scientific Research Programmes." In I. Lakatos and A. Musgrave, eds., *Criticism and the Growth of Knowledge*, Cambridge: Cambridge University Press, 1970.

Lenin, V. I. "Imperialism the Highest Stage of Capitalism." In *Selected Works of Lenin*. Moscow: Progress Publishers, 1977.

Light, Margot, and A. J. R. Groom, eds. *International Relations: A Handbook of Current Theory*. Boulder, CO: Lynne Rienner, 1985.

Linklater, Andrew. *Men and Citizens in the Theory of International Relations*. 2nd edn. London: Macmillan, 1990.

Beyond Realism and Marxism: Critical Theory and International Relations. London, 1990.

Locke, J. *The Second Treatise of Government*. Indianapolis: Bobbs-Merrill, 1952.

Louche, J. *Explanation and Human Action*. Oxford: Basil Blackwell, 1966.

Lyotard, J. *The Postmodern Condition: A Report on Knowledge*. (Trans. G. Bennington and B. Massumi.) Minneapolis: Minnesota University Press, 1984.

McClelland, C. A. *Theory and International System*. New York: Macmillan, 1966.

Mackie, J. *Ethics: Inventing Right and Wrong*. Harmondsworth: Penguin Books, 1981.

McKinlay, R. D. and R. Little. *Global Problems and World Order*. London: Frances Pinter, 1986.

Marx, K. "A Contribution to the Critique of Political Economy." In T. B. Bottomore and M. Rubel, eds., *Karl Marx: selected Writings in Sociology and Social Philosophy*. London: D. C. Watts, 1963.

Capital. London: Dent, 1972.

Mayall, J. "International Society and International Theory." In Michael Donelan, ed., *The Reason of States*. London: Allen and Unwin, 1978.

Mitrany, D. A. *A Functionalist Approach to World Politics*. London: Martin Robertson, 1975.

Morgenthau, H. *Politics Among Nations*. New York: Knopf, 1973.

Moynihan, Patrick. *On the Law of Nations*. Cambridge, MA: Harvard University Press, 1990.

Nardin, Terry and David Mapel. *Traditions of International Ethics*. Cambridge: Cambridge University Press, 1992.

Navari, C. "The Origins of the Nation-State." In Leonard Tivey, ed., *The Nation State*. Oxford: Martin Robertson, 1981.

Nicholson, M. *Rationality and the Analysis of International Conflict*. Cambridge: Cambridge University Press, 1992.

Nozick, R. *Anarchy, State and Utopia*. Oxford: Blackwell, 1974.

Nye, Joseph, ed. *Nuclear Ethics*. New York: The Free Press, 1986.

O'Brien, W. V. *Conduct of Just and Limited War*. New York: Praeger, 1981.

O'Brien, William V. and John Langan (eds.). *The Nuclear Dilemma and the Just War Tradition*. Lexington, MA: Lexington Books, 1986.

Oakeshott, M. "The Language of the Modern European State." *Political Studies* 23 (December 1975).

Onuf, Nicholas Greenwood. *World of Our Making: Rules and Rule in Social Theory and International Relations*. Columbia SC: University of South Carolina Press, 1989.

Organski, A. F. K. *World Politics*. New York: Alfred Knopf, 1968.

Paine, T. *The Rights of Man*. London: Dent, 1979.

Paskins, B. and M. Dockrill. *The Ethics of War*. London: Duckworth, 1979.

Passmore, J. "Logical Positivism." In Paul Edwards, ed., *Encyclopaedia of Philosophy*, New York: Macmillan, 1967.

Pateman, C. *Participation and Democratic Theory*. Cambridge: Cambridge University Press, 1970.

Pennock, J. R. *Democratic Political Theory*. Princeton: Princeton University Press, 1979.

Pettman, R. 'Race, Conflict and Liberation in Africa." In Ralph Pettman, ed., *Moral Claims in World Affairs*. London: Croom Helm, 1979.

State and Class. London: Croom Helm, 1979.

Phillips, R. L. *War and Justice*. Norman: University of Oklahoma Press, 1984.

Plamenatz, J. *Consent, Freedom and Political Obligation*. London: Oxford University Press, 1968.

Pogge, T. *Realizing Rawls*. Ithaca: Cornell University Press, 1989.

Poggi, G. *The Development of the Modern State*. London: Hutchinson, 1978.

Popper, K. *The Open Society and Its Enemies*. London: Routledge and Kegan Paul, 1945.

Pratt, V. *The Philosophy of the Social Sciences*. London: Methuen, 1978.

Price, Richard. "Interpretation and Disciplinary Orthodoxy in International Relations." *Review of International Studies* 20, 2, (April 1994): 201–4.

Pridham, G. "Terrorism and the State in West Germany During the 1970's." In Juliet Lodge, ed., *Terrorism: a Challenge to the State*, Oxford: Martin Robertson, 1981.

Quine, W. V. O. "Two Dogmas of Empiricism." In W. V. O. Quine, ed., *From a Logical Point of View*. New York: Harper and Row, 1961.

Quine, V. O. and J. S. Ullian. *The Web of Belief*. New York: Random House, 1978.

Rabinow, Paul and William Sullivan. *Interpretive Social Sciences: A Reader*. Berkley, CA: University of California Press, 1977.

Rawls, J. *A Theory of Justice*. London: Oxford University Press, 1972.
"The Idea of an Overlapping Consensus." *Oxford Journal of Legal Studies 7*, 1 (1987).
"The Law of Peoples." In Stephen Shute and Susan Hurley, eds., *On Human Rights*, pp. 41–82. New York: Basic Books, 1993.
Reynolds, C. *Theory and Explanation in International Relations*. London: Martin Robertson, 1973.
Reynolds, P. *An Introduction to International Relations*. London: Longman, 1976.
Rorty, R. *Philosophy and the Mirror of Nature*. Oxford: Blackwell, 1980.
Rosecrance, R. *International Relations: Peace or War*. New York: McGraw Hill, 1973.
Rosenau, J. *The Adaptation of National Societies: A Theory of Political System Behaviour and Transformation*. New York: McCaleb-Seiler, 1970.
Rosenau, J. N., G. Gartin, E. C. McClain, D. Stinziano, R. Stoddard and D. Swanson. "Of Syllabi, Texts, Students and Scholarship in International Relations." *World Politics* 29, 2 (January 1977).
Rosenau, James. "Thinking Theory Thoroughly." In Paul R. Viotti and Mark V. Kauppi, ed., *International Relations Theory: Realism, Pluralism and Globalism*, New York: Macmillan, 1993.
Rosenau, P. "Once Again Into the Fray: International Relations Confronts the Humanities." *Millennium: Journal of International Studies* 19, 1 (Spring 1990): 83–110.
Rosenberg, Justin. "The International Imagination: IR Theory and 'Classical Social Analysis' ". *Millennium: Journal of International Studies* 23, 1 (1994): 85–108.
Rothstein, Robert L. *The Evolution of Theory in IR*. Columbia: University of South Carolina Press, 1991.
Rousseau, J. J. *The Social Contract*. London: Dent, 1973.
Schwarzenberger, G. and E. D. Brown. *A Manual of International Law*. 6th edn, London, 1976.
Sewell, J. P. *Functionalism and World Politics*. Princeton: Princeton University Press, 1961.
Singer, J. D. "The Level of Analysis Problem in International Relations." In K. Knorr and S. Verva, eds., *The International System: Theoretical Issues*. Princeton University Press, 1961.
Human Behaviour and International Politics. Skokie: Rand McNally, 1965.
"The Behavioural Science Approach to International Relations: Payoff and Prospects." In J. N. Rosenau, ed., *International Politics and Foreign Policy*. New York: The Free Press, 1969.
Smart, J. J. C. "An Outline of Utilitarian Ethics." In J. J. C. Smart and Bernard Williams, eds., *Utilitarian Ethics: For and Against*. Cambridge: Cambridge University Press, 1970.
Smart, J. J. C. and Williams, B. *Utilitarian Ethics: For and Against*. Cambridge: Cambridge University Press, 1970.

Bibliography

Smith, Steve. "The Development of International Relations as a Social Science." *Millennium: Journal of International Studies* 16, 2, (Summer 1987): 189–206.

"Paradigm Dominance in International Relations." *Millennium: Journal of International Studies* 16, 2 (1988): 189–206.

Stankiewicz, W. J. *In Defence of Sovereignty.* London: Oxford University Press, 1969.

Taylor, C. "Neutrality in Political Science." In Alan Ryan, ed., *The Philosophy of Social Explanation.* London: Oxford University Press, 1973.

Thorndike, T. "The Revolutionary Approach." In P. G. Taylor, ed., *Approaches and Theory in International Relations.* London: Longman, 1978.

Truzzi, M. *Verstehen: Subjective Understanding in Human Sciences.* Reading, MA: Addison-Wesley, 1974.

Tuchman, B. *A Distant Mirror.* London: Macmillan, 1979.

Tugwell, M. "Politics and Propaganda of the Provisional IRA." In Paul Wilkenson, ed., *British Perspectives on Terrorism.* London: Allen and Unwin, 1981.

Vincent, A. "The Hegelian State and International Politics." *The Review of International Studies* 9, 3 (July 1983): 191–207.

Vincent, John. *Human Rights and International Relations.* Cambridge: Cambridge University Press, 1986.

Viotti, Paul R. and Mark V. Kauppi. *International Relations Theory: Realism, Pluralism and Globalism.* New York: Macmillan, 1993.

Walker, R. B. J. *One World Many Worlds: Struggles for a Just World Peace.* Boulder, CO: Lynne Rienner. 1988.

Walsh, W. H. *An Introduction to the Philosophy of History.* London: Hutchinson, 1967.

Waltz, K. N. *Man, the State and War.* New York: Columbia University Press, 1959.

Theory of International Politics. London: Addison-Wesley, 1979.

Walzer, M. *Obligations: Essays on Disobedience, War and Citizenship.* Cambridge, MA: Harvard University Press, 1970.

Just and Unjust Wars: A Moral Argument with Historical Illustrations. New York: Basic Books, 1977.

Thick and Thin: Moral Argument at Home and Abroad. Notre Dame: University of Notre Dame Press, 1994.

Watt, D. C. *A History of the World in the Twentieth Century.* London: Hodder and Stoughton, 1967.

Weber, M. *Theory of Social and Economic Organization.* (Trans. A. Henderson and T. Parson.) London: W. Hodge, 1947.

From Max Weber. (Eds. H. H. Gerth, and C. W. Mills.) London: Routledge and Kegan Paul, 1970.

Wight, M. *Systems of States.* Leicester University Press, 1977.

Power Politics. (Eds. Hedley Bull and Carsten Holbraad.) Harmondsworth: Penguin Books, 1979.

International Relations Theory: Three Traditions. (Eds. Gabriel Wight and Brian Porter.) Leicester and London: Leicester University Press/Royal Institute of International Affairs, 1991.

Williams, B. *Morality: An Introduction to Ethics.* Cambridge: Cambridge University Press, 1972.

Winch, P. *The Idea of a Social Science.* London: Routledge and Kegan Paul, 1958. *Ethics and Action.* London: Routledge and Kegan Paul, 1972.

Windsor, P. "The Justification of the State." In Michael Donelan, ed., *The Reason of States.* London: Allen and Unwin, 1978.

Wright, M. *The Theory and Practice of the Balance of Power.* London: Dent, 1975.

Wright Mills, C. *The Sociological Imagination.* Oxford: Oxford University Press, 1959.

Index

CAMBRIDGE STUDIES IN INTERNATIONAL RELATIONS